Eccentric Wealth

The Bulloughs of Rum

Alastair Scott

BIRLINN

First published in 2011 by
Birlinn Limited
West Newington House
10 Newington Road
Edinburgh
EH9 1QS

www.birlinn.co.uk

ISBN 978 1 84158 955 8

British Library Cataloguing-in-Publication Data
A catalogue record for this book is available from the British
Library

Extracts from *Bare Feet and Tackety Boots* by Archie Cameron
reproduced with permission of Luath Press Ltd.

Hi-arts supported this book with a research grant.
HI~ARTS

Printed and bound by CPI Cox & Wyman

To Catherine Duckworth and Thomas Krebs

CONTENTS

LIST OF ILLUSTRATIONS

Sir George in his Rhum tartan

Monica Charrington (née Ducarel), who married Sir George in 1903

Monica posing nude

Monica's sitting room in Kinloch Castle

Kinloch Castle today from the north

Sir George on the cover of *Sport Pictures*

A childhood drawing on *The Public School Latin Primer*

Sir George in later life

The majestic beauty of Harris, west Rum

The final resting place of John, Sir George and Lady Monica Bullough

AUTHOR'S NOTE

I first went to Rum in 1972 with a school camping expedition. The experience made a profound impression on me and Rum has lured me back many times since. Over these decades the spelling of the island's name has changed from 'Rhum' to 'Rum' – the details are given in the narrative – but to avoid confusion I should point out here that both refer to the same place.

The more I learned about Rum the more incredulous I became that no one had written a biography of Sir George Bullough or troubled to investigate the intoxicating rumours of extravagance. My priority with this book has been to create a factual, and above all readable, account and to this end I have given reference sources for major or controversial quotes, but not for the minutiae. To keep footnotes to a minimum I have included an Appendix on some of the Bullough family who played a part on the fringes of Sir George's life, and added a timeline so that the chronology of events can be followed with greater ease and clarity.

Sir George died in 1939, Lady Bullough in 1967 and their daughter Hermione (Countess of Durham) in 1992. There will be many people who knew them personally, and more who heard about them indirectly through others. I would be delighted to hear from anyone who would like to share memories or recall incidents involving them. No biography can ever be considered 'complete' and many gaps remain in this one, despite three years of research. This book is my best attempt using the archive material available. If any of my facts or theories are wrong, I welcome the opportunity of correcting them.

I can be contacted through my website: *www.alastair-scott. com.*

ACKNOWLEDGEMENTS

George Randall and Ewan Macdonald founded the Kinloch Castle Friends Association (KCFA) in 1996. In the pages that follow I pay tribute to the enormous impact this organisation has had in bringing the plight and importance of the castle to public attention. I hope this book inspires many more to lend support. Details can be found on *www.kinlochcastlefriendsassociation.org*

Catherine Duckworth is the font of knowledge on all aspects of the Bulloughs in Accrington, and much more besides. Without the information she provided and ideas she inspired, this would be a much leaner volume. Her support and proof-reading were invaluable and to her I owe my biggest debt.

Thomas Krebs has left a well-trodden trail between Rum and his native Switzerland, where he alone has uncovered the Schmidlin strand of this story and eagerly passed on his findings. Thanks also, Thomas, for guiding me around the Giessbach.

George Randall is a leading authority on the Bullough family and castle. I am grateful to him for sharing some of his research in the KCFA Newsletters. At the outset these informed much of my own understanding and provided me with springboards into unexplored pools.

Other KCFA members who assisted were Douglas King (for the post-Bullough period), Mary Wardle (the Uddingston connection), John Bullough, Graham Bullough and Julian Mackenzie-Charrington.

Thanks to Scottish Natural Heritage – in particular, David Frew, who could not have been more obliging in allowing me access to the castle archives, and Tom Cane for readily answering emails choked with questions.

To Rita Boswell (Harrow School Archives), Gill Parker (recollections of Percy Hill's family), Josephine Pemberton (red deer), Patrick (the Fujiya Hotel in Japan), the staff of the *Oban*

Times, Lancashire Record Office and many libraries including Accrington, Skye mobile, Highland HQ, Perth, Fort William and the National Library of Scotland – also thanks.

Permission to use extracts from published works is gratefully acknowledged for the following:

p. 17, Pen and Sword Books for *Aspects of Accrington, Discovering Local History*, edited by Susan Halstead and Catherine Duckworth, Wharncliffe Books, 2000.

pp. 30, 45, 156, 172 and John Love, *Rum: A Landscape without Figures*, Birlinn Ltd, 2001.

p. 54, *Debrett's Peerage and Baronetage*

p. 135, Garry Otton (author) and John Hein (editor) have both given permission for this passage to be quoted from *Scotsgay Magazine*, Issue 53A, September 2003.

p. 146, *Country Life*, 9 August 1984, from an article by Clive Aslet.

p. 153, *The Scots Magazine*, December 1978, article by Archie Cameron.

p. 157, Derek Cooper, *Hebridean Connection*, Routledge & Kegan Paul, 1977, page 85.

pp. 154, 163–171, 179, 186, 214, 224, Archie Cameron, *Bare Feet and Tackety Boots*, Luath Press Ltd, 1988.

p. 211, Alastair Dunnett, *The Canoe Boys,* In Pinn, 2007. First published under the title *Quest by Canoe*, 1950.

Despite every effort I have been unable to contact the following copyright-holders:

p. 158, Bridget Paterson, Kinloch Castle Friends Association newsletter no. 4, April 1998.

p. 210, Donald Cameron, W*hile the Wild Geese Fly: Tales of a Highland Farmer and Auctioneer*, privately published by Glen Nevis.

p. 221, Alasdair Alpin MacGregor, *An Island Here and There,* Kingsmead Press, Bath, 1972.

p. 221, *Scotland's Magazine*, 1959, from an article by Sir John Betjeman.

Sport Pictures for the 'Golden Ascot' photograph

Hi-Arts awarded me a Scottish Arts Council research grant which allowed me to penetrate deeper and further afield than I ever would have done at my own expense, and I'm grateful for the considerable bounty of fact and detail added to an important facet of social history.

Final thanks to Birlinn, namely: Hugh Andrew, for believing in this book and Tom Johnstone, for adding fluency to my prose.

Best wishes and prosperity to the Rum Community. *www. isleofrum.com.*

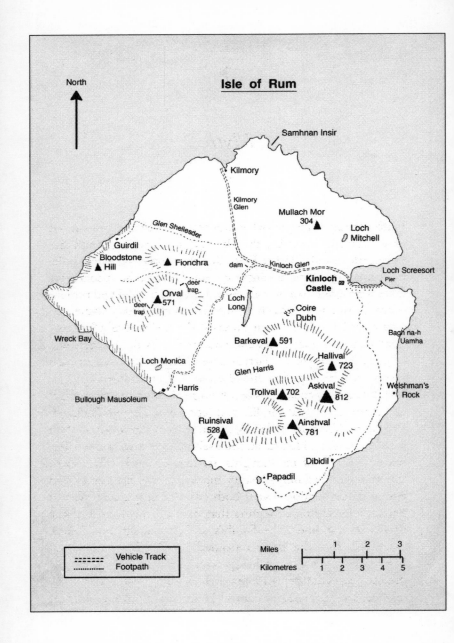

1

Myths

With a theme of rags to riches, this story spans three generations of a Lancashire family, the Bulloughs. There is grandfather James, the founder, father John, the augmenter and – much the most mysterious and fascinating – son George, the spender. He takes high living to a new extreme. Divorce, scandal and rumour – always rumour – attach themselves to the family name and a cupboard door falls open to reveal the skeleton of a lost son. The Great War intervenes and effectively kills the Golden Age of partying. But what a party it was! Its legacy endures. Around George and his beguiling life of excess a legend is born.

Like most legends it has become a glorified concoction of fact and fabrication. That the life and legacies of George Bullough have so readily transcended logic and entered the realm of myth is not surprising. He was an intensely private man and left few written records of his thoughts, feelings or deeds. More than this, though, the family's history appears to have been concealed with a determination that is both odd and suspicious. Were it not for the newspaper reports that have provided most of the details in this book, the family's self-effacement would have succeeded, and the story remained irretrievably enmired in hearsay. George's nearest living descendant, a single grandson, declines all contact with researchers. The few other close relatives I've managed to contact have evaporated the moment my subject is mentioned. Where voids exist in the foundation of a visibly ostentatious lifestyle, imaginations run riot. The Bulloughs were fertile ground for gossip.

One possible explanation for their secrecy may be gleaned from a reflection on the times. Although the story in its Scottish context took place long after the most brutal and repellent instances of landlords evicting their tenants for motives of profit, one member of the family conducted his own small-scale clearance. The family's wealth came through the effects of the industrial revolution which is associated with abuses and exploitation. There may have been retrospective embarrassment over these involvements, or others of an even more sensational kind which will be referred to later.

Briefly, here is the popular version of the story in its most lurid, scurrilous and *least trustworthy* form.

George Bullough was fourteen years old in 1884 when his father, John, married for the second time. By then John was a man of exceptional fortune, a manufacturer of cotton-processing machinery in Accrington, Lancashire. John's father had started the business and transformed himself from a mill urchin into a successful inventor and entrepreneur. John exceeded his father's accomplishments in both areas and, in 1884, was rich enough to buy a large sporting estate in Perthshire. This was the venue for his marriage to a Stornoway girl, Alexandra; he was forty-six, she nineteen. George attended the wedding, completed his schooling at Harrow and became a cavalry officer in the Guards. He was tall, handsome and athletic. His step-mother was pretty, vivacious and only a few years older. Before long they were caught in bed together. Thunderously displeased, John banished his errant son on a world cruise in the family yacht. To console himself, John added a new playground to his portfolio, the Hebridean island of Rum.

George's voyage was planned to last five years, and as an incentive not to curtail it, he was given an unlimited spending allowance. *Rhouma* was no ordinary vessel but a luxurious steam yacht 221 feet in length. Cricket matches were held on her deck. Her crew of forty included an orchestra and personal photographer. Along with a few friends George set out on a route determined by the whim of the moment: South Africa, India, China, Japan, Australia, America and various places in between. The photographs he returned with bear witness to a remarkable journey: there he is on an elephant in Rajasthan, here, apparently, standing among a carnage of heads and decapitated torsos after a mass execution during the Boxer Rebellion; there, perhaps, posing in the up-ended roots of a giant redwood, and here, surely, leering from behind his photographer's shoulder at sixteen bare-breasted wives of African Chief Usibeppo.

He met the Tsar of Russia and the Emperor of Japan. At an auction in Kyoto he outbid Emperor Meiji for a life-sized ivory eagle. The emperor wanted it to make a matching pair for his collection and, having failed, he subsequently lost interest in his lone eagle and sent it to the Tsar of Russia as a wedding present. A magnanimous gesture, for his country had just defeated Russia in war; the peace treaty was signed on board *Rhouma*, and for accommodating this George was presented with a bronze monkey-eating eagle weighing many tons. These and many other souvenirs were loaded onto *Rhouma* and taken back to Britain, somewhat sooner than planned, as news reached George that his father had died. The date of his death was 25 February 1891, and the celebration of his twenty-first birthday, three days later, was a suitably muted affair. After the funeral and the revelation of his inheritance, he discovered just how rich he had now become.

George's annual income was suddenly in excess of £300,000. Comparative values are hard to compute, but in terms of purchasing power this equates to many million pounds today. He wasted no time in putting it to use and commissioned the building of a castle on Rum. No expense was spared. Disliking the colour of local sandstone, he imported the rich red of Arran's deposits. Puffers by the hundred landed their cargoes on the rocky beach at Loch Scresort, including 250,000 tons of Ayrshire topsoil for the Japanese gardens and golf course. Three hundred workmen and forty master carpenters laboured for three years to create the splendour of Kinloch Castle. It boasted every innovation of the times. Glasgow was the first place in Scotland to install electricity, Kinloch Castle was the second. Windows incorporated a unique system of double-glazing, the internal telephone system was found in few other stately homes anywhere in Britain and revolutionary showers produced 360 degrees of jets with variable functions and phases. Outside, fourteen gardeners transformed the grounds. In acres of glasshouses a tropical paradise was replicated with palm trees and free-flying humming-birds. They flitted among crops of peaches, nectarines, figs and grapes: below them, in separate ponds, turtles and alligators basked apathetically prior to becoming soup for those extra special occasions. So it is said, so it is said.

While the castle was being built, the Boer War started and George offered to fit out *Rhouma* as a hospital ship and take her to Cape Town. The offer was accepted and for the year that such facilities were needed, many wounded soldiers experienced a level of comfort that was probably never again matched in their lives. For this service George received a knighthood. That at least is one explanation. The other is more popular and irresistibly salacious.

George had met a society belle called Monica Charrington. Not one to let a decade of unhappy marriage cramp her style, Monica was reputed to have had a string of affairs among London's rich and famous, and been a mistress of Edward VII. The liaison threatened to breach what little respectability the future king retained, and to avert a public scandal, George stepped in to take Monica off His Highness's hands. It was George who was cited as co-respondent in Monica's divorce rather than the Prince of Wales, and for this he earned royal favour and a knighthood. Sir George married Monica at Kinloch Castle in 1903.

The parties now began in earnest. Sir George and Lady Bullough preferred to enjoy separate lives when visiting Rum, each with their own choice of guests and lovers. Monica had a nude portrait painted and hung outside her room. Erotic French prints leered down from the walls of her drawing room and she had the castle refashioned to suit her tastes. George filled his library with pornography. Gaiety Girls and prostitutes were transported by special trains to Oban and thence by the versatile *Rhouma* to the shores of Rum. On the lid of the Steinway piano in the Great Hall you can see the scratches caused by the high-heels of one who was lifted up on it to dance. On several occasions a secret attendee was Edward VII. Not content with these affairs – so the tittle-tattle goes – George indulged a lust for all-male parties too. When the castle was being built he paid the workers extra if they wore kilts; the better to admire their physiques. When the castle was vacated in 1957 a sado-masochism cage was found in the cellar. Or so they say.

Deer and trout were imported to improve the quality of trophies, and the Bulloughs and their guests spent the days 'sporting'. French chefs cooked their meals and they were summoned to eat by the Orchestrion, a mechanical marvel that simulated a forty-piece orchestra and was played like a jukebox. Only six were ever made, and this one, built for Queen Victoria who died before it could be delivered, cost him one-third of his annual income. A real orchestra played in an upper recess in the ballroom, screened by a thick curtain from the antics below. Drinks were served through a double-doored hatch that excluded any glimpse of the life beyond. The dancing, and whatever else ocurred, took place below a ceiling studded with little lights to emulate a galaxy of stars. Squads of roadmen were employed to maintain the tracks over which George and his friends raced Albions at Le Mans speeds to the other side of the island. Additional staff were needed to care for his pack of twenty-four hounds. The pack lived in heated kennels, whereas the living quarters of the housestaff were unheated. Thus the stories go.

These then were the heydays of castle life. Then came the war. The decline set in. The Bulloughs' visits became less frequent, less prolonged. The glasshouses were abandoned, the humming-birds and turtles died, the alligators were shot. *Rhouma* was sold and replaced by a slightly smaller superyacht.

Kinloch Castle had never been anything other than a holiday home, used for a few weeks each year. Despite reduced expenditure on Rum the Bulloughs' lifestyle after the war continued much as before. They returned to Rum each autumn for the stalking season. The veil of secrecy concealing their private lives there was preserved and Rum assumed the reputation of the 'Forbidden Island', where outsiders were denied a landfall. The Bulloughs spent more time circulating round their other homes in London, Worcestershire and their specially commissioned house at Newmarket, where George indulged his passion for owning and breeding racehorses. He seemed to attract success. His horses won the Grand National and the Ascot Gold Cup. His dogs took prizes at Crufts. He was Master of the Ledbury Hunt. Sir George and Lady Monica continued to travel. The font of their income never dried. The parties they began continued, and continue. Their superyacht still sails the seas. Their castle is preserved. Their footwear still rests by their beds. They were never allowed to die. Large in life, they just kept growing larger in the mind.

* * *

For decades visitors to Rum have been regaled with the more sensational accounts of the castle and the Bulloughs' lives. When indolent writers feed off the regurgitated output of their predecessors, then inevitably the same half-truths and inversions are repeated and exaggerated until they emerge with the apparent bloodline of fact. Few seem to have questioned, for example, how George Bullough heard about his father's death in 1891, broke off a world tour in Salt Lake City (where the photograph albums abruptly end) and managed to arrive back in Accrington in time for his father's funeral a week later. Nor how he managed to sail round the world in *Rhouma* and return with photographs dated 1894, when he didn't purchase *Rhouma* until the end of 1895. His travels certainly took place and *Rhouma* did indeed make extensive voyages, but here, as in many other areas of a saga rife with conjecture, truths have been wrenched out of context and chronology and manipulated into a different tale.

This book's intention is to set the record straight. Many of the most extreme elements are true. Others are plausible but unsubstantiated. Some are pure fabrication. The George Bullough story is lustrous enough based on the known facts.

2

Weft Fork and Slasher –
James Bullough

Accrington (a 'town surrounded by oaks' in Saxon times) all but fills a long, abrupt valley high in the Lancashire dales. The oaks have long gone, but the odd copse of trees breaks the horizon where a fringe of farms and fields make a last stand against the upthrust of houses. These form an impressive symmetry of parallel terraces running steeply down to the town centre. Once a dense amphitheatre of smokestacks, the town's notable landmarks now are an abundance of churches, the finest market hall in the county and the railway line which straddles the centre on a viaduct. The air of decline is heavy. The heart is a shopping centre, the pulse weak. Lancashire wit and friendliness remain irrepressible, but the sense of abandonment is unmistakable, as if all the locals have really got left is their football club. Accrington Stanley's fame rests on being very old, unwilling to succumb to destitution and failing to recognise when it should be defeated by superior teams. 'Th' Owd Reds' seem to bear a double burden of the community's pride and hopes.

For its survival in the age of emerging industrialization, Accrington was fortunate in its geology and geography. The Burnley coalfield extended to the town's limits and provided both fuel and mining employment. The surrounding hills were a source of gritstone for building and mudstone for the 'Accrington brick' that brought initial and enduring commercial fame. A reliably wet climate ensured the river Hyndburn flowed strongly through the town's centre, and this was harnessed for both power and washing in the new processes of cotton manufacture. The Leeds-Liverpool canal looped the outskirts of the town and railways brought connections east, west and, crucially, south to Manchester. When technology led to the building of factories, then inevitably Accrington was poised to take full advantage of its commanding position. There was abundant labour to move into town from the rural cottage industry of handloom weavers, now becoming redundant, and enough creative vigour in the community for Accrington to spawn its own inventors and radically alter the wider world. What was to distinguish this town from a plethora of others which enjoyed similar advantages and growth was the breadth and diversity of its industrial base. The cotton industry dominated, but around it was formed a solid bastion of related and unrelated manufacturers.

At school certain names and dates were drilled into the minds of pupils in connection with the development of the weaving industry. In my case, little of what we learned remains except a vague recollection of Hargreaves and something wonderful called a spinning-jenny. In researching this book I have had to address that deficit.

In fact it was an earlier inventor, a clockmaker called John Kay, who is credited with the first revolutionary idea. In 1733 Kay dreamed up the flying shuttle, which exponentially increased weaving speed and enabled wider bolts of cloth to be woven. In 1764 came the spinning-jenny, supposedly invented by Lancastrian James Hargreaves. The tale persists that when his daughter, Jenny (coincidentally also an old name for an engine), accidentally knocked over his spinning wheel it gave him the idea for a way of activating eight, later eighty, spindles from one turning wheel.

The reality is somewhat different; Hargreaves was given, and later claimed as his own, the preliminary plan for the spinning-jenny by a man called Thomas Highs, a brilliant inventor who never had the funds or acumen to protect his ideas. The spinning-jenny's flaw was that the threads it produced were coarse and weak and could only be used for the weft (the threads woven at right angles to the length of the warp). This problem was also solved by the unfortunate Highs. He discovered that sets of paired rollers turning at different speeds would produce the much-desired, fine, strong thread. The problem was how to power the machine. The 'Frame', as it was called, was too heavy to be turned by hand. Highs adapted it to the principles of the millwheel and harnessed the power of water. His Water Frame was adopted by wigmaker Richard Arkwright, who joined forces with John Kay. Kay had been all but bankrupted by litigation fees when trying to enforce his patents for the flying shuttle. Together they turned the Water Frame into a commercial success and are credited with inventing it.

So, two inventions revolutionised spinning and one weaving. The other famous figure in cotton manufacture is Edmund Cartwright, a clergyman, who is recognised as the progenitor of the first power loom, despite never having made a viable model. His best effort of 1786 provided the breakthrough and others redesigned it into a successful machine.

Nowhere in the history of weaving during the industrial revolution do James or John Bullough feature prominently. Yet it is arguable that their inventions and enterprise over the years contributed as much to the advances in output and efficiency in the cotton industry as any of their celebrated predecessors. What has been recognised is that its local sources of both genius and prototype machinery allowed Accrington to lead the world for decades, and without them, the Lancashire cotton industry would have died in its infancy. What differentiates the Bulloughs' inventions from those of Kay, Hargreaves, Arkwright and Cartwright is that theirs were not revolutionary changes but incremental improvements of existing processes. Radical they certainly were, and they numbered many dozens, and they carried technology to new heights over a long period.

In a thoroughly unreliable family tree the earliest mention of the Bullough origins in Lancashire dates back to *c.*1200, with a 'Stephen Bulhalgh' resident in Kirkdale. The family surname metamorphosed through various forms, some Norman – de Bulhalgh, Bulhaigh, Bulhaighe and Bulowghe – to the first recorded 'Bullough', born around 1580 at Little Hulton in the Parish of Deane. This was close to Bolton, some fifteen miles south of Accrington. Over the next seven generations the family migrated no further than five miles away and, in 1799, the future co-founder of the world-dominating Globe Works was born in the hamlet of Deane. He was named after his father.

His parents, James and Anne Bullough, were a typical working-class couple of impecunious means. Life for the masses was still a crude struggle for existence. Candles and oil lamps provided light. The penny post had yet to appear, universal education did not exist and the rush to steam power was decades away. James senior was a handloom worker in what was still predominantly a cottage industry. Powerlooms had been invented, but their use was not widespread, although several small spinning factories using water power had started up in nearby cities.

The young James was seven when he was apprenticed to a handloom weaver in nearby Westhoughton. Despite his lack of schooling he possessed the natural gifts of an inventor's eye and an engineer's mind. While progressing from hand-weaving through a series of mill jobs he noticed how much time and material was lost whenever the weft broke. Using some of his sister's plaited hair and linking it to a bell, he adapted his loom so it sounded a warning each time the weft tension slackened. The Self-Acting Temple, as it became known, was his first major success. Although the financial rewards were small, his ability was recognised and he soon became an 'overlooker' (foreman) at mills in Bolton and Bury. In 1824 he married Martha Smith.* The following year he became manager of a small factory, where he introduced his latest improved hand-loom, the Dandy Loom.

---

* Most sources give her maiden name as Smith, but one as Millar.

James Bullough's innovations did not meet with universal approval. This was an era of inflammatory discontent as traditional weavers saw their livelihoods threatened by technology. Aged thirteen, James Bullough may have witnessed the notorious Luddite riots which swept Lancashire and Yorkshire in 1812. Now seen as a marked man, accelerating the pace of change, his position was precarious, but his drive for new inventions never wavered. His biggest breakthrough came in 1841, with the joint patenting of the Roller Temple and Weft Fork for powerlooms. The effect was dramatic and produced the famous Lancashire loom which, with subsequent modifications, was to remain the workhorse of the weaving industry for over a century. The effect was equally marked in the public outrage it caused. Employers were threatened with violence and walkouts by their workers if they showed any interest in the 'professed improvement of the loom, introduced at the Brookhouse Mills in Blackburn'.

Another depression had set in, and such was the hostility to innovation in the streets that, for at least the second time in his life, James had to flee Blackburn for his personal safety. The troubles continued and reached a climax in August 1842, when 700 Special Constables failed to prevent crowds storming one mill after another, destroying boiler plugs and rendering the weaving machines useless. This incident entered history as the Plug-Drawing Riots. Bullough's Brookhouse Mill was specifically targeted and another petition was brandished by protestors, denouncing the Lancashire loom for which 'the patent was considered to be an evil in all its bearings'. Not that he knew it then, but this was the last major resistance the indomitable James Bullough had to face. Thereafter the populace was forced to move to the inevitable quickstep of change.

In 1845 James ended fifteen years at Brookhouse and moved on to other mill-owning partnerships in Oswaldtwistle, Waterside and then Baxenden. Now trading as James Bullough & Son, with two sons actively involved in the expanding business and a third, John, completing his education, James spent more time indulging his passion for invention. His list of patents had grown long, and included such mystifying names as the Weft-Stop Motion and the Loose Reed, but the admirable fortune they had amassed for him to date was rendered insignificant by the revenues of the next one, the Slasher.

The year was 1852, and the Slasher was a collaborative achievement with two employees* whose names also appeared on the patent; James Bullough played fair in all his dealings. The Slasher was an advanced system of sizing and starching the warp, producing a three-fold increase in output over previous machines. It proved to be an instant success. Up to this point James had operated mills and introduced all the benefits of his ingenuity, but he had never owned a factory which produced the machines he designed. This was about to change through another stroke of luck in his charmed life.

In 1853 a 38-year-old engineer from Bury called John Howard started a loom-making enterprise with a little-known individual, James Bleakley. They chose Accrington for this modest venture, comprising four employees in a huddle of wooden huts. The wages bill for the first week totalled £5 17s 9d. For unknown reasons Bleakley soon pulled out, and left his partner without any working capital. Howard struggled on until 1856, when his failing business caught the eye of James Bullough. He saw the potential at once. The two men were a perfect match. Howard had the engineering skills, Bullough had the ideas and a very deep pocket. Soon Howard & Bullough, Globe Works, Accrington, manufacturers of looms, outgrew their huts and were launched into a continual process of expansion.

Despite the turbulence caused by his inventions, James Bullough was a popular man. All his life he worked hard, and it was not uncommon to find him toiling through the night in his office or workshop. Indeed it was said that he 'slept on his looms'. As a child he had only ever worn wooden clogs, and in

---

* David Whittaker and John Walmsley.

later life he never wore any other footwear, his only concession to respectability being a top hat, which made him a somewhat incongruous character. In his pockets during summer he habitually carried peas from his garden and handed them out to children as if they were sweets, and would often linger to join in a game of marbles. Despite his wealth he preferred the company of his colleagues and less privileged friends. Above all he was a quiet unassuming man who valued his privacy and avoided publicity – quite unlike his youngest son, John, who had been selected to succeed him.

James's remarkable life ended on 31 July, 1868, at Ibrox Terrace, Govan. He was visiting his daughter who lived there. Dying on holiday came to be a perverse idiosyncrasy of many of the Bulloughs, but it was perhaps most unexpected in James's case. He was rooted in his native Lancashire and had never travelled far afield, at least not in physical distance. In every other respect, his sixty-nine years had been an epic journey.

3

Sin, Shame and a Prodigious Talent

Written into the contract drawn up with John Howard was the provision that James's youngest son, John, would join the management of the company when he came of age. Early in life John must have shown signs of unusual ability for his father to favour him over his older brothers. James once told a neighbour that he'd made provision in his will for his two eldest sons, Jim and Will (he left each of them a cotton mill), 'but the Globe is for John. An' if ee won't make it do, then it won't do'.

Clearly regarding his own lack of education as a drawback, James was determined to give his most promising son the best opportunities to study and learn. John was sent to Queenwood College in Hampshire, which was one of the first schools to specialise in teaching science and agriculture. It was an experimental institution founded by Robert Owen, the visionary humanist and philanthropist, most famous for creating the model community of New Lanark (1800–25). His philosophy must have made an impression on John, for it was to feature in his own style of business management.

From Queenwood he went to Glasgow University to study arts but did not graduate. Perhaps the future challenge of making the Globe Works 'do' was too absorbing, and rendered the completion of a degree in abstractions irrelevant. At face value arts was a strange subject for a natural engineer to take up, but less so when seen from the perspective of a family aspiring to belong to the upper echelons of society, where an appreciation of music and literature could not only be indulged but was rapidly becoming the essential fashion of empire.

John's date of birth, and consequently his age at all landmarks in his life, is a source of confusion. The family tree, inscription on his sarcophagus, obituary notices and entry in his marriage register all conflict with one another. His Swiss marriage certificate gives the earliest birth-date of 14 November 1837, whereas the age engraved on his tomb computes his year of birth as 1839. Any discrepancy is not particularly important and 1837 is the date I have assumed to be correct. As his parents married in 1824 John was relatively late on the scene, yet four sisters were born after him.

Despite his low ranking in the male order, John joined Howard & Bullough and served his managerial apprentice at the top. His father retired in 1863 and a new deed of co-partnership was drawn up with the original founder, John Howard. When Howard died three years later, John Bullough found himself in sole charge of the Globe Works. He was twenty-nine years old.

The population of Accrington in 1801 had been 3,000. By 1868 it had increased to 20,000, and 500 of these now found employment at Howard & Bullough's Globe Works. The annual wages bill was £8000. Within three years of his taking over as manager this had risen to £30,000, and by 1874 to almost £40,000. John Bullough was certainly making the Globe 'do'. He was every bit as hard-working as his father, and his genius for invention equally luminous. Between 1866 and 1888 he filed no fewer than twenty-six patents.

His masterstroke, however, came from someone else's invention, whose potential he was quick to recognise. In 1876 he crossed the Atlantic to attend the American Exhibition held in Philadelphia. Here he spotted the Rabbeth Spindle, a device whose special system of bearings allowed it to carry unbalanced loads and run at 'unlimited speeds', certainly in excess of 20,000 revolutions per minute, when conventional spindles seized at around 7000 rpm. The 'ring' spindles took less power, so one machine could drive more of them. The ramifications, Bullough realised, were enormous, even though it meant he had to persuade the industry to move from the standard 'mule' frame to a new ring frame.

F.J. Rabbeth, a skilled machinist at the Remington rifle armoury, was reluctant to part with the rights to his spindle and Bullough found him to be a shrewd negotiator. In the end Bullough won, and purchased the patent 'for a considerable amount of money'. Along with the legalities the price included working models of the spindles and the necessary tools and machinery to copy them.*

If Rabbeth came away feeling he had done well, Bullough knew he had done better. As George Randall explained in *Aspects of Accrington,*

> In 1878, the manufacture of the Rabbeth Ring Spindle commenced at the Globe Works and its success spurred a massive extension and reconstruction programme, including moulding shops and timber yards. New and larger engine houses, a dozen in all, were required to drive ever more machinery as production increased and the workforce grew to over 2,000. Within a few years, many millions had been produced for the home and world market, turning Globe Works into the truly global empire its name implies.†

The Rabbeth Spindle was to stand alone as the most import-

---

* This remuneration left Rabbeth rich enough to devote the rest of his life to an obsession with rifles and shooting. Aside from becoming a champion marksman, usually with rifles of his own creation from cannibalised parts of the leading brands, he became recognised as an authority on all aspects of the sport. His experiments with the most effective bullets for hunting certain species led him to introduce two new calibres, the 0.25 and the 0.28, neither of which were ever produced commercially.

† *Aspects of Accrington, Discovering Local History.* Edited by Susan Halstead & Catherine Duckworth. Wharncliffe Books, 2000.

ant single development in the cotton industry for decades.
John Bullough not only had turned a small family factory into
the driving force behind world cotton production, but he had
introduced a style of progressive management that was to endure
long after his death. The scale of his ambition was matched by
his ebullient personality.

His obituary revealed that 'discipline was one of Mr Bullough's
cardinal principles and the Globe Works was no place for the
lazy or indifferent workman'. Tough and uncompromising as
he was in attitude and opinions, John was nevertheless not one
to exploit his workers – at least when judged by the standards
of the times. The Factories Act of 1833 was intended to protect
children from excessive work regimes and decreed that:

1. No child under nine years of age should be employed.
2. Children between nine and thirteen years of age are not to
    work more than nine hours per day.
3. Children between thirteen and eighteen years of age are not
    to work more than twelve hours per day.

In reality many factories disregarded the Act, and there were
insufficient inspectors to enforce it. Mines were excluded from
its restrictions, and it was not uncommon for children as young
as five to be found working fourteen-hour days underground.
Not until 1840 did it become illegal to use boys as chimney
sweeps. The Factories Act *was* enforced at the Globe Works, and
in 1871 John Bullough became the first Accrington employer to
extend the nine-hour working day to all employees. The six-day
working week was thus reduced from the standard seventy-two
hours to fifty-four.

For this voluntary adoption of what had become known as
the 'Nine Hours Movement', he was presented with an ornate,
coloured 'Testimonial' by his grateful workforce on 5 December
1871. It begins: 'Dear Sir, IT is with feelings of deepest gratitude
that we take this opportunity of expressing to you our heartfelt
thanks for the very handsome manner in which you have given

us, unsolicited, the boon of fifty-four hours working time to constitute a week's work without reducing our wages . . .'

What a remarkable turn-around from the days when James Bullough had to flee his workforce for his 'professed improvements'!* While not in the league of Robert Owen, who transformed an industrial community with schools, wholesome food and free healthcare, John Bullough showed distinct philanthropic traits. He established Howard & Bullough's Technical School – among the first of its kind for the development of employee skills – and the Accrington Mechanics Institution, was elected President of the Accrington and Church Industrial Co-operative Society and poured generous funds into the coffers of ailing churches. His vitality must have been extraordinary, because his sponsorship and presidencies extended from the Lancashire Football Association to local football and swimming clubs. One newspaper obituary later observed that he 'was fond of sport and "somewhat aggressive". Generous, and an excellent judge of character and ability in others. He was robust in health, "full of life", courageous and determined. He could not suffer defeat in racing, boxing, wrestling or cricket.'

He kept a championship loft of racing pigeons, and was passionate about shooting, horse-racing, cock-fighting, boxing, dogs, music and unfortunately – as will be demonstrated later – writing poetry.

But his interests did not end there. Unlike most industrialists of the period who were Liberals, John was a fervent supporter of the Conservative and Unionist Party. He was a firm believer in capitalism pure and simple, and abhorred any act of government interference. He founded, and largely funded, the town's first Conservative Club. He served as its chairman and

---

* And five years later, on 5 February 1876, a further Testimonial in similar vein was drawn up by the Millowners of Accrington. It pays tribute to how his innovations and those of his father have brought 'pecuniary . . . advantages to millowners and manufacturers and inestimable blessings upon the working classes in this and other countries of the world'.

was selected to stand for parliament, but in the end declined because of business commitments. Such was his esteem in the community that invitations to make speeches arrived frequently and were rarely refused. His addresses were widely reported by the press on such subjects as, 'Why a working man should be a Conservative' and 'Licensed victuallers versus teetotalers.' He was also a regular writer of Letters to the Editor, sounding off on a wide variety of issues. These give a penetrating insight into his character and prejudices.

Letter to the Accrington Gazette, *on the subject of the Proposed Free Libraries*

22 March 1887.

Sir,
As to a free library, whilst I admit the pleasing sound of the name and one eminently suited as a catchword to tickle the ears of all of us who are in the philanthropic fashion of the day, I don't think the project can stand investigation. I believe some seventy per cent of the books which these readers take out of these libraries are novels. I've no particular objection to novel reading, except to the trashy sensational sort; but I hardly think the rate-payers are in any way called upon to supply novels to novel readers. The circulating libraries, for a very small annual subscription, enable anyone to obtain as much and more of this class of literature than is good for him or her. As to those who wish to read serious books – books requiring to be studied rather than read for solid instruction – few books will suffice for them; they can therefore buy them for themselves and they will think better of them when they have thus acquired them ... Therefore you will see that I am no enthusiastic supporter of free libraries at the expense of the ratepayers.

I am, yours faithfully
John Bullough

Sin, Shame and a Prodigious Talent

Letter to the Accrington Gazette, *'Lady County Councillors'*

May 11, 1889.

If I know my own mind at all I speak out of respect for women and because of that respect I would save them if I could from mixing in the rough-and-tumble world of politics ... Such work will impair their best feminine qualities. In measure as they ape man and approximate their natures to his in the same measure they will forfeit that claim to chivalrous treatment which is theirs so long as they remain women, and which it is men's duty and pleasure to extend to them when in their legitimate sphere.

But do these fine ladies imagine that they can enter the rough and rude arena of politics and contend with men and not receive their share of hard blows? If so, they are sadly mistaken. If they don't act as women they can't be respected as women. When they themselves disclaim their weakness and enter the strife as men's equals, there is no room for chivalry – they forfeit all claim to special consideration. For my part I hate strong-minded women. I think they are enemies of their sex. They are the products of, and the associates of, weak-minded men. In proportion to my hatred of them is my respect for woman in her true sphere exercising her legitimate influence. I don't like to see my ideal destroyed and transformed into a repulsive creature 'half-Margaret and half-Henry'.

Apart from haranguing editors, delivering orations, funding good causes, running a business empire, producing twenty-six inventions and indulging a myriad interests ... he also had a family to consider.

On 11 February 1869, barely six months after his father's death, John Bullough, then thirty-two, married German-born Bertha Schmidlin in her adopted Switzerland. Bertha was the daughter of Eduard Schmidlin, director of the famous Grandhotel Giessbach near Brienz.* She was twenty-one and already widowed, her husband having died four months after their wedding. How John and Bertha met is not known, but

* Eduard's remarkable life is outlined in Appendix B under 'Bertha Schmidlin and her family'.

it seems likely that Bertha had returned to work at her father's hotel to rebuild her life, and John stayed there while on business or holiday. The marriage took place at the Reformed Church in Brienz, a pretty lakeside town set below towering mountains. Given the qualities John expressly admired in women, one can only imagine that Bertha knew her 'legitimate sphere' and was not strong-minded – in the beginning, at any rate.

After their honeymoon the couple returned to John's then home, the Laund, in Accrington. The following year, on 28 February 1870, a son was born. He was christened George in Christ Church. A daughter followed two years later and was named Bertha after her mother. The Bullough family soon moved home to Oswaldtwistle, just outside Accrington, where they leased Rhyddings Hall. This stately home, set in its own park, had been built in 1845 by Robert Watson, a former partner of James Bullough and by then a wealthy mill-owning magnate. It was here that George, the central figure in the story that follows, and his sister Bertha spent their childhood.

Life for their mother, moving from a spectacular and cosmopolitan home in the Swiss mountains to industrialised Accrington, proved to be insufferable. She must have spent considerable periods alone, despite accompanying her husband on occasional business trips as far afield as America and Europe. How willingly she went is not known, for John turned out to be a violent bully from their very first night together. Their divorce proceedings, discussed later, list an appalling catalogue of his abuses. Bertha walked out in September 1879, and yet matrimonial relations *appear* to have continued until early summer that same year, for nine months after that a second son, Edward, was born.

Edward is one of the mysteries in the saga. His name does not appear in any Lancashire records. He is not mentioned in his father's will. No newspaper articles report his relationship to his father except at the very last, a fleeting reference without comment in his obituaries. He was deliberately expunged from the family tree, the 'Pedigree of Bullough', hanging in Kinloch Castle. Effaced from *Burke's Peerage* and from all family chronicles, it is only in the last five years that his existence as one of John's sons has been rediscovered.

Swiss records show that he was born at the hotel then managed by his grandfather, the Bellevue, in Thun on 28 March 1880. In the UK census of 1881, three of the family are shown as resident at Rhyddings Hall: John Bullough, his wife Bertha and their daughter Bertha. Also listed are a maid and cook (both Scots*). George was presumably at boarding school. There is no mention of Edward, now aged one, or of a governess. Edward had presumably been left in Switzerland while her mother was attending the legal process for ending her marriage.

* * *

Edward's story provides an interesting sideline – none of the Bulloughs can ever be considered to have led dull lives.

He spent little time in Thun after his mother divorced, for she moved to Dresden where he attended school. In 1902 he completed a four-year Master of Arts in French and German at Trinity College, Cambridge, and stayed on to teach. His gift for languages was exceptional. He had obviously picked up English either from his mother or grandfather, and he rapidly added Russian, Italian, Spanish and Chinese to his native German. His degree of fluency can be gauged by the fact that Cambridge awarded him a professorship in his 'fourth' language, Italian. He was one of two principal collaborators on the production of Cassell's *German Dictionary*. As well as teaching he delved deeply into a study of aesthetics and psychology. There is a

---

* Catherine Duckworth points out that many wealthy Lancashire families had Scottish servants. The governess tended to be French, the cook Scottish and the maids frequently from Scotland or any other part of Britain, but *not* local girls. The Lancashire attitude was that to be in service was the lowest form of employment and beneath their dignity.

suggestion he may have worked as a spy in the Great War –
he certainly served as a Lieutenant in MI5, or, officially, the
Intelligence Department of the Royal Navy Volunteer Reserve.
He was highly regarded for his abilities, and not only was he a
member of the mission which arranged for the surrender of the
German fleet, he was also asked to interpret at the signing of the
Peace Treaty in Kiel. In later life he was an ardent freemason.
Then, never having shown any inclination towards established
churches before, in 1923 he converted to Catholicism and, after
retiring from Cambridge, devoted himself to serving the Church
as a Dominican Tertiary.

He married Enrichetta Checchi, the only child of the
internationally famous Italian actress, Eleanora Duse. They had
two children who both joined the Dominican Order, undertook
vows of chastity and adopted the names of saints (Brother
Sebastian and Sister Mary Mark), thus adding another layer to
the veils of secrecy begun by John Bullough.

According to the given facts Edward was a full brother of
George Bullough, who was to enjoy immense wealth from his
inheritance. Edward inherited nothing, but seems to have been
palmed off with a relatively paltry settlement. What might the
feelings of these two brothers have been towards each other?
They certainly knew of each other's existence, but it is doubtful
whether their paths crossed much. George and Edward probably
did meet later in life, for sometime in the 1920s Edward and
Enrichetta were on holiday in Scotland and visited Rum. (There
were no tourist opportunities to visit the island then, so it must
have been 'by arrangement'.) They toured Kinloch Castle and,
so their daughter recalled towards the end of her life, were
surprised to notice that Edward's name did not appear on the
framed 'Pedigree of Bullough'. Allegedly Edward shrugged
it off, bemused that anyone could stoop to such pettiness.
Brother Sebastian and Sister Mary Mark never met their cousin
Hermione (George's daughter), but as children they 'exchanged
Christmas cards'. Thus some contact was maintained between

the two sides of these estranged families, and the 'poor' relatives were always aware of the 'rich' branch, but eschewed all claim, interest or favour.

Yet some settlement had been made by John Bullough. Brother Sebastian's obituary noted that 'the Bullough family fortune enabled Edward [Brother Sebastian's father] to be educated at the very prestigious Vizthum Gymnasium at Dresden'.

Edward Bullough, the 'forgotten son', died at Woodchester Priory from septicaemia following a minor operation in 1934. He was fifty-four.

Before John and Bertha's divorce papers were discovered, it was assumed that Edward was disinherited because he was born into the bitter context of a failed marriage. It now seems more likely that it was because John was *not* the father of Edward after all. In 1882 he composed a poem entitled 'To Little Bertha'. This three-stanza dedication to his daughter begins by describing how her ten years of life have been filled with happiness and an absence of tears. It then warns that this is now ending and her 'hour of trial' is about to begin. The second stanza reads:

> *Sin and shame we cannot name*
> *Now forever her parents sever:*
> *Of sin and shame she's no discerning*
> *But for the absent kiss a yearning.*

If this were *his* sin and shame I do not imagine he would be writing poetry about them. If they were Bertha's, then this would be symptomatic of John feeling that he was the wronged party. The name Edward may also be a clue, this being a Schmidlin name, not a Bullough one.

If we take Bertha's evidence in the divorce proceedings (*Bullough* v. *Bullough & Nentwig*), she claims that over a ten-year period from her wedding night until they separated, her husband struck her, insulted her and treated her with cruelty to the detriment of her health; that his aggression caused her to lose a child after five months of pregnancy; that he regularly and repeatedly committed adultery with their housekeeper; that he committed adultery and contracted a venereal disorder while travelling in Russia in 1872; that he committed adultery at a house of ill fame at Troy, USA, in 1873; that he tried to strangle her on a railway platform near Venice in 1879.

John denied the charges, then prevaricated and said these acts had been condoned by Bertha, and then he charged Bertha with 'frequently having committed adultery' with one Albert Nentwig. Both Bertha and Nentwig denied the charge and the judge found in their favour, awarding them costs. The marriage was dissolved on the grounds of 'John Bullough's adultery coupled with cruelty' on 16 January 1883.

That John was not the father of Edward seems to me the most plausible explanation for what happened but the theory is far from watertight. At no time in the divorce proceedings does John question the paternity of Edward. Edward's Swiss birth certificate lists John Bullough as the father. (Curiously, the birth was not registered until three months after the event.) His mother chose to raise Edward in Switzerland and Germany with the surname of Bullough. Was this a face-saver for her? Did John Bullough make a sizeable settlement in favour of his wife's 'illegitimate' child only because he had no proof of Nentwig's genes? Possibly. Their divorce sent shock waves through Lancashire. Divorce was rare in that stratum of society and it had already caused him huge public embarrassment. If this was the true course of events, he must have made a settlement to end the matter, but he certainly did not want Edward in the family tree.

* * *

Thus around early 1881 John Bullough's family was reduced to son George (11) and daughter Bertha (9), and a life that had always been lived under tight control was stripped of its illusions. Out of the disintegration of his marriage came the realisation that he, John, needed space and a change of routine. Scotland and the 'sporting life' beckoned. For two years he had already been making forays to the west coast of Scotland, but now a new phase in his life was about to begin in which work would take a back seat behind leisure.

That John Bullough, from an industrial town in Lancashire, should end up residing on, and writing eulogies about, one of Scotland's most remote and rugged islands is, on face value, astonishing. However, these were perverse times in the Highlands, where a façade of romantic imagery could still provide cover for savage deeds and all sorts of men were drawn to exert their power over the land and the people who occupied it. The most notorious clearances were long over, but evictions continued, and despite being on a smaller scale, the grief and trauma they inflicted was no way less destructive, the methods used no less barbaric. The original motive had been to make profit from sheep. Now there appeared a generation of exceptionally wealthy men who bought land *not* for its potential yield, but as private kingdoms. They sought wildernesses to own as sporting playgrounds, where they built mock castles and created closed communities of selected employees to cater for their personal pleasure. Some of these lairds were blue-blood aristocrats who had managed to retain title and wealth, but many more were the new breed of commoners-made-good, men of 'trade', such as Clark of Clark's Threads, Jesse Boot the Cash Chemist . . . and Bullough of the Globe Works.

There was one specific connection which led John Bullough to Rum, and that was his politics.

4

Stormy Magnificence and Rude Mountains

There is a great deal of stormy magnificence about the lofty cliffs, as there is generally all round the shores of Rum; and they are, in most places, as abrupt as they are inaccessible from the sea. The interior is one heap of rude mountains, scarcely possessing an acre of level land. It is the wildest and most repulsive of all the islands. The outlines of Hallival and Haskeval are indeed elegant and render the island a beautiful and striking object from the sea . . .

John MacCulloch (1820), a surgeon-turned-geologist who made annual tours of the Highlands from 1811 to 1821 and later published copious letters sent to his friend, Sir Walter Scott.

Rum is the largest of the so-called Small Isles in the Inner Hebrides. None is particularly small, but Rum rises above them all in much more than just stature. On the map it appears vaguely diamond-shaped, almost round, eight-and-a-half miles long from north to south and eight miles wide. Its coastline of twenty-eight miles consists largely of cliffs, rising almost to a thousand feet, but also giving way to several rocky or sandy beaches. A single sea loch, Scresort, penetrates a little over a mile into its eastern flank, but much of its length is surprisingly shallow. This is the only anchorage, generally safe in all wind directions other than the rare easterlies, though it is far from ideal and prone to katabatic blasts in gales.

Rum's nearest neighbours are: Canna (coast to coast three miles away), Eigg (four) and Skye (seven). Today it is served almost daily by a Caledonian MacBrayne ferry from the mainland port of Mallaig (17 miles) and in summer also by a private one from Arisaig. Historically the links were not nearly so good, the main port then being Oban, and on occasions Strome Ferry (for a short time the nearest rail link).

In many respects Rum *is* different, in some it is unique. To its neighbours' hill, it is mountain – in places so awesome it appears to have fallen off the adjacent range as a disjointed vertebra of the Skye Cuillin. To the Small Isles' pasture, it is largely bog. To the common characteristic of Gaelic place names, Rum has Viking terms for its most prominent features. Erosion has left it as one of the most exposed Tertiary volcanoes in the British Isles. The location of the earliest evidence of human habitation yet found in Scotland is on Rum. This island holds the largest colony of Manx shearwaters found anywhere in the world, comprising an estimated one-fifth of the total population. And – taking the superlatives to another extreme – it is the only known habitat of the species *Ceratophyllus fionnus*, a flea dedicated exclusively to the nests of Manx shearwaters on Rum.

The evolution of Rum began some 3000 million years ago, and what we see today is a sculpted mixture of some of the oldest and youngest known rocks in the world. Side by side are a girdle of Torridonian sandstone, a remnant of the Earth's ancient crust between 800–1100 million years old, and multiple intrusions of igneous upstarts of only 60-odd million years. The latter appeared as a late life crisis when Rum bulged into a volcano and erupted. As it cooled it split along its north-south length (now called the Loch Long fault) and over thousands of millennia the outer sheaths of ancillary rock have been eroded to reveal the process of the landscape's creation. Here volcanists can view the internal plumbing of a volcano. Such is the unique nature of Rum's geology that it continues to attract scientific study and has a reputation as internationally important.

The Ice Ages brought glaciers to deepen and smooth the glens and deposit strange egg-like erratics about like a careless hen. When the ice melted the land rose, leaving raised beaches that are most prominent at Harris about fifty feet above current sea level. Tundra vegetation developed into heaths, grasses and finally forests, despite the minor setback of a localised Ice Age 12,000 years ago.

Excavations of a Mesolithic or Middle-Stone-Age site close to the head of Loch Scresort – just a few good spear throws from where George Bullough would build his castle – made an unprecedented discovery. Over three seasons archaeologists gathered 138,043 pieces of worked stone. Many were microliths – small barbed heads for the tips of arrows and tools – and, equally exciting, hazelnuts that could be accurately carbon-dated. The nuts were found to have been collected and roasted 8,500 years ago, making them the earliest positively identified evidence of human activity yet unearthed in Scotland. Habitation continued through the subsequent Neolithic period, though it has yet to be established whether it was unbroken. One of the chief attractions of Rum in this period was its small but distinctive source of bloodstone, which was prized as a substitute for scarce flint.

With the advent of the Bronze Age, farming developed and land was cleared for cultivation. In his definitive book on the island's history, *Rum: A Landscape Without Figures*, John Love describes another intriguing revelation from this period:

> a dark fibrous smear on the inside of one of the pottery fragments [was revealed to be] pollen grains of heather . . . meadowsweet, royal fern and a few cereals . . . plants all normally associated with fermentation, so the pot had probably contained some form of mead . . . Dated at 3890 years BP this is one of the earliest discoveries of an alcoholic beverage in British prehistory – a particularly appropriate distinction for an island that rejoices in the name of Rum.

Gradually, it seems Rum's population left, or occupation became extremely intermittent. Eventually the Picts moved in and constructed several primitive forts, whose grassed-over remains can be found on the coast. Then came a more peaceful people. The first named resident was a hermit, St Beccan, who died on the island around AD 676. A distant relative of Columba, he had been a monk at Iona before seeking deeper isolation. Although the exact location of his hermitage is not known, it is believed to have been near a cliff-top lochan on the south of the island, the place Vikings later named Papadil, 'the dale of the priests'. Another possible location is in the extreme north at Kilmory, 'the church of Mary'. No remnants of a chapel have ever been found. A third possibility is Bàgh na h-Uamha, a coastal indentation south of Loch Scresort where there is an intricately carved stone cross which dates back to the seventh or eighth century, somewhat later than St Beccan, but it shows early Christians had a continuing interest in Rum.

The Vikings too shared that interest, but theirs was more of a passing nature. They must have been canny for they left little behind – a gaming piece of narwhal ivory and a burial cist, both found close to Kilmory – but no traces of regular occupation. They appear to have regarded Rum predominantly as a stopping-off point in their travels. This is conjecture and questionable. Why would visually insignificant places like Papadil, Guirdil and Dibidil attract their attention, if not for occupation? However, in general they do appear to have honoured the most prominent landmarks with Norse names: the mountains Barkeval, Hallival, Askival ('Spear Hill', the highest at 812m, 2,664 feet), Ainsival, Ruinsival, Orval and Trollval. Trollval, sometimes spelled 'Trollaval' or 'Trallval', has prompted speculation as to whether the superstitious Vikings may have climbed this peak after dusk and heard eerie noises or stumbled on the 'caves' of their nemesis, for 'Troll's Hill' has the greatest concentration of shearwater burrows on the island!

As Norse domination declined, descendants of the great Scottish warrior Somerled won control of the Small Isles. They were tossed from clan to clan as booty in their interminable feuding, but were eventually settled under the ownership of Clanranald. Rum soon slipped from his grasp and was claimed by Maclean of Coll. In 1549 the island was described as 'a forrest full of heigh montanes and abundant little deires in it'. Another account, *c.*1677, is a delight of detail:

> Rhum is one big island being on the Westsyde of Eig and on the southeast syde of Canna ... The island is verie profitable for there is abundance of butter, cheese and milk in this island ... it is full of maires, mosses, glenns, hills and verie bigg mountains ... there is verie manie deare in this island and certain foullis which will be taken in the mountains and are exceedingly fatt, of the fattest birds or foullis which is in all the sea. They are no bigger than a dove or somewhat les in bigness. Some what gray in coloure of their feathers being of the most delicate birds to be eaten that is bred within the whole island, except that doe taste olyd [oily or wild].*
>
> Timothy Pont, *Geographical Collections Relating to Scotland*

But things were changing rapidly. By the time the *Statistical Account* of 1796 appeared, the 'verie manie deare' had been wiped out a decade earlier. Evidence of the crude traps into which they had been driven and slaughtered still remains. Trees were suffering a similar fate. Birch, hazel, alder and oak were the main species, but their destruction was almost complete despite the *Statistical Account*'s use of the ancient appellation *Riogach na Forraiste an Fiadhach*, 'kingdom of the wild forest'. When John Bullough set foot on the island some eighty years later, not a stand of trees remained save one apologetic and decorative plantation of sycamore. The climate too was deteriorating, as

---

* Manx shearwaters are sleek black-and-white petrels which migrate at astonishing speeds to the South Atlantic off Brazil and Argentina. They spend all their lives at sea apart from coming ashore to raise their young in burrows. These are usually made on coastal cliffs, but Rum's colony, believed to be over a thousand years old and estimated at 60,000 birds, is unique in occupying high inland peaks. Early ornithologists considered them related to the puffin, an error that stuck, for the species is still known by the scientific name *Puffinus puffinus*.

the petulant John MacCulloch noted: 'If it is not always bad weather in Rum, it cannot be good very often; since on seven or eight occasions that I have passed it, there has been a storm, and on seven or eight more in which I have landed, it was never without the expectation of being turned into a cold fish ... it possesses a private winter of its own, even in what is here called summer.'

Visitors to Rum today may find it hard to believe, but the weather has improved since then. Contemporary Loch Scresort looks forward each year to no more than eighty-five days of gales, and averages forty. Three metres of rain is the mean annual fall, but this is misleading, for the localised variations are extreme: five metres lands on the trolls in the mountains, but only 140 centimetres at Harris in the west.

Despite all the grim conditions, MacCulloch loved the place. 'If I am wrecked anywhere I will choose Rum', he wrote, recalling

> one of those occasions when I could not keep the sea, and knew nothing about the land ... I met a young man in the usual shepherd's dress, and accompanied him to his house, to remain as long as it should please the elements of Rum. When shall I go into such a house in England, find such manners and such conversation under such plaids, and see such smoky shelves, covered not only with books of the ancients but of the moderns; books too not lying uncut, but well thumbed and well talked of.

The population of Rum in 1796 was 443, a surprisingly large community, though Pennant had remarked on its relative poverty twenty years earlier. The people grew oats, bere barley and potatoes in 'lazy beds' – so called because the thin, infertile soil required so much hard labour – and kept cattle and sheep. Fish were also a staple in their diet. They paid their rent to the absent lairds, the Macleans of Coll, one of whom had forced the island to become Protestant when the neighbouring islands continued with Catholicism.

1826 was Rum's year of grief. Short of money after the collapse of the kelping industry (which produced valuable alkali while the Napoleonic wars disrupted normal supplies), the laird leased Rum to a kinsman, the despised Dr Lachlan Maclean. Maclean promptly gave the population of 350 a year's notice to leave, to be replaced by 8,000 blackface sheep. On 11 July 1826 the evictions took place, and three hundred people were forced into two emigration ships. An observer described the scene: 'The wild outcries of the men, and the heart-breaking wails of the women and their children filled all the air between the mountainous shore of the bay.' The ships, ironically named the *Dove of Harmony* and the *Highland Lad*, sailed to Port Hawkesbury, Nova Scotia, where their reluctant passengers were disembarked into the unknown.* Fifty souls remained on Rum. Two years later they too 'elected' to leave, and boarded the *St Lawrence* on assisted passages to the New World.

Dr Maclean's success in clearing the island seemed to take him by surprise, for Rum's population now consisted of himself, the family of a single shepherd and 8,000 sheep. Desperately short of labour, Maclean had to intercept five families being cleared from Bracadale, Skye, and persuade them to transfer to Rum. For a while he remained optimistic and built a solid lodge, Tigh Mor, later known as Kinloch House. The times were not favourable for his enterprise. Mutton and wool fell into decline. By 1839 he was bankrupt. Yet the *New Statistical Account* records his time there with high praise and bravado. This is not surprising, for it was written by Dr Lachlan's brother-in-law, the Reverend Donald Maclean.

They were to make a pathetic pair. Dr Lachlan became an alcoholic, was himself evicted from Rum, emigrated to Australia, returned a few years later to Oban where he set up a medical practice and, when this failed, became a farmer in Mull. Here he ended ninety-two years of blighted struggle. His brother-

---

* Cape Breton's population in 1815 was 6,000. By 1838 it had soared to 35,420.

in-law fared worse. In 1834 the Rev. Donald's career came to a spectacular climax when he faced simultaneous charges of neglect of duty, adultery, indecent exposure, attempted rape, assault and drunkenness on both foot and horseback! His case dragged on for four years, and when summoned to appear before the General Assembly to answer for himself, he turned up drunk. Not surprisingly, he lost. He died the following year.

In 1845 Rum was put on the market and bought for £24,455 by James Gascoyne-Cecil, the second Marquis of Salisbury (whose son, Robert Cecil, would serve three terms as Prime Minister). His style of ownership was seen as 'irascible, high-handed . . . egotistical, domineering and quarrelsome. He had little respect for the opinion of others and a high respect for his own.' He immediately imposed a new regime whereby anyone not in his employment had to leave the island. One-year contracts were introduced. Private plots were reduced to eliminate those of independent means and islanders were forbidden to keep sheep because Lord Salisbury believed it would encourage theft from his own flock of 5,000 head. By 1851 the island's population had recovered to 161. Salisbury considered this excessive, and asked for a list of around sixty names to be drawn up for 'assisted voluntary emigration'. When this seemed interminably delayed, he wrote to his factor, Mackenzie, demanding 'a definite list from which, when approved, I will allow no variation . . . They must leave the island or any that cannot provide themselves elsewhere will be treated entirely as paupers and put in such houses as may suit me, not allowed to keep cows etc. Mind to explain that I have a desire that they should emigrate. It is a favour I do them to assist their wish.'

Fearful that they might change their mind if the ship arrived in Loch Scresort, Salisbury paid the fares of the fifty-eight émigrés, first to Glasgow and thence to Nova Scotia. The bill for this obligatory 'favour' came to £291 3s. 6d. Once again a laird of Rum found he had exported his best shepherds and had to recruit new ones, this time from Mull. Much of Salisbury's reign in Rum was marred by his recurring phobia of sheep theft. When ninety head of sheep were missing from the gathering in 1855, Salisbury erupted. 'As it is we have the satisfaction of showing that we are the laughing stock of every Scotch farmer for our losses,' he lamented to his factor. Then he instructed him to dismiss every shepherd and find new ones. Only later – too late for those dismissed – was it discovered that an error in counting was largely to blame for the discrepancy, and a higher than average death-rate through over-grazing, an inevitable consequence of the unrealistic numbers imposed by Salisbury. Unrepentant, he found a new scapegoat. A dozen eagle traps were ordered in 1852. At least two eagles were killed by these means and eight were shot in 1866, these being white-tailed eagles and among the last of their kind. By 1920 the species had become extinct in Scotland.

On the credit side, Salisbury embarked on a building spree which produced some lasting benefits. Houses and shooting bothies were built, roads extended, paths improved (largely by a Welshman who showed daredevilry in cutting steps round a cliff at 'Welshman's Rock') and a solid pier was constructed in Loch Scresort, accessible at high tide. He reintroduced deer and attempted to create a salmon run for fishing.

The failure of the latter enterprise was the straw that finally broke his back. The project centred on Long Loch, and the intention initially was to construct two dams: one to block off the loch's outlet to Harris, and a second to raise the overall level and redirect the outflow eastwards to the Kinloch River. Salmon introduced to the loch, would, it was hoped, start a new cycle of return. Three hundred men were employed on the project throughout the summer of 1849, and the level of the loch was successfully raised by early October. In the first week of December 'an unusually heavy flood from the hill' washed the dam away. Four years later another dam had been completed, this time creating a new loch to feed the Kinloch River. Within two weeks it too had disintegrated in a maelstrom of rock and whitewater. In his record book Salisbury listed the projects accomplished and concluded each with his signature and a gratuitous annotation that calls into question his state of mind: 'All done by me!' At a cost of £1700, the dams did not receive gold star comment, and they extinguished his interest in this unsubmissive land.

He had conveyed the legal ownership of Rum to his eldest son in 1850, but the latter showed no interest in the island and predeceased him by three years in 1865. Ownership thus passed to the 3rd Marquis of Salisbury, the prime minister, who was probably too busy to remember he had it. He let the grazings to a Captain Campbell for a few years and then sold the island for an undisclosed figure in 1870 to one Farquhar Campbell of Aros, in all probability the full name of Captain Campbell. The island's population was now a relatively static eighty. Campbell built a small sporting lodge, the White House, and let this out with sporting rights for £800 per annum.

Doubtlessly enlightened as to Rum's existence through its association with Prime Minister Salisbury and inspired to follow in the footsteps of his Tory hero, the person who took up the lease in 1879 was John Bullough, Machinist, Accrington.

* * *

As a young man, John had been a university student in Glasgow. His aunt Margaret lived there. It is likely he had visited Loch Lomond and seen some of Scotland's wild grandeur, but nothing can have prepared him for his first trip to Rum. The *Hebridean*, carrying him away from the deepening darkness and scandal of his impending divorce, must have sharpened an appreciation for whatever was new, remote and of 'stormy magnificence'.

He loved it from the first. In verses that would have made McGonagall cringe, he wrote:

There's a land in the West
'tis the Isle I love best;
there the lordly stag doeth roam
and the eagle makes his home.

Among Rum's population (90) in 1881 the census returns
record an eighteen-year-old mechanic and engineer, William
Bullough, and John Ashworth, gamekeeper, residing in the
leased White House. John 'Hookey' Ashworth was to remain a
keeper on Rum for over twenty years. (In Accrington he had
worked in a mill using a hook to drag bales of cotton about,
hence his nickname.) Already John Bullough was bringing in
staff and introducing Rum to his relatives and friends. One of the
most important among the latter, from an historical perspective,
was a lame poet, Edwin Waugh, 'the bard of Lancashire'. His
book *The Limping Pilgrim on his Wanderings* (1883) is now a rare
and unique account of life on the island at that time. From the
vitality of his prose and the absence of pathos there is nothing to
betray the fact that he was ill and dying.

Waugh describes how Scresort Bay presented a straggling
hamlet of eight to ten thatched cottages referred to as 'The
Town'. Kinloch House, built fifty years earlier by Dr Maclean
was a 'plain, strongly-built stone house with a steep roof and
with a porch, and with a small wing at each end. The rear ends
of the house are shaded by trees, and the lawns in front slope
gently down to the shore of the bay. The south side of the lawn
is flanked by the garden, and the north side partly by trees'. Fruit
bushes were laden with berries. Maclean's stand of sycamores
looked healthy and struck him as 'evidence of what might be
done in bare mountainous Hebridean islands by plantation'. The
midges were horrendous. On Sundays about twenty worshippers
attended church, including shepherds with their dogs which lay
under the pews or came and went through the open door.

Waugh spent hours talking to those he met and collected
their stories. One concerned the tragic diphtheria epidemic

which had struck a little over ten years earlier. Murdo Matheson was a shepherd at Kilmory where he lived with his wife Christina and their eleven children. Determined to give them the best education possible, he taught them himself, bought second-hand books and encouraged a nephew studying Divinity to act as occasional tutor. It was rumoured that an article of clothing washed up on the beach was carried home by one of the children. Whatever the source, diphtheria manifested itself in their household late in the summer of 1871. Five children died within three days between 7 and 9 September. A stone in Kilmory graveyard gives their names and dates. Broken by grief, the Mathesons sold up and emigrated to New Zealand. A daughter died shortly after arrival. Having previously suffered the death of a child in infancy, Murdo and Christina buried their seventh child in the soil of the land in which they had invested all their hopes for better things.*

John Bullough had no such worries on his leased island. On his annual sporting forays he immersed himself to the very hilt of Victorian sentimentalism in nature. Writing poetry about eagles was one thing, but his keepers were still endeavouring to eradicate them, while doing everything possible to assist the 'lordly stag' in its recovery. Lord Salisbury had imported specimens from English parks, both fallow and red. At the end of 1862 the total population was estimated at around a hundred fallow and sixty red. The fallow were ill-suited to the climate, in decline and never again recorded after 1886. The red deer on the other hand were thriving, and their population had grown to about 600 by the time Bullough raised a gun to them. Edwin Waugh recorded that the trophy heads were sent to Dugald of

---

* The eldest son, Dougald – of whom more later – had worked on fishing boats and in an uncle's chandlery in Skye. Hoping one day to become a sea captain, he had studied navigation and been taught logarithms by his father. On the 88-day passage to New Zealand he practised his astro-navigation and whiled away the time by checking the vessel's progress, recording a three-mile error on arrival at Port Chalmers – an astonishing degree of accuracy by any seaman's standards.

Glasgow to be stuffed. There were game birds too, and fishing – modest-sized brown trout and sea trout, but enough for city folks' entertainment.

Was John Bullough really so content with this simple life? Did he not yearn for a property that might offer greater comfort and prestige? The answer appears to be that he wanted everything. He was forty-six years old and wealthy enough to buy complete satisfaction of his desires. On 27 September 1883, while maintaining the lease on Rum, he purchased at auction the magnificent 50-square-mile Meggernie estate in Perthshire. Its original sixteenth-century tower-house with turrets and corbie-stepped eaves dominated a conglomeration of later add-ons, which had converted it into a 27-bedroomed stately home. The bidding opened at £90,000 and rose in thousands to an unprecedented £103,000. This excluded the value of timber, so John forked out a little short of £150,000 for complete ownership of 32,129 acres at the western extremity of Glenlyon. At the time it was the largest Scottish property to have been sold by auction in England. The seller was William George Steuart [sic] Menzies of Culdares.

Glenlyon is Scotland's longest glen and one of its most spectacular for mountain scenery. Meggernie Castle stood proud in a carse at the end of a two-mile drive of lime trees, and came complete with gardens, stables, dog kennels, a ready workforce in estate houses ... and a somewhat chequered history as a Campbell stronghold. An early owner was Mad Colin, who never recovered from a knock on the head as a child and subsequently devoted his life to violence and blood-letting. Around 1580 he caught a band of MacDonalds of Glencoe raiding his cattle, and promptly hanged thirty-six of them outside his front door. When confronted by the Privy Council and asked whether he would put his hand to a deed admitting he had executed these men unlawfully, he replied that he would happily put not only his hand but his foot to the paper as well. And Meggernie Castle had belonged to Robert Campbell until the debts incurred by a lifetime of drink and gambling forced him to sell. Within a few years, reduced almost to destitution, he took the fatal step of accepting a commission in the Earl of Argyll's regiment, and thus found himself in command of the soldiers sent to perpetrate the 1692 Massacre of Glencoe.

If there were ghosts at Meggernie, *The Times* made no mention of them in the notice of sale: 'It seems the very place for a wealthy man of the world, who is doubtful as to whether or no he is weary of its vanities ... The real attraction would be that a man of taste might have carte blanche in his own private wilderness, where all the elements of the picturesque are mingled in the wildest profusion'.

John already rented a private wilderness, but Meggernie was all his, and its accommodation provided levels of comfort and status surpassing those at his main residence in Accrington, Rhyddings Hall. Never one to do anything by halves – and now having been divorced for almost two years – he barely allowed time for the door-hinges to be oiled before Meggernie Castle became the grand venue for his wedding. His new bride was Alexandra Marion, the 'youngest daughter of Kenneth Mackenzie, Esq, agent for the National Bank of Scotland, Stornoway' and his wife Margaret. In the register of Saint David's Episcopal Church, Weem, dated 8 September 1884, Alexandra signed her full name, though she usually called herself 'Alec', and gave her age as nineteen. Perhaps conscious of the extreme difference in age, John gave his as forty-six when more likely he was forty-seven. It is not known how or where they met.

The People's Journal for Perthshire recorded that the service was taken by the Rev. R. Smith, vicar of Tintwhistle, Cheshire. Mr Tom Bullough was best man. Miss Mackenzie (Alec's sister) was 'best maid'. Among the party was Edwin Waugh, Master George Bullough and Miss Bertha. 'The service was not choral but as the happy pair walked down the aisle the organist played the "Wedding March" ... The déjeuner was served in the Weems

Hotel ... The bride and groom left by the evening train from Aberfeldy on their honeymoon amid a shower of rice and other symbols of good luck.'

At the reception at Meggernie before leaving for the railway station, John in his wedding speech attempted to ingratiate himself into this new society:

> If I am not a Highlander myself, at least my better half is; however, you must take me as I am, a degenerate southerner, and if there is any capacity for improvement in me, I have no doubt you will see it develop during the time I shall spend amongst you here ... But Gentlemen, the name of Bullough has some attraction for Scotland. Out of five weddings that have taken place in our family, four of these are what I may call 'Scotch' weddings – three sisters have married Scotch men, and I myself have married a Scotch woman; so that I and my family have got as closely connected to Scotland as we can.
>
> I am not only exceedingly glad to see my tenantry here, but I am glad to see such a fine-looking lot of men. I embrace this opportunity of making your acquaintance and now that the sporting season is nearly over and I shall have more time on my hands, I hope I shall make a more personal and closer acquaintance with you all, by and by.

It was an encouraging start and augured well. Alas, it was not to last. Getting to know his tenantry better was to poison their relationship. For the time being, however, the newly-weds settled into a comfortable routine split between Rhyddings Hall, where John continued a lesser role in running the factory, and, for longer periods, the country pursuits of Meggernie and occasionally Rum. Alexandra immediately found herself stepmother to George, who was fourteen at the time of the wedding and just days away from his first term at Harrow, and Bertha, who was two years younger and probably attending school in Accrington. The family was soon to increase, for in February 1886 Alexandra bore a son, christened John, always referred to as Ian but privately known as 'Ion'! Two years later Ian's sister, Gladys, entered the world. Both children were born at Meggernie, a sign of how much more time the Bulloughs were spending in their northern home.

In the year of Ian's birth, 1886, a notice in *The Times* of Saturday 5 June read:

> Island of Rum – Magnificent Sporting Island on the West Coast of Scotland for Sale. Messers J Watson Lyall & Co, Land Agents, are instructed TO SELL by AUCTION at The Mart, Tokenhouse-Yard, Bank of England, London on Tuesday 15th day of June 1886 at two o'clock precisely, unless previously sold, the magnificent sporting island of Rum which being the most picturesque of the islands which lie off the West Coast of Scotland is altogether a property of exceptional attractions. Its sporting capabilities are unsurpassed, and as a sporting estate it has at present few equals. Besides the sporting amenities it yields a very handsome rental. The population, some 60 or 70 in all, is composed of shepherds and workmen and their families, employed by the sheep-farmer on the estate. There are no crofts. The extent is about 27,000 acres, of which about 300 acres are arable, 150 acres lochs and rivers, 530 acres of foreshore and about 26,000 acres forest and moorland. The game consists of red and fallow deer, grouse, partridges, woodcock, snipe and the great variety of wildfowl of the West Hebrides. The fishings are excellent ...

In the fuller description given in the particulars the agent's hyperbole grew ever more florid. Messers J. Watson Lyall had clearly never visited the place. The lodge became 'the Mansion House of Kinloch' situated below a sheer cliff face and 'a most beautiful cascade ... while on the Western shore of the island towers "Bloodstone Hill" (1272 feet) flashing in the sunset, green as emerald from base to summit.' Some of the hills were 'covered with the finest grass and well sheltered'. Communications, they asserted, were excellent. 'The Steamer *Hebridean* from Glasgow, via Oban and Tobermory, calls every week, summer and winter, with mails, passengers and goods, and to receive livestock or whatever else may be sent from the Island ... There is a large stone pier.'

Of course the bay was too shallow for the *Hebridean* to use the pier, and Edwin Waugh's experience of the service just four years earlier was somewhat different, as he recalled in *The Limping Pilgrim*. 'When the steamers call at Rum – which is always by special arrangement – they call at such irregular times that their coming can never be calculated upon to anything like a nicety; and, as they generally come in the night time, they have to sound a kind of hoarse horn, or whistle, to let the sleeping inhabitants know that they are in the bay ...'

One person interested in purchasing Rum, who was also familiar with the island and would not be deceived by the glowing report, was a leading Scottish naturalist, John Alexander Harvie-Brown, who lived near Stirling. With undisguised excitement he wrote to his agent, Andrew Forester, for his opinion and advice on the value. He received the following withering reply:

> I have read with much interest your memo as to Rum and I cannot find in it one redeeming feature. Road bad. Peats ditto. Lochs inaccessible. Rivers spoilt by artificial endeavour to improve on nature. No salmon. Difficulty of access. Climate abominable and generally everything uncomfortable. Ugh, ugh. I wouldn't live on the place tho' you gave it me for nothing ... I hear there was an offer of £70,000 last year for it which was refused. I don't believe a word of it!

Either the auction never took place on the 15th June, or it failed to raise an acceptable figure. Another two years were to pass before Rum fell under the hammer. The incumbent owner, Farquhar Campbell of Aros, may have encountered legal problems over the sale which his death two months later in August merely exacerbated. As an absentee proprietor, Campbell left little trace on the island of his ten years of stewardship. Tenant sheep farmers from Skye stayed in Kinloch House and employed many islanders as shepherds and labourers. John Bullough had the use of the White House and the sporting rights. Rum passed to a nephew, another Campbell, about whom little is known except that he came from Ballinaby in Islay. Along with Rum he also inherited his late uncle's estate of Ormsary in

Argyll. His greatest distinction appears to have been the chaos at his funeral, years later. He was a wealthy landowner and the last of his line, and his funeral was abandoned halfway through as mourners ransacked his house hoping to find a will made out in their favour. As John Love records in *Rum: A Landscape without Figures*, 'They did not find the will but they did find the whisky. The coffin was not remembered until ten o'clock that night, when they finally took it down to "bury the poor man decent, and there was no good came of it".'

Whatever the cause of the delay in selling Rum, the island came back on the market in 1888 and John Bullough bought it early in May for £35,000.

Of particular interest in the sale particulars is the reference to the absence of crofters and crofts on Rum. Crofts trace their existence back to around 1800. The clan system had disintegrated and the land once held in common for the people had been claimed by former chiefs or had passed through illicit transactions into private ownership. When the Napoleonic War interrupted the trade in industrial alkali (important in the manufacture of soap, amongst other things) and seaweed was found to produce an acceptable alternative, coastal landlords were quick to recognise this as a double blessing. By moving their resident populations from the more fertile straths they had traditionally occupied to small parcels of poorer ground by the sea, specifically designed to be too small for subsistence, they achieved the clearance of the best ground for bigger flocks of sheep, and created a dependent workforce close to the sea to collect kelp.

The kelp market brought the landlords handsome profits for about fifteen years and then collapsed. This marked the beginning of the worst phases of the clearances. Crofts, however, continued to be occupied and created, and were not limited solely to coastal regions. Crofters paid rent but had no rights whatsoever. They could be, and were, evicted on a whim, and their rents set at any level a landlord's factor chose. Not until after many brutally suppressed protests was a law enacted – coincidentally, three weeks after the original date set for the auction of Rum – on 25 June 1886, which at last guaranteed crofters rights of tenure, fair rents and fair recompense for improvements (as well as the right to cut peat and collect seaweed). Thus to advertise Rum as having no crofts or crofters was considered a significant incentive for potential buyers.

Where John Bullough developed his rancour against crofters is hard to know, but it ran deep. Once roused he was not easily mollified, and like so many before him, he mistook for laziness the all-pervading disincentive that is engendered by the deprivation of security of home, land and produce. When even a tree planted by a crofter (right up until the 1970s) remained the property of his landlord, who but the uninformed would criticise the crofter for not planting trees? John Bullough, however, had his own black-and-white view. On 28 January 1888, shortly before he secured Rum, *The Times* published his 'Letter on The Crofters' Question'.

> Sir, We have long had an Irish Question. We now have a Crofters' Question. In dealing with it we are going on the old plan which we have found to answer so admirably, of yielding to clamour in the futile hope of pacifying those who are determined not to be pacified, as long as there is any hope of extorting what is left. Each concession is accepted and forthwith denounced as miserably inadequate. Meanwhile, the well-clad, well-fed, pampered crofter continues to loaf away his time while his wife does the work, reserving his small stock of energy for attacks on his neighbours' property and demonstrations against the offices of the law.

> [It ends]: I sign myself truly as one who admired the crofter at a distance, but who lost his respect for him on closer acquaintance; as one who has often watched him stalk along the side of his wife bent double under a creel full of potatoes; as one too who has seen her carry him across swollen brooks on her back; and finally, and truly, as one who is ready to help him as soon as he shows a disposition to help himself in a lawful way.
>
> I am, yours faithfully, John Bullough.

Doubtless the fact that Rum was void of thieving, loafing crofters with their newly-won concessions made the purchase of his new domain more attractive and certainly made it possible to implement his most pressing change – a clearance of all but three families. The tenant sheep farmers, John Ferguson of South Uist and Donald Ferguson of Lochboisdale, who had used the main residence of Kinloch House, now had to vacate the building for the new owner and see out the remaining eleven years of their lease in the farm house and steading. Besides them there were three or four shepherds and their families living in remote parts of the island, and around eight blackhouses were inhabited in the main hamlet on Scresort Bay. Some of these were occupied by a single elderly person. The exact numbers or description of those forced to leave is unknown, only that three of the original families were allowed to remain. The population of between sixty and seventy was thus reduced to fifty-three (1891), the majority of these being replacement workers chosen by the new laird. There may well have been an argument for dismissing lazy or dishonest individuals, but the scale of the changes and the speed of their implementation suggest more an eviction as ruthless as all the others before. Whatever philanthropy the head of the Globe Works exhibited in Accrington, in Rum he reverted to his callous, wife-beating alter ego.

It is far from clear how much time John Bullough spent on Rum once it was under his ownership. The next phase of development suggests a considerable commitment on his part, but the varied projects could have been completed without his presence. His absence from the shooting records is striking. *The Isle of Rum Deer Forest Book* was started in the year of his acquisition, even though he had been shooting on the island for the previous eight years. Along with its companion volumes for game birds and fish (started several years later) these leather-bound books with their entries inked in exquisite italic scripts are now unique records. Not only are they are a valuable source of wildlife statistics, but they also comprise the only known

'Visitors' Book' – the proviso being that only those who made a kill are listed; poor shots or those of Buddhist tendencies remaining anonymous. The first entry for deer was made on 2 December 1888, when 'George Bullough' shot a six-pointer, twelve-stone stag in Harris Valley under the guidance of stalker Peter Maclean. Eighteen-year-old George appears to be on Rum with his older cousins, Tom (32) and William (24). There is no mention of John Bullough, not in this year nor in any of the subsequent three (and after that he was dead). Either John did not visit Rum, did not shoot or did not hit anything, all of which are hard to believe, given his professed love of the place.

> *And year by year as round we come*
> *to greet our grand old Father Rum,*
> *. . . and with rifle, rod and gun*
> *there let my race be run.* *

He was an autocrat, opinionated, prejudiced and with an arrogance that was perhaps an inevitable consequence of self-made wealth founded on a privileged upbringing, but his childish expressions of love for the Isle of Rum were genuine. So I imagine he did visit the island during these last few years of his life. *The Scotsman* reported his shooting activities at Meggernie in 1888, giving the days' bags and the observation, 'A lot of barren birds and several cheepers† were seen'. Why then did he not pick up a gun on Rum? Perhaps his fitness or aim were failing, despite him being described as 'robust' all his life, or possibly he devoted his island days to 'improvements'. Despite his apparent preference for Meggernie, he certainly injected large doses of

---

* Three volumes of John Bullough's speeches and a small selection of poems were published by his widow soon after his death. In her introduction, Alec (Alexandra) wrote: 'The verses are in the rough, just as he brought them home after his day's shooting, for they were nearly all written on the hillside near some bonnie Highland burn and during the enjoyment of his after luncheon cigar. Alec Bullough, Meggernie, Christmas Day, 1891.'

† Cheepers are juvenile grouse. If seen after the start of the shooting season they indicate a later hatching than usual.

adrenalin into Rum. Stone shooting lodges were constructed at Harris, Loch Papadil and Kilmory. He also transformed the wilderness which Edwin Waugh described thus: 'seen from a distance, Rum looks as bare as rock over which green moss has crept, here and there . . . [apart from the cluster of trees around Kinloch House] there is not another tree nor bush in sight; indeed, as far as I have seen yet, there is not another tree on the island.'

Into this scene John Bullough brought none other than the naturalist Harvie-Brown, who had wanted to buy the island himself. On the latter's advice Bullough planted 80,000 trees. He imported red deer from Windsor, including ten fine stags. Two did not survive, but he noted with pleasure that 'stags already introduced from the south of England took to the hill in October and proved more than capable of holding their own. They fought with and conquered the native wild stags.' In addition, each year he trapped four or five deer at Meggernie and sent them to Rum.

He also introduced more ptarmigan, partridge (noting how they clung close to the shores and would not settle inland), pheasants which appeared to be happy enough in the heather for want of trees to roost in, and grouse by the hundred from Yorkshire. 'What is remarkable is how they assume the characteristics of the native birds. One can always get within shot, while in Yorkshire and Meggernie they are so wild that one cannot get near them in winter . . . the new blood has done wonders for the grouse. We could kill 600 brace any season now, and three years ago the place would with difficulty yield 200.' None of these comments sound as if they come from a man who has lost interest in guns or who can no longer control them.

In 1890 he purchased the 55-foot, 24-ton cutter *Mystery* to improve the ferry service to Rum. The *Mystery* was able to intercept the daily ferry between Oban and Mallaig which passed the island at a distance.

In what proved to be his last letter to Harvie-Brown, written three months before his death, Bullough wrote about the 80,000 trees: 'they are doing exceedingly well and in January 1891 we begin planting again at Kinloch, Kilmory and Harris, probably over 500,000. They will embellish the island, and [if they] pay a small interest in twenty years, I am satisfied.' In fact the trees eventually failed. Not one survives to this day, despite the admirable endeavour. The partridges and pheasants struggled on in the alien environment for twenty years before succumbing. The grouse did well, but as the annual bags increased drastically their numbers suffered corresponding decimations. The deer, however, were an unqualified success and assumed the finest reputation in the land.

John Bullough spent Christmas 1890 at Meggernie with Alexandra and their two children, Ian, who was four, and Gladys, three. Early in January they travelled back to Accrington where John was to attend a Conservative Bazaar. During the journey he caught a chill which turned into a lung infection. His confinement at Rhyddings Hall failed to produce any improvement and so it was decided that he would head for a warmer climate.

John had travelled widely on the continent on business but he had never been to Monte Carlo, where he chose to go now. The family left Accrington in mid-February, according to one of his obituaries, but appears to have aborted the journey in London. Little Ian's hopes of spending his fifth birthday on a Mediterranean beach were dashed, and it was celebrated in a particularly grim capital choked by fog. Yet John appeared fit to everyone who met him, maintained a lively correspondence and accepted invitations to dinner, one at the home of Baroness Burdett-Coutts who found him 'in perfect health'. He was making plans to return to Accrington in time to celebrate another family birthday, this time George's 'coming of age' twenty-first.

His decline was sudden. Congestion of the lungs set in and he lapsed into a three-day coma from which he never regained consciousness. He died in his bedroom at the Hotel Metropole on Wednesday 25 February 1891. He was no older than fifty-four, possibly fifty-two.

A first-class coach was reserved for Alexandra, Ian and Gladys and the coffin placed in the centre. In what must have been a gruesome journey with the coach being uncoupled, shunted around and recoupled to each connecting train, they arrived at Accrington at 4.25 p.m. on 27 February. George and his sister Bertha were waiting to meet them along with hundreds of locals who had each paid one penny (the cost of a ticket to the nearest station) to gain access to the platforms. Newspaper reporters were there too, observing how Mrs Bullough 'was almost prostrated with grief, and had to be practically carried through the throng on the platform by Mr George Bullough and two ladies'. The Globe Works' flags were set at half-mast, as were those throughout the town, and Howard & Bullough foremen stood by as pallbearers to carry the coffin to the hearse.

It was estimated at the time that a thousand homes in Accrington derived a wage from the Globe Works. The weekly wages bill was £2000, and although this represented an average wage of only £2, people were grateful for it and extremely anxious for the future now that the town's dynamic figurehead was no more. Thousands of people lined the streets as the cortège passed.

The family had hoped for a private funeral but that was clearly impossible, and they acquiesced in the overwhelming presence of the public. Sixteen hundred crammed into Christ Church for the service, led by the Reverend Greensill. Afterwards the coffin, 'of lead, enclosed in very plain oak' and inscribed 'John Bullough, Died February 25th, 1891, Aged 52 [sic] years', was placed in the family vault alongside the remains of his parents. His company there was to prove only temporary.

As the public gate-crashing of the funeral had been a spontaneous event, an official procession and commemorative service were enacted the following Sunday. Two hundred employees of Howard & Bullough set off from the Globe Works, and on the way to the church picked up the local fire brigades and 250 members of local Conservative Clubs, headed by the Primrose Reed Band playing the 'Dead March'. Once again the streets were lined with spectators, and the church achieved a new record attendance. The Reverend Greensill took as his text for the sermon, 'Be ye therefore ready also; for the Son of Man cometh at an hour when ye think not' (*Luke*, 12, 40). They sang the hymn, 'O God our help in ages past, Our hope for years to come ...' after which, sensing that many were burdened with a sense of impending gloom, the Reverend Greensill made special mention of the fact that the deceased had put in place the finest managers possible who, he was sure, would safeguard their livelihoods; he advised them to take comfort from the words they had just sung.

His address was surprisingly diverse and included references to John Bullough's excessive tendencies ('if he hit hard, he hit fair'), the latest output figures at the Globe Works ('70 to 80 machines of all kinds each week') and the following intriguing titbit about the deceased's previously unknown trade as a butcher; 'Like many other English gentlemen, he was passionately fond of shooting, and his prowess as a sportsman was testified by the numerous deer and hundreds, perhaps thousands, of rabbits and hares which he sent to Accrington [from Scotland] for sale in aid of the funds of the new Conservative Club.'

At Accrington Stanley's next football match, the Reds wore black crepe armbands in memory of their late president.

At the reading of the will, a peculiar and carelessly-worded testament drawn up only three months earlier, the family discovered that John had left a personal estate with a net value of £1,091,835 10s 1d. Financial provision was made for his wife and two daughters, though the latter's shares were subject to pedantic conditions and perversely unfair; Alexandra received £75,000, Bertha, the eldest daughter, £30,000 (interest for life, capital to revert to the estate on her death) and little Gladys, £50,000 (to be invested until the age of 21, then £20,000 in cash and £30,000 invested, interest for life). Nephew Tom was bequeathed a handsome figure but this was annulled because he had witnessed the will – an indication that John, in contrast to his acumen as a businessman, had arranged his will hastily and without competent advice. Numerous court cases would ensue to sort out its contradictions and vagaries.

To George and Ian fell the lion's share. (There was, of course, no mention of the forgotten son, Edward.) They received a fifty per cent share of the capital in Howard & Bullough, and a Highland estate each. Curiously, five-year-old Ian was left the prize property of Meggernie, which had cost £150,000 at purchase, while the eldest son, George, was left Rum, half the land area, lacking any comfortable accommodation and which had recently cost a mere £35,000.

Why this bias? Is it possible that John had discovered an intimate relationship between George and Alexandra and this was his way of 'punishing' him? If so, then why was he so anxious to return to Accrington for George's birthday at the risk of his health? What seems more likely is that John appreciated how easy it was to love Meggernie over Rum. Perhaps he knew how much George appreciated the island and hoped he would 'make Rum do', whereas his infant son's preference was harder to gauge and for him it was safer to go with Meggernie. Whatever the reason, Ian inherited Meggernie and his mother Alexandra was allowed the enjoyment of it, but 'that enjoyment shall cease on the day that she shall marry again'.

So George inherited Rum and all that it contained, including the cutter *Mystery*. If he yearned for the island, it was not discernable. If he set foot on it over the next sixteen months, his visit is not recorded apart from one perfunctory pilgrimage. What he craved was freedom from all ties and obligations. Yet he was prepared to wait and settle matters properly. He had buried his father the day before his twenty-first birthday. He would bury him again within six months, and later for a third time before they could both rest in peace.

5

George Comes of Age

In the archaic and barely intelligible language of heraldry, the Bullough coat of arms is described in *Debrett's Peerage and Baronetage* as: 'Arms: Per chevron gules and erminois, a chevron counterflory argent, in chief two bull's heads caboshed of the last. Mantling gules and or . . .' In simpler words, set against a background of red and white foliage are a shield topped by a knight's helmet surmounted by what looks like a matron's extravagant hairstyle but is in fact a beehive. The shield is red and gold, divided by a white chevron and in the upper red half are two bull's heads, mouths agape as if bellowing. The knight's helmet is black with the visor open, and the tall beehive which grows out of it has three bees upright around its base and a larger one standing proud at the top. The bulls have obviously been rounded up from the family name to stand for strength and virility, while the bees represent industry. The coat of arms does not look particularly old, more like an artistic representation of tradition imbued with Victorian virtue.

Grandfather James, the founder of Howard & Bullough, would certainly have shown little interest in such frippery. Father John would probably have relished such decoration and might even have had it designed with himself represented as the queen bee on high. Yet despite his love of making speeches and his prominence as a leading businessman, he appears to have shunned the showy side of success. 'Any honour the town could give might have been his for the seeking,' preached the Reverend Greensill at the memorial service, 'but those who knew him best tell us that such honours he did not, and would not, seek'.

Son George, however, the quietest and most private of all, did value such things. A flashy coat of arms was a worthy accompaniment, if not a fundamental requirement, of a knighthood and entry into Debrett's. In his future castle he would hang this coat of arms and the Pedigree of Bullough. In the castle's huge Ratner safe, whose key was lost and which remained unopened until 1998 – fifty-nine years after his death – would be found some unexceptional glassware and two scrolls: the certification of his knighthood and that of his baronetcy. Sir George valued honours and status.

He was born in Accrington on 28 February 1870 at the family home, The Laund. It appears he may have learned some German from his mother, Bertha, because the odd German word (e.g. *wichtig* – 'important') appears in some of his travel telegrams. When he was two years old, his sister Bertha was born.* Around 1877 the family moved house a short distance to Oswaldtwistle, a town still proud of its identity but now joined to Accrington, where they rented Rhyddings Hall. (Neither of these homes exists today, though the grounds of Rhyddings Hall were presented to the public as a park which is still in use.) The house was a modest mansion with a secluded garden in open parkland. A permanent staff of around four cooked, cleaned, served and tended the grounds. George and Bertha enjoyed a privileged upbringing, but can have seen little of their father who was frequently travelling abroad, and they must have long been aware of their parents' acrimonious relationship. By 1879 their father had taken on the lease of Rum but it is unlikely that he ever took his young family there.

---

* The assumption that George learned German is supported by the fact that Bertha, who also shared an early exposure to their mother's native language, went on in later life to translate a German version of the classic *Danaid* into English. It was published in 1902 under her married name, Bertha Young.

The following year their mother was pregnant with Edward when she decamped to her father's home in Thun to bear the child. She returned for brief visits to attend to the formalities of her divorce, but had left England for good by 1883, when George was thirteen and Bertha eleven. Despite being the innocent party, Bertha was not given custody of her older children. Whether they ever saw her again is not known, but it seems likely that George would have visited her nine years later on a trip he made to the continent shortly after his father's death. What a devastating void this must have left in their young lives!

Then came the purchase of Meggernie in 1883, and the excitement of a new playground with its own castle and stables. This was followed soon afterwards by their father's second marriage and the introduction of a stepmother, only five years older than George himself. Yet he had little time to get to know her, for the week following the wedding in September 1884, aged fourteen, he was sent off for his first term at Harrow.

His textbooks can still be seen in the castle library. Clearly he found them tedious. *An Introduction to the Study of Greek* is covered in doodles. *White's English-Latin Dictionary* has a rash of ink blots and has been tortured with pencil perforations. He practised his signature twelve times and wrote his initials twenty-two times on the title page of Euclid's *Elements*. A simple ink sketch of a man racing a horse across the frontispiece of a *Public School Latin Primer* shows where his thoughts really were, on a theme that would prove central to his life.

George was tall for his age and supposedly 'made a reputation' at school for his love of sport and riding. Unfortunately many of Harrow's records from that period are missing or were destroyed. First team selections for rugby and cricket have survived, but nowhere does George feature in them. A love of sport does not necessarily indicate prowess in it, so it is possible George enjoyed taking part but did not excel. He must certainly have been a very competent rider and probably a reasonable shot, but such minority sports were seldom accorded the same status in

English public schools as rugby and cricket. Equally likely is that he played squash keenly enough, for later he would build a squash court on Rum. Neither has he left any trace of his academic ability. Probably he muddled along getting low passes. In keeping with his minimalist approach to writing later in life, he made no literary contributions to *The Harrovian*. However, one of his qualities *was* immortalised in song.

George joined The Grove (a boarding house) and his housemaster was Edward Bowen. Bowen had written the words to many of the school songs, including one called 'Giants' which he had composed in 1874. Sometime during George's schooldays he added the following extra verse for his house to sing:

> *There were singers of force and fire, you know,*
> *. . . With Bridgeman (C.) and with Bradley (O.),*
> *Who sang the carols of years ago,*
> *And best of the warblers here, Bullough!*
> *But we have the voice of a sulky crow,*
> *And shouldn't improve the choir!*

George left school in 1887. He was a striking figure, six foot five inches tall (some even say six foot eight inches), lean and unusually good-looking. Dark-haired and with the moustache of the period which accentuated a habitually serious expression, he poses in photographs with a strict sense of formality. His air is always self-assured but impatient, as if already bored with the interruption and wanting to move on. The eyes betray a spark of mischief, but of the wild, relaxed, laughing George known as the constant instigator of the most outrageous parties and drinking sprees, there is not an image to be found. The camera was clearly for recording respectability. He is dapper, always to be seen in suits of the most expensive cut or immaculate plus-fours, a man meticulous about his appearance. It is easy to imagine him on a horse or walking up a pheasant beat, impossible to visualise him in a rugby scrum or fording a bog. Yet obviously this is a façade, for later he would trek for weeks on horseback through rugged stretches of New Zealand, and wade through Indian swamps in pursuit of game. The serious exterior does not reflect the inner life. He probably had to learn to act a part as a defence against his father.

The accepted story is that after leaving school George joined the cavalry and became an officer in the Scottish Horse. The Scottish Horse was not formed until towards the end of the Boer War in 1901, so this is patently wrong. Neither did he join any other regiment. Instead he succumbed to what must surely have been his father's wishes, and took on an apprenticeship in the company he was being groomed to inherit. The *Accrington Observer* would later report: 'As a youth he spent a considerable part of his time in the works doing the duties of an ordinary apprentice so as to acquire a practical knowledge of the business.' Such an approach would fit in with John Bullough's style of management.

Being the eldest son, George doubtless carried the hopes and expectations of his father that he would follow the family footsteps into the business. The choice of Harrow as a school seems unusual in this respect. Whereas John himself was sent to a school specialising in science and technical skills, he selected a school better known for making gentlemen and building connections between the rich and noble for his son. Probably he hoped that the technical skills would come later. The outcome was a disappointment. George showed scant aptitude, let alone interest, in managing the empire his father and grandfather had nurtured from nothing. In the final version of his will, signed three months before his death, John acknowledged the futility of expecting George to cope with it. He specified that the Globe Works was 'to be sold or converted into a limited liability company and the whole of the money accruing shall be divided equally between my son George and my son Ian'.

This then was the situation on George's twenty-first birthday, the day after his father's funeral. His apprenticeship at the Globe Works ended instantly. As co-owner of the business with his five-year-old step-brother, he was now in charge. Following his father's recommendation, he gave instructions for Howard

& Bullough, as it was still officially known, to be turned into a private company limited by guarantee. (The conversion was completed that August.) He and his brother did not sell out, but retained their controlling interests.

Aside from this he appears to have told the managers just to carry on as they had been doing before, and left them to it. In these men John Bullough had chosen well. Many were later ranked amongst Accrington's greatest 'Captains of Industry': names such as E. W. Horne, who served for thirty years, T. Gordon, forty years, Alfred Hitchon, W. Smith, John Redman and the indefatigable company secretary, Joe 'Brentwood' Grimshaw. Grimshaw's correspondence fills two fat ledgers, at first as facsimiles in flowery italics and later as typed carbon copies, and ranges in subject from dealing with orders to dispatching cigarettes and cigars to George at Meggernie.*

The census of 5 April 1891 shows Rhyddings Hall was occupied by a somewhat pathetic family group of George ('Head of Household, Occupation: Machinist'), his three-year-old half-sister Gladys and two favourite cousins who were visiting, Tom and William. They are outnumbered by a staff consisting of Gladys' German nurse, a cook, waitress, kitchen-maid and two housemaids. There is no mention of Alexandra and Ian. George's full sister, Bertha, is also absent, but this is not surprising because she had been intent on carving out a life of her own away from her disrupted family. Two weeks after the census, aged nineteen, she married Charles Young of Melbourn, Cambridge, and slipped – thankfully, one imagines – out of the Bullough saga and into a more stable environment.

For George there followed what must have been a period of adjustment to the realisation of his new responsibilities, and to finding the quickest way of off-loading them. He acquired a personal secretary, Robert Mitchell from Keighley, who, over the best part of a decade, would be George's constant companion

---

* Typewriters are being used occasionally with carbon copies in 1891, and have largely replaced handwriting by 1894.

and chronicler of their extraordinary journeys across the globe. Mitchell must have worked at Howard & Bullough and may well have been John Bullough's personal secretary prior to being delegated to George, for he is mentioned in the introduction to *John Bullough's Speeches*. 'I must here thank Mr Mitchell for his very kind assistance in collecting the speeches ... Alec Bullough'. Mitchell was thirteen years older than George and the only photograph in which he can be readily identified shows him to be a squat figure with a face tending towards jowls, a thin layer of receding hair combed back and the heaviest of walrus moustaches. He too looks serious and presents the phlegmatic air of authority expected of the English abroad, but the impression may be tainted by the fact that he is sitting in a howdah on the back of an Indian elephant.

Doubtless it was Mitchell who organised George's 'Coming of Age' party for Howard & Bullough's workforce on 5 September, some six months after the event. Everyone was given the day off, two shillings and sixpence spending money (one shilling and sixpence if under twenty-one) and a return ticket for a day at Blackpool. Bunting flew, brass and 'Do-da' bands played (including a special rendering of 'A fine old English gentleman' as a tribute), and 2,000 workers boarded three trains for what was heralded as Accrington's 'greatest picnic' ever. The English gentleman didn't attend. He was stalking at Meggernie.

There are only two references to Rum around this time, 1891, the first being an announcement in the papers that, for the first time in its history, and apparently at George's 'insistence', a post office was to be opened on the island in May. As George had owned the island for less than three months and negotiations for a new post office must have been more protracted than that, either the credit must go to his father or George had been managing the island as part of his wider 'apprenticeship'.

The second, in *The Blackburn Standard,* is a report that shortly before midnight on Sunday 2 August, under conditions of secrecy, John Bullough's coffin was removed from an Accrington graveyard and reached Rum two days later.

6

When My Bones Are Laid To Rest

John Bullough's coffin had been placed in the family vault at Christ Church. In his will he did not leave instructions about where he wished to be buried, but in one of his poems, though not expressly concerned with the disposal of his earthly remains, he is clear about the place he would like to haunt.

> *When my bones are laid to rest,*
> *God grant me one request,*
> *That my spirit still may dwell*
> *In the Isle I love so well.*

This doggerel was written on the west beat of Meggernie in August 1889. George Bullough appears to have given this poem priority as an indication of where his father should be buried. He overlooked the fact that John had shunned Rum for the last three years of his life in preferring Meggernie, and the later poem called 'The River Lyon', one of the last ones he wrote, on 11 August 1890, states explicitly where he would like his final resting place to be. It concludes:

> *When brooding cares around me gather,*
> *And life's whole span is arched in gloom,*
> *Let me by that river wander,*
> *And on its banks, oh! build my tomb.*

So it was river versus isle, and isle won. On the southwest side of Rum lies the abandoned settlement of Harris, the principal township before the clearances. It is the most fertile ground on the island, a green cloak wrinkled by lazybeds sweeping down from the mountains to a long and prominent raised beach, and, fifty feet below it, lies a rocky shore once prized for its role as a source of driftwood. It is a beautiful spot, but exposed to the prevailing wind, which can reach storm speeds of over 120 mph. This was where George had shot his first stag and it remained his favourite part of the island. Here he chose to build a mausoleum for his father.

Near the north end of the bay was a rock face suitable for excavating a 'subterranean groin vault', effectively a horizontal tunnel in the shape of a cross. Allegedly, it was thirty feet high and eighteen feet across the transepts, though the visible remains suggest a much smaller structure built against the hillside, not into it. The interior was faced in the palest of blue tiles and colourful mosaics depicting floral patterns and the monogram 'JB'. An iron grid sealed the entrance. To have completed an enterprise of this scale in a remote area within six months was an astonishing feat and George must have begun the work immediately upon his father's death.

On 4 August 1891, John Bullough's body reached Rum aboard the *Hebrides* and was placed in a sarcophagus at the centre of the vault. The Bishop of Argyll and the Islands performed a service and George presented him with a silver cross in gratitude.

The *Oban Times* made scant reference to the event – perhaps bodies were always passing here and there through its streets – but fortunately New Zealand's newspapers took more interest in the island. One in 1902 refers to this mausoleum, saying it cost £50,000 and used only the finest Italian ceramics. The reference is in a gossip column, so its reliability is dubious. However, the groin vault proved to be a short-lived resting place. John Bullough's travels were not over yet.

7

Illicit Affair and Escape

What is clear is that after his father's death George preferred his step-brother's inheritance to his own and was spending most of his time at Meggernie. He was there for the grouse shooting in August 1891, for the autumn stalking and for his cousin Tom's wedding, which the castle hosted that October. Alexandra would have been there too. Meggernie, after all, was her home.

What of the suspected relationship between the two? George was tall, elegant and extremely handsome. At eighteen, say, he would have been a typical hot-blooded youth confined to a boring routine and living at home. His stepmother would have been twenty-three, married to a much older man who spent considerable periods of time away from home. She was attractive and lively, and probably lonely. The opportunities and incentives for them becoming clandestine lovers were undoubtedly there. None of the Bullough men were conventional according to the social mores of the time. That there was such an intimate bond between George and Alexandra may have been based on nothing but gossip but I suspect there was fire beyond the smoke.

It seems to me unlikely that the relationship, if it took place while John Bullough was alive, was discovered by him. He does not come across as someone so forgiving as to treat a faithless wife and treacherous son generously in his will, nor to have forsaken a trip for his health to be there for the latter's 'coming of age' party when the event had already been celebrated in his absence, and at his expense. If they were lovers before the old man's death, they kept their secret intact. After this they had all the freedom they wanted to share each other's company away from the eyes of servants and Alexandra's young children. If their chemistry and personalities matched it might be more realistic to assume that a passionate bond was inevitable rather than just possible.

In November 1891 George and Mitchell departed on their first 'grand tour', which, according to one of Joe Grimshaw's letters, involved 'travelling on the Continent in connection with business'. The business element was the official line which bore no resemblance to George's intentions. His father's empty office be damned – he was out to experience life and enjoy himself. The itinerary is unknown but it may have taken in a few mills besides the pleasures of Europe, and probably included a visit to his mother, who had remarried and moved to Dresden.

The travellers returned some eight months later at the end of July 1892. By the Glorious Twelfth they were at Meggernie, and Grimshaw had been instructed to despatch to them '12 boxes (50 in each) of cigars and 6 boxes (100 in each) of cigarettes'. With 1200 smokes on hand, the party spirit was obviously taking hold.

Any relationship George had with Alexandra must have cooled during his long winter tour and – unless new levels of promiscuity were involved – been terminated by the next development. In early May 1892 Alexandra became engaged to Lieutenant-Colonel John Beech, marrying him on 1 December at St John's, Princes Street, Edinburgh. By the terms of the will her enjoyment of Meggernie terminated on that day and she moved out of the castle into Fasgath Lodge on the edge of the estate. Presumably little Ian and Gladys moved with her, though the comings and goings between Fasgarth and Ian's inheritance-in-trust must have been frequent. This may have left George as the nominal trustee looking after his step-brother's interests, but he was not about to let any such commitments stand in the way of his next project. His plans had been hatching for some time. He and Mitchell were about to set off for as long as it took to see the world. By the time Alexandra remarried, they were gone.

There were a few last minute details to see to, one shedding light on the employment of servants. On 24 September Grimshaw wrote to Mitchell at Meggernie seeking clarification that George had 'taken out licence for four servants at Meggernie'. A Mr J Scott of Ballinluig was enquiring and threatening prosecution if the matter was not resolved. Grimshaw's next letter is to Mr Scott advising him that 'Mr Mitchell had taken out licences for 3 carriages (2 of which are here & 1 was sent up to Meggernie) and 2 dogs, but had omitted to take one out for the gardeners'. A third letter applies for licences for '2 male gardeners to put the matter right'.

With Grimshaw adding these administrative duties to his role as company secretary, George then arranged power of attorney over his affairs to be invested in his cousins Tom and William, along with his solicitor, Charles Costeker of Darwen. Tom was to prove another strong personality in the subsequent family history, his expensive lifestyle falling far short of George's but being its nearest rival. However he combined this with loyalty to Howard & Bullough, regularly attending meetings and warming a seat in the office in his capacity as chairman.

By then Howard & Bullough was the world's largest producer of ring spindles, having sold millions of them since John Bullough had acquired the patent. Created a private limited company in 1891, three years later it became a public limited company. It was exporting machinery to countries as far afield as Brazil, Russia and India, and was about to open a factory in Rhode Island, USA. Yet there was no room for complacency, as competition for business was hotly contested. Messrs Brooks & Doxey, Dobson & Barlow and the Platt Brothers, to name a few, supplied much of the domestic market, and had the lion's share of the overseas market. These competitors might be paying Howard & Bullough royalty fees, but this was not enough to secure the company's future. H&B appeared to be holding their own in India, but the market was expanding rapidly and their rivals were in there vying for such business as that of Jacob Sassoon's Bombay Mill, 'which, when full, will contain 100,000 spindles and 2,000 looms'. Japan too was opening up to foreigners, but H&B's representation there was poor. Of the first ten mills operating in the 'Celestial Empire' (China), where expansion was described as 'something like phenomenal', H&B's machinery was found in only one. Sales were to increase rapidly in the mid-1890s, but in the early part of the decade the picture was anything but rosy.

If George Bullough packed an order book in his luggage for the impending world tour, then it can scarcely have been exposed to the light of exotic lands. Nevertheless, he must have sold the idea that this was a sales trip to Grimshaw, at least. Shortly after George and Mitchell departed, Grimshaw – perhaps sarcastically, because he was no fool – penned a letter to Mitchell. It is dated 1 December 1892, but no address is given (though it transpires the travellers were in Bombay at the time). 'I often wonder how you are getting on,' he begins, somewhat enviously. He continues with details of bank transfers on their behalf, and devotes a paragraph to how gloomy the business outlook is. He ends: 'Trusting that this finds you & Mr George in the best of health and good spirits ... and that your sojourn round the World may prove beneficial to Howard & Bullough Ltd, with kindest regards to both of you, Joe Grimshaw.'

In the sixteen months since George's father had died, he had spent eight months abroad and around five months at Meggernie. He would do anything, it seems, to avoid Accrington and the Globe Works. (Years later, when he compiled his entry for *Who's Who*, there would not be a single mention of Howard & Bullough or any business interests.) Now he was setting out on a journey that would last a little short of three years. His annual income was said to be around £300,000, a self-perpetuating fortune of scarcely imaginable proportions. He was twenty-two years and six months old.

8

The World Tour, 1892–1895

George Bullough's world tour has long been shrouded in mystery. For decades visitors to Kinloch Castle have been shown twenty beautifully-bound photograph albums containing 740 images. Slightly under two hundred of these are not photographs but etchings printed as postcards. The remaining 553 images are mostly full-plate (6 ½″ x 8 ½″) *contact* prints; no enlargement took place, the prints are the same size as the original glass negatives. This has produced photographs of outstanding detail and quality, superior to anything the average camera today will create. Almost every one has a caption, but only a handful specify a date (1894 or 1895). They appear to be ordered in the sequence of a journey rather than strictly chronologically. There are two sections of blank pages annotated in pencil 'For Karachi' and 'For Madeira' and there are odd mistakes: a scene from Jaipur has ended up in Malaysia, and that familiar post-holiday amnesia ('Where on earth did we see that?') has struck over the Iolani Palace in Honolulu, which has been called 'Palace, Batavia'. The collection depicts famous landmarks, scenery, streets, buildings, customs and portraits. Commonly recurring themes are battle memorials or sites of atrocities, and modes of punishment. One remarkable aspect is that, although some of the world's largest and most progressive city centres are shown in detail, there is not a single motorised vehicle to be seen, and only a few bicycles.

The baffling aspects of this journey centre largely on when it took place, the exact route, the means of transport and the striking absence of anything personal in the photographic content. Castle visitors have always been told that George, having been caught in bed with his stepmother, was banished by his father on a world voyage in the family yacht, the 221-foot *Rhouma*, returning three years later on his father's death. If the journey ended on his father's death (1891), how can he have brought back photographs dated 1895? If he took his own photographer, why is it that George can be identified in only two out of 553 images? If he travelled in *Rhouma*, why is there not a single image of the ship when there are numerous other steamships featured? Did the photographs represent not one grand world tour but several smaller ones?

Shipping registration records proved frustrating as many have inexplicable gaps in the relevant years, but eventually I confirmed that *Rhouma* was purchased by George on 7 October 1895. Yet the *Game Books* on Rum showed George 'sporting' each autumn from 1895 onwards, which excludes the possibility of an extensive voyage to such far-flung destinations as Japan and Hawaii. He was, however, absent from the *Game Books* during the first five years of the 1890s.

Some of the photographs depict hotels, so I emailed the ones still in existence (remarkably there were four) asking if, by chance, they still had visitors' books from that period. Only the manager of the Fujiya Hotel in Japan responded: 'I found his signature as G. Bullough on May 28th–May 31st, 1895. He stayed in the same room as Robb Mitchell. The room was number 40 or 41.' This laborious detective work was rendered obsolete by a visit to Accrington Library, where Catherine Duckworth (see acknowledgements) mentioned that there was a large collection of newspaper articles a colleague had recently discovered on George Bullough's world tour. She produced copies, and suddenly the journey snapped into focus. At least the first third did.

Between 2 May and 12 December 1896 the [*Accrington*] *Gazette* ran a weekly series of reports on the tour, several months after its conclusion. The first was written by a journalist who admitted that initially George Bullough had been reluctant to allow any details to be published, but had relented. The journalist summarises the route and then describes the exotic souvenirs now to be found in Rhyddings Hall. Thereafter each article is reproduced verbatim after a standard introduction: 'Mr Robert Mitchell, continuing the description of his tour with Mr Bullough, said: ...'

It was the newspaper's intention to cover the whole journey, but after twenty-six episodes, covering one year of their travels, the feature was terminated without explanation. The editor's decision is not surprising. Robb (as he appears to sign himself) Mitchell's reports start with entertaining descriptions and show great interest in everything he experiences but lapse more and more into heavy treatises on history and politics. Mitchell was a Tory – a companion chosen by George to reflect perfectly the views he was immersed in as an adolescent and had adopted from his father – and was writing for a Tory newspaper, but his views progress towards an extreme that may have proved too rabid for general consumption. However, his observations constitute a vivid social comment on the times and illuminate in quirky detail a world long gone. And given that his employer consented to these articles, it is fair to assume that Robb Mitchell's words found a common resonance in the character and mindset of George Bullough himself.

Passenger lists indicate that a valet, W. Cockburn, may have been present for some stages of the journey, but the newspaper articles never mention him. On 29 September 1892 the two, possibly three, travellers went to Gravesend and boarded the ss *Oceana*, 'one of the most comfortable and best equipped steamers running to the Australian colonies'.

* * *

Ceylon, India

Mr Robert Mitchell, continuing the description of his tour with Mr Bullough, said: . . .

> It may be interesting to mention that the crews carried by the P. and O. boats are composed of coloured sailors, called Lascars, whose appearance added much to the picturesque scene. The whistle (siren) is blown three times as a signal, for those who have to return to the shore, to depart . . . many touching farewells taking place around one which would stir the feelings of the hardest hearted man . . . we steamed slowly down the river, amidst the waving of hats and handkerchiefs, and ringing cheers, which were alternately repeated from on shore and aboard.
> . . . [Amongst the purser's duties was] to arrange the seats at table. This latter is most trying of all; for, in spite of balloting for places, there is always an endless amount of arranging, changing, and grumbling, especially among a certain class of passengers, who always want to sit at 'The Captain's Table'.

Once in open sea many passengers felt queasy, but Mitchell reported smugly:

> Having the good fortune never to be seasick, we were able to appear on deck every day, and to fully enjoy the trip . . . The indefatigable Purser called a meeting of the passengers, and an 'amusement committee' was formed. The Admiral of the Australian Station, Admiral Bowden Smith . . . was chosen Chairman of the Committee, Mr Bullough was elected a member, and I was selected to act as hon. sec. £90 was raised in subscriptions, and this sum was devoted to defraying the expenses of concerts, and formed also the prize fund for the sports which were instituted and lasted until the end of the voyage. A gratifying feature in this matter is the fact that 10 per cent of the money raised is handed over to seamen's philanthropic organizations . . . Tournaments were inaugurated, including all games playable on board, chess, draughts, etc, there being 14 different competitions on at the same time, giving the passengers constant employment and entertainment.

In the evening he was gratified to note that passengers 'always appeared at the dinner table in evening dress'.

They stopped briefly at Gibraltar, where a coal hulk caught fire and almost torched the *Oceana*, narrowly drifting by to become stranded on the Algeciras shore where it burned for three days. Their passage across the Mediterranean was calm and pleasant except for the scorching sirocco wind. They made stops at Malta and Brindisi, the latter being the collection point for oriental mail which was sent overland from Britain. They found Port Said 'as miserable a hole as can be found ... The great feature of Port Said is its coaling ... Up and down these planks the natives run with the coal, which is carried in small sacks, in one continuous stream, yelling and singing as they go. When seen at night, as we saw it, amidst the glare of huge torches, it looked like a veritable inferno, and the howling of these black beings flitting about made the scene even more uncanny.'

They passed through the 99-mile-long Suez Canal, which had been in use since 1869 but had not accepted the ships of all nations until 1888, and which, as Mitchell remarked, 'reduced the distance from London to India from 11,379 miles to 7,628 miles'. The heat of the Red Sea proved oppressive on the 1,200-mile leg to Aden.

> As an example of the discomfort, one gentleman, in dressing for dinner, had to change his collar three times in five minutes, and the meals were gone through in a state of perspiration which would have been intolerable were it not for gentle puffs of wind caused by the Punkhas. The Punkha is a machine for fanning a room ...
>
> Arriving at Aden our Indian passengers and mails were transhipped to smaller boats for Bombay.* Here, as at Aden, the swarming natives came round the ship in their little canoes ... These small boys are magnificent swimmers and divers. For a sixpence any youth will dive from the upper deck right under the ship.

---

* To remain true to the original source I am preserving Mitchell's rendering of place names even though many of these, particularly in India, have shed their colonial connotations and changed.

Mitchell and Bullough were heading for Ceylon.

During the voyage to Colombo two fancy dress balls, besides ordinary dances, took place on board, and it was really astonishing what admirable fancy dresses were worn ... The dresses had to be made out of almost anything that came to hand, yet everyone, with the exception of the skipper, wore fancy dress, and the scene on deck, which was specially decorated with flags and lighted by electricity, was brilliant in the extreme.

Athletic sports were also held on board before we got to Ceylon. The sports were of especial excellence owing to the large number of good athletes on board, some of whom had just come from Oxford and Cambridge, and were on their way to the Colonies. The sports of course included events for both ladies and gentlemen, and were keenly contested throughout. Perhaps the most amusing and interesting even to the general passenger was the obstacle race and this is also one of the most difficult competitions. Starting from a line, the competitors have to first climb through a suspended life buoy, then creep under a piece of sail cloth which is tightly nailed to the deck; suspended barrels have next to be passed through, after which a wind shoot (and some of these are thirty feet long) is met. A wind shoot, I may explain, is used to convey fresh air to the firemen and engineers working below, and is circular in form, being like a long sack without bottom. The shoot is besmeared inside with flour or soot, and to creep through all this flour and soot without losing one's breath is not a very easy matter, and a laughable sight is presented to the spectators when the competitors emerge – black or white – from the end. The final and most amusing obstacle, however, is a huge butt of water, which is placed at the bottom of one of the companion ladders. The men coming down the ladder have to plunge into the butt and swim across, being played upon all the time by a sailor with a hose pipe. The exertion required and the pitiful objects the competitors present after the obstacle race is sufficient evidence as to the difficulties they have to face. The sports included the usual potato races, egg and spoon races, putting the weight, flat races, etc.

We had a most enjoyable passage from Aden to Colombo, reaching the latter port on October 23rd, 1892.

They stayed at the Grand Oriental Hotel (still going but now far from grand) and had a wretched night owing to heat and mosquitoes. But Ceylon's tropical foliage 'made it look like a land of paradise'. There were some difficulties, however, resulting from the 'peculiar dress of the native Cingalese ... The men are of a very effeminate cast of features, and wear white flowing robes, so that to an unpractised eye they are really very difficult to distinguish from women.' They, of course, avoided such confusion: 'The clothes worn here by Englishmen are trousers and coat (no vest), made of white cotton, or thin flannel and a hat called a tope ... made of pith, is of a light colour, often white, and constructed as to protect the nape of the neck from the sun ... If a man wants to go across the street he hails a Gharry, as the vehicles are called.'

Another 'very easy and comfortable way of travelling about Colombo is by vehicles called jhinrickshaws (usually called "-rickshaws"). They are like a two-wheeled perambulator [and] are dragged about by native "Rickshaw boys", as they are termed, and it is really surprising what a lot of ground they can cover in a day ... Rickshaw boys have been known to drag a person 60 and 70 miles in a day in one of these machines.'

Their city tours were to develop a pattern which included visits to any available racecourses and botanical gardens. Bullough's interest in trees and flowers was profound, and may well have been inspired (through Bertha) by his grandfather, Eduard Schmidlin. They admired the 'beautiful yellow alamanders, the lovely purple bougainvilleas' on the road to Mount Lavinia, passing 'through small villages, which are swarming with native children, who run about almost naked, and follow every carriage as fast as their little legs can carry them, begging for pennies.' Here they had lunch and made an observation which indicated that Bullough was already collecting design ideas for his future castle. 'The hotel at Mount Lavinia is famous for its Sunday lunches ... Live turtles are kept on the premises, so that a fastidious eater can choose his own turtle for his soup.'

They also discovered a new drink. 'It is very interesting to watch the natives climb the high cocoa nut trees and extract the milk from the nuts. The milk is fermented into a kind of spirit called toddy, which is drunk by the natives when they are on a spree. The manufacture and sale of this "Toddy" is under Government supervision. Even the trees on which the nuts are grown are marked for duty purposes.'

They embarked on the dizzy feat of engineering that is the Colombo to Kandy railway, peering into 'a gorge over 1,000 ft deep' and admiring views fragmented into tiered paddy fields below and tea plantations above. From Kandy they made a horseback tour of tea plantations and then 'visited the famous Peradeniya Botanical Gardens, which cover 150 acres, and are said to be the second finest in the East (some claiming that the Batavia Botanical Gardens are the first).' This was followed by a walk to 'the Buddhist temple, where Buddha's tooth is exhibited once a year to the people who flock in thousands. This tooth is held in the highest veneration, and is about two inches long, judging from which Buddha must have had a pretty big mouth, and a very rough time of it when troubled with toothache.'

On Friday November 4 we went aboard the British India steamer 'Taroba' which was to carry us to Madras. Arriving on board, we found no less than 20 missionaries, along with their wives and children, who had come from America, and were bound for rural Bengal to Christianise the natives. [One of these] in the course of his remarks said they had left America for ever, and were going to live and die in India. Curiously enough, two years after this we met this very same ship in Colombo Harbour [and asked the captain about the missionaries]; 'Oh, yes,' he said, 'the American missionaries didn't like Bengal – they have all gone back except two, and these are aboard my ship now, on their way home.'

They stayed with friends in Madras, 'the third city of the Empire in size and importance. 'The chief streets are wide, and well planted with trees, especially in the European quarter ...

There is a splendid gymkhana club and a good racecourse.' Gaining temporary membership of the Madras Club, 'which is only for males … and reckoned the finest in the East', they were introduced to the city's leading residents, occasionally meeting the fairer sex at the Adyar Club, 'for some very good times in the evening boating and dancing.' On a less salubrious note, 'Here in Madras we noticed for the first time that peculiar disease known as Elephantiasis.'

> Whilst sitting on the verandah of our friend's bungalow, we were visited by an Indian 'juggler'. Pulling out of his basket a small worsted ball, about one and half inches in diameter, he made a few passes and mystic signs, and in the space of a very few seconds he produced from this ball of worsted a plain handkerchief, which he held over the ball, and a pretty little bird cage with about 12 very tiny and beautiful birds inside. These jugglers have loose sleeves, bare to the elbows, and perform their tricks within two feet of their audience, so that the latter have a good chance of seeing how the tricks are done. But they don't discover them … In [another] trick he took packets of red, white and blue sand, mixed them all together, and put them into his mouth. He would then blow from his mouth either absolutely white, red, or blue sand, whichever was asked for.

From Madras they headed south on their first experience of Indian trains, hanging their water bottles wrapped in wet flannels out of the carriage window. 'Of all the arrangements that run on wheels, the Southern Indian Railway stands pre-eminent for its speed. It crawls along at the wonderful rate of about nine miles an hour, when it does not stop to rest, and if anyone is troubled with a mania for travelling by train, they could not do better than try this line.' They visited temples, suffered 23 mosquito bites on their feet alone one night and then undertook one of the most dangerous sorties of their entire trip – a night journey by cart through bandit country.

> Our host told us the route from Tinnevelly to the foot of the Travancore Hills, where we were going, had been in times past

infested with Dacoits, and was not yet altogether free from these robbers. He asked us if we had any arms, and we replied in the negative, having left our arms in Madras. We told him we had only got two walking-sticks, and he said he thought we should get there all right but as for himself, he always carried a revolver ... We were met by a man who had two bullock bandies (carts) ready to convey us to our destination, a distance of 23 miles. The night was pitch dark. Packing our luggage in one bandy, and ourselves in the other we started our journey, having only one small oil lamp to each bandy. [Ours] was barely large enough for the two of us, and we could only just lie down side by side, packed like sardines, our feet dangling over the hinder part of the cart – a position anything but comfortable, and one which absolutely prevented us from getting anything like sleep ...

After journeying for some time they were accosted by a group of men brandishing sticks who stopped the carts and argued with the driver. Fearing for their lives, the two Europeans started to drive them away with their sticks and the two drivers joined in. George Bullough at six foot five inches must have made an impressive sight lashing out, for 'the whole of the men, about nine in number, took to their heels. We [reached safety], having done the 23 miles in a little over four hours, which constituted a record for that style of travelling in the district.'

In a club which resembled a 'superannuated hen pen' the pair had a hot tub and travelled to Bangalore, where they bumped into some fellow passengers from the *Oceana*:

the Viceroy's son and his friend, who informed us that they had just come from Mysore where they had been entertained by the Maharajah of that state to a series of hunting expeditions, during which they had each of them been lucky enough to kill a tiger. These vice-regal shooting parties are, however, very different to the ordinary ones ... hundreds of men are earlier sent out into the jungle who thoroughly search the district until they come across the tigers which are then driven into a convenient district and a cordon of men set round about to prevent the animals disappearing. The place is then driven by beaters, and the guests being placed in good positions seldom or never fail to get some sport. The case of the ordinary sportsman is very different indeed, for, having provided himself with men, tents, etc he may search the jungle weeks, or it may be for months, before he is lucky enough to get a shot.

Howard & Bullough had been supplying Gokak Water Mill since its founding about five years earlier, and this was Bullough and Mitchell's next stop, having been invited to stay by the owner, Mr Kerr. It proved to be a most unusual place overlooking magnificent waterfalls.

Scores of miles away from any European civilisation, Mr Kerr has by his own energy, ability and ingenuity used the forces of nature in such a way that he has turned a dense wild jungle, inhabited a few years ago only by wild beasts, into a thriving little community, which is most complete and unique. The machinery and iron materials used in the buildings have all been dragged for hundreds of miles by bullocks over a country without roads, and which in the rainy season was absolutely impassable for any heavy traffic ... In spite of all this, Gokak can boast a mill, lit by the electric light, which would grace any Lancashire town, a suspension bridge, of which any eminent engineer might well be proud, a system of rope driving as well laid out as anything we have in Britain ... Special provision has been made by him to supply the village with good, clean, pure drinking water ... A medical dispensary, under the charge of a specially qualified native, is open to all the villagers, a school where English is taught ... This genial gentleman has so inspired the people with a sense of his high character ... that the children and grown-up natives gather round when he goes out for a walk, to try and touch the hem of his coat, hold his hand ... more in the light of a god than a man ... It is just such examples as these which give England her wonderful power in foreign countries, and make her, what she undoubtedly is, the greatest colonizing power the world has ever seen.

So impressed was Bullough that on his return to England he bought shares in the mill.* It was a happy time for him, 'sitting

---

* Gokak Mill is still working and is one of the most modern mills in India.

on the verandah ... watching the hundreds of monkeys of all sizes playing about on the rocks, and in the garden ... also to see the vultures, blue-rock pigeons and hawks flying continually overhead; to hear the scream of the wild peacock and grunt of the wild pig, and look down the 300 ft into the river below and watch the crocodiles at play'. Despite the brutal needle grass which invaded their clothes and skin, they spent most of the time hunting with the guns they carried in their luggage. 'One day report came that a buffalo had been seen some little distance away. Our host immediately accompanied us, and after an exciting crawl through the thick undergrowth the brute was brought down by Mr Bullough's rifle; a very pretty and rare deer also rewarded our efforts that day. Unfortunately we were not in luck's way as regards panthers.'* A monkey was also shot here and skinned, joining other trophies sent back to England for later installation in Rhyddings Hall and Rum.

The railway line from Poona to Bombay was another 'marvel of zigzags, a reversing station and eight viaducts in its 119-mile length, and costing, we are told, an average of £41,188 per mile.' In Bombay they visited the Yacht Club, 'the most beautiful of all', where a fine military band played on the lawn three times a week. They spent days riding ponies round the Ghaut mountains near the 'well-known sanatorium "Matheran"', and visited the Bombay Natural History Museum. The Chief Director showed them a 26-foot python having its fortnightly meal, a live drake, and his collection of cobras, which revealed another cruel custom:

> Occasionally it is necessary to advertise for cobras for the museum. In this case the natives invariably bring their specimens with their lips sewn up ... The cobra having been purchased, then comes the difficulty and danger of undoing the stitches,

---

* Indian panthers are actually melanistic leopards with varying degrees of spots and varying shades of darkness. There are estimated to be 14,000 leopards remaining in India today, some in national parks but the rest in shrinking habitats. Indian tigers are also an endangered species.

and this the director said was the most difficult and dangerous thing he had to do.

One evening we had the pleasure of dining with one of the greatest big game shots in India ... We counted no less than 50 tiger skulls on his sideboard, and saw some of the finest heads of buffalo, and some other big game, that have ever been shot. The chairs and carpets were furnished with skins of tigers, panthers, bears, wolves and other kinds of big game. In the middle of one large room he had constructed a splendid piece of rock work, with flowing water, in which he had half a dozen young crocodiles, whose habits he was studying ... Only a very small portion of these trophies were in these rooms, the greater part of them having been sent to his home in Scotland. [He was not named.]

For all his wealth, Bullough apparently declined to follow the usual practice of his race: 'Most English people travelling in India hire a native servant whom they call their "boy" to accompany them on their travels, and he pilots them through the country. We, however, preferred to pilot ourselves, and managed very well indeed.'

And so they piloted themselves to Jeypoor, where Mitchell once again demonstrated an obsession with the width of streets. Usually he was content to label them narrow or wide, but here he excelled himself. 'Jeypoor, the capital of Rajputana, is a splendidly laid out city. Its main streets are 37 yards wide, the side streets are 18 yards in width, and even the back streets or slums are fully nine yards wide. Thousands of natives with their many-coloured clothes thread their way amongst scores of bullock carts, horses, camels, elephants and donkeys ...' The grounds of the local palace they found stocked with 'three hundred horses, each horse having a groom, who sleeps in a recess in the wall just above the manger. Besides these there are some 80 elephants, and some hunting cheetahs and leopards, all of which, together with his troops, join in the processions when the Maharajah is out on state occasions.'

One of the Maharajah's chief advisers 'gave us a real Indian dinner, which he served himself. This dinner consisted of about ten courses of sweetmeats ... So sickly was this ... the feat became an ordeal which we prayed might soon come to an end.' After dinner they were treated to a performance of the celebrated Nautch Dance.

> Four of the Maharajah's best girls had been procured for the occasion, and were supposed to be very beautiful and talented. As far as their beauty was concerned, I am afraid we did not appreciate it, and as regards their dancing, it did not appeal to us in the slightest degree. The dancer simply uses one foot to mark time, and turns herself slowly round while the other is kept on the ground.
>
> Having obtained permission from the British Resident, who kindly placed one of the biggest of the Maharajah's elephants at our disposal, we spent one day on a visit to the ancient City of Amber ... Our elephant was awaiting us, covered with a magnificent cloth, and carrying a seat called a houdah to carry four. Mounted on this huge beast we began to climb up the hill. It may here be incidentally remarked that although we were wearing sun hats to prevent sunstroke, the weather was so cold that we were obliged to wear our thickest overcoats.

Two photographs were taken of the party and these are the only two in the collection in which Bullough and Mitchell have been identified. There they are in ties, waistcoats and overcoats, wearing their sun hats in one picture and removing them for the second. Only on a few occasions during the entire journey do they appear to have a personal photographer, and the likelihood is that either one of their hosts had a camera or they hired a local photographer, as the profession was growing in popularity. For the most part Bullough purchased images sold in the neighbourhood of most tourist centres. In India they bought many taken by Bourne & Shepherd, a much-published duo whose work now constitutes the most detailed archive among early photographers in the sub-continent.

The journey continued to Agra, where they stayed at Laurie's Great Northern Hotel and met 'a party of jovial bookmakers, who had come over from England to Calcutta to earn an honest penny at the races' and were enjoying a break sightseeing. The Taj Mahal was a never-to-be-forgotten 'poem in marble', and in a shop they spotted a 'representation of the Taj, worked in red plush with silk and gold. This single piece had occupied several workers nearly five years. It was intended to send it to the Chicago Exhibition, the price being £400.' George didn't hesitate and added it to his collection.

In Delhi the pair risked a Turkish Bath, where

the visitor is treated in a manner he is not likely to forget. As soon as he enters a stalwart attendant takes full possession of him. These native attendants are very wiry and strong, and instead of rubbing with their hand they use the soles of their feet, which, being about as rough as the soles of tennis shoes, make a great impression. To say that these men roll the subjects up into almost every conceivable position, knead, skate, and slide over all parts of the body, and then finish up by pounding them out of breath, would only give one a bare idea.

Sadly, the photographs of Karachi are missing. They might have included some of the frenzied scenes encountered on a day trip into the Khyber Pass.

Caravans to and from India go through twice a week in times of peace, but at the time of our visit relations between the Ameer of Afghanistan and the Indian Government had been somewhat strained, and no caravans had passed through for a least three weeks ... we made our application at once to Col R Warburton, the Commissioner for the Khyber Pass, who told us that a caravan was going through the following day, and he would make arrangements for us to accompany it ... The caravansary, a huge square where the caravan starts from, was packed with camels, horses, bullocks, donkeys, etc, and men who were busily engaged preparing and packing up merchandise for the morrow's journey. The men in charge were a wild, fierce looking lot, with their long, uncombed greasy hair hanging down on their shoulders, and were made to look even more fierce by their shaggy beards and the fact that each carried a huge knife in his belt, and often a couple of revolvers. They were extremely dirty, and dressed in very coarse cotton cloth like sacking, their coats being made of the skins of goats. We found the various animals being loaded with a large variety of merchandise, amongst which may be mentioned rock salt, Manchester goods and corrugated iron for roofing, etc.

In one corner of the large square we came across the unique sight of an Afghan playing the Scotch bagpipes, he probably having learnt them from some of the Scotch regiments who have been stationed in the district.

[They set off in a trap at 9.30am.] After three miles the mountains close in, then half a mile later the pass narrows to 150 yards . . . then to 30 yards, the rock rising in sheer precipices from 60 to 100 feet on each side and the pass keeps narrowing until Ali Musjid is reached, where the width is only 15 yds wide and the mountains on each side rising over 1,000 feet . . . It was a wonderful sight to see the long line of about 300 camels interspersed with horses, mules, donkeys and bullocks, all with heavy loads, slowly wending their way along the Pass, accompanied by their fierce looking drivers, each of whom . . . seemed ready either to repel an enemy or cut a throat. The tinkling of the bells carried by the camels, and the wild unearthly yells given by the drivers when urging on their beasts, together with the constant jabbering and shouting kept up by these wild, hairy-looking people made up a scene never to be forgotten.

In 'Kurachee' they come across an example of alligator (in fact, crocodile) baiting.

The natives kept calling out 'See fight, See fight', and on enquiry we found that it was the habit of some visitors to give these wretches a couple of rupees to throw one of their live goats amongst the alligators, for the fiendish pleasure of seeing the poor kids torn to pieces by the reptiles whilst fighting to possess it. The natives seemed to be much surprised when we flatly refused to accede to their requests, evidently not being able to understand where the cruelty came in.

In January 1893 they boarded the ss *Kapurthala* from Karachi to Bombay, and from there took trains across India to tour battle sites of the Indian Mutiny, which had taken place some

thirty-five years earlier. The horror of the Cawnpore (Kanpur)
Massacre clearly still haunted them, and several of the relevant
photographs in the albums have been mounted in black borders.
Perhaps looking for solace, in Lucknow, they found a surprising
interest:

> There are also a fair number of drink shops and so-called
> opium dens ... We took every available opportunity of visiting
> these opium dens in all parts where they were to be found ...
> [they were] as a rule quite as clean and well kept as any of the
> surrounding shops or dwellings, and often more so. The opium
> smokers we found to be perfectly quiet and peaceful, who
> smoked their pipes with the greatest decorum, and in no single
> instance did we see anything approaching the disgusting scenes
> published by some of those biased writers. On the contrary we
> came away with the distinct impression that the use of opium
> is productive of far less misery and crime than drink in our
> country ...

Another surprise in Lucknow was to find that

> Lord Hawke, with his team of English cricketers, arrived and
> played a match with a team picked from the district. Lord
> Hawke's team going in first ran up the score of 315. The district
> players made a very indifferent show, scoring only 76 in the first
> and 92 in their second innings ... The match was attended by
> all the chief Europeans of the place, and the game was watched
> with intense interest by crowds of natives, who evidently enjoyed
> seeing the Englishmen run after the ball. The ordinary natives
> of their own free will would never deliberately set themselves
> to chase a ball up and down a field under a hot sun, when they
> would be so much more comfortable sitting under the shade
> of the trees and enjoying a nice smoke.' [How Mitchell would
> wince at contemporary international standings in cricket!]

'Sacred, stinking Benares' was their first impression of that
holy city, although later they admitted that 'one of the most
wonderful sights in India is to be seen any morning at Benares
by taking a boat and rowing slowly down the river, and watching
the colourful crowds'. However, 'it was quite common to see

pieces of partly burnt flesh floating about among the bathers who, not content with drinking the water whilst bathing took it home to use it there'.

Calcutta's squalor depressed them too, and their mood was not helped by the discovery that 'the Great Eastern Hotel was so full that we could only be accommodated with a tent on the roof until some of the guests left to make room for us.' Chowringee Road was more to their taste: 'After four in the afternoon the wealth and beauty of Calcutta may be seen, both native and European driving along, accompanied by the picturesque Syces (grooms). These Syces carry a Yak's tail to flick off the flies and mosquitoes from the horses.'

On 9 February 1893 the Indian leg ended and they boarded the ss *Africa* for Rangoon.

BURMA

Rangoon's 'exceedingly wide' streets were bound to delight Mitchell and they did. Once again the travellers mingled with the elite of European society, who had nothing better to do than walk about between the hours of 4 and 7pm, and the Cantonment Gardens and Dalhousie Park were

> as pretty bits of scenery and recreation grounds as it is possible to find. A striking feature of Burmah is the use to which elephants are put. It is quite a sight to visit the saw mills of Moulmain and Rangoon. These ponderous but sagacious beasts move about the timber yards dragging huge tree trunks along and placing them with the greatest exactitude in the position required of them ... The elephant has his little joke with the men and boys, but when their teasing becomes too much for him he watches his opportunity, and quietly filling his trunk with sawdust simply smothers his teasers. We saw one man get a terrific storm of sawdust blown into his face by an elephant which he had been teasing. These useful beasts have their regular meal times like the

men, and from the amount of green stuff they can stow away at a meal, would make short work of any of our greengrocers' shops.

A visit to the Rangoon jail, where over 3,000 prisoners are kept, was very interesting ... One building with a passage straight through is furnished with well-lighted cells closed by iron gratings. These are the condemned cells, and contained at the time of our visit two men, a Burmese, quite a young fellow, and a Hindu. The Hindu on seeing us made the most abject obeisance, while the Burmese was snoring soundly, quite unconscious that the morrow would see his life's lamp snuff out. The life sentence prisoners were kept in a building divided into small workshops. Here all kind of wood carving was being done – most beautiful work, which is sold to order. The attendant informed us that prisoners coming in quite raw, never having used a chisel before, became expert wood carvers in a few months. Another building for life sentences was occupied by shoemakers and tailors, amongst which was the only white prisoner. This man had killed a native girl and her mother, and had been condemned to death, but had his sentence commuted to imprisonment for life.

They took a train to Mandalay, where a walk through an unmarked military firing range almost cost them their lives. Here they boarded a boat to travel downriver to Prome.

The Irrawaddy Flotilla Company run very good river steamers. Their boats are two deckers, the upper one being used for 1st saloon passengers, and the lower one for natives and cargo ... The skipper was a most interesting man, having been engaged in his present occupation during the late war. He, together with his first officer and engineer, all Englishmen, were taken prisoners during the war by one of King Theebaw's officers and conveyed to Mandalay. Arriving at Mandalay they were stripped naked, chained to a bullock cart, and in this condition made to walk through the streets under the broiling sun. Several times they were led out to be executed but as the person who had seized them claimed the right to the fiendish pleasure of killing them, and as some of the other officials disputed that right, the sentence was put off from day to day, when happily the entry of the British into Mandalay set the prisoners free. The exposure and the terrible anxiety, however, caused the death of one man, sent the second to a lunatic asylum, whilst the captain himself lost for ever the sight of one eye.

The journey was full of interest, watching the transfer of cargoes – rice and kutch ('a resinous substance like pitch used for dyeing fishing nets') – but at night the flies were awful, oil lamps in the dining room having 'heaps of flies all round to the depth of five inches'. They passed the village of Migingyan where the notorious photograph of crucified dacoits was taken. It is not known whether the victims were cut down before or after they died.*

On 23 February 1893 they embarked on the ss *Shropshire* for Ceylon, intending to make immediate onward passage to Australia. Unfortunately the *Shropshire* ran fast on a sandbar in a ferocious lightning storm, causing a seven-hour delay which resulted in them missing their pre-booked connection. A week later they left Colombo on the ss *Orient* for Australia.

Australia, 1893

After a 'severe tossing while rounding Cape Lemoin' our travellers reached Melbourne on 23 March.

> The capital of Victoria is undoubtedly the best laid out city in the Australian Colonies. [It] is threaded with an excellent system of cable cars ... there is a constant succession of theatrical and operatic companies from England and America visiting ... and the street cries, especially the newsboy's call of 'Doily piper' reminds one strongly of the London street arab, whilst the slightly nasal accent given to some words, together with the self-satisfied know-all sort of air, which is so common amongst ordinary Colonials, brings to mind the pronounced American.

---

* This punishment was not of Burmese origin but instigated by the British who claimed 'it was the only means of maintaining authority', according to other captioned photographs of the period.

The racecourse, however, they considered second to none. 'Our visit to Australia happened just at the time of the financial crisis, and ... during our stay eight banks failed, and hundreds of families who had been living in affluence were suddenly plunged into the greatest poverty, some of them having absolutely nothing to buy clothes with.' Long queues formed as people tried to extract their savings, some carrying them off in wheelbarrows only to fall foul of thieves, while the bank doors remained 'closed pending reconstruction'.

Somehow unaffected by the cash crisis, they visited what appears to be an early version of an Australian 'dude ranch'. Cloven Hills Station at Camperdown was owned by an early settler from Yorkshire, 'one of those dear old English matrons whose sweet and kindly nature endears them to everybody.' To everybody, that is, who wasn't black. Racism was rife. She and her husband came to Victoria

> when the whole country was overrun by the Aboriginal blacks ... who wandered about from place to place and never would settle down to any work ... Of a very low type, which resisted all the efforts of missionaries to Christianise them, lazy and shiftless, they furnish a good illustration of the theory of 'the survival of the fittest'. The thieving habits of the Aborigines often led them into trouble with the settlers. One settler got so exasperated at the loss of so many of his sheep and cattle that he collected his men and drove a lot of natives into a ravine where he shot them down as though they had been rabbits. Public feeling got so strong against him for this action that he had to leave the country shortly after. The rich black volcanic soil of this part ...

That this horrific act was tacitly condoned by Mitchell and of no greater note than the soil type illustrates the ugliest twisting of morality under the guise of colonial superiority. In India Mitchell was appalled by the atrocities perpetrated against British prisoners during the Indian Mutiny, yet a massacre of Aborigines was equated to the eradication of vermin. He, and Bullough, recognised cruelty in throwing live goats to crocodiles, but would deliberately wound a kangaroo to avoid damaging the pelt.

Aside from railing against the Australian workers' propensity to strike, their hosts told them about

> that peculiar class of men called 'Sundowners' ... similar in dress and appearance to our tramps ... Their chief occupation seems to be 'looking for what they don't want to find' and that is work ... He generally maps out his route so that he will be at a station at night fall, or 'sundown', as it is called. Arriving at the station he is sure of a shelter for the night, with a supper and breakfast. For these provisions he is supposed to do some work in the morning before leaving, such as chopping a bundle of sticks, etc. Ninety per cent of these people, however, having been born tired, sneak off after doing as little as possible, and make tracks for the next station, taking a good sleep on their blankets in the middle of the day, in some shady nook to wile away the time. At all stations this provision is made for 'Sundowners', and as it very often happens that as many as eight or 10 will put in an appearance at once, they become a nuisance. If a station owner refuses to give them food, being of a very benevolent disposition they either take the liberty to leave a gate or two open ... or, maybe, they will kindly drop a lighted match and leave the station owner with a bush fire to put out.

In Woolloomanatta they had good sport amongst the rabbits, quail ... and parrots. '[The latter] have a very beautiful plumage and are capital eating, being very difficult to distinguish from quail when cooked.'

After this they boarded the ss *Austral* bound for Sydney. A photograph in the albums shows 'The *Austral* as She Appeared When Sunk in Sydney Harbour' [11 November 1882]. Mitchell notes 'She was accidentally sunk by having too much coal put on one side which caused her to overturn'. She was successfully refloated, and the travellers found her comfortable enough eleven years later, and not all damp!

The banking crisis must have eased, for Bullough signed a bank draft for £300 in early June, some of which went to settle the bill at the Australia Hotel.

This hotel is a magnificent building, and is the largest hotel in the Australian colonies. When one observes the huge granite pillars flanking the wide entrance which leads into the splendid hall, and sees the beautiful marble staircases and costly furnishings, one is not surprised to learn that it cost £300,000 to build [the same as Kinloch Castle would cost]. It is run on the American plan, the smokeroom, billiard-room, and bar being all open to the public. This is a great drawback from an Englishman's point of view, because visitors are denied the privacy they naturally expect to get in an hotel, which is their home for the time being.

In their eyes Sydney justified itself as the prettiest harbour in the world.

On holidays steamers carry thousands of people to the various pretty bays and inlets with which the harbour abounds, and hundreds of sailing craft of all kinds may be seen flitting about ... sudden gusts of wind are apt to sweep down the various valleys and overturn small boats. This, however, does not deter the Sydney youngster from going out in all sorts of weather, and though the harbour abounds in sharks, he seems to take no heed of them, or of being upset, but swims about the overturned boat as though no sharks existed ... We had some good sport fishing for shark and schnapper.

The Botanical Gardens and Randwick racecourse delighted. the pair, but overall the city did not pass muster. To the list of Aborigines, strikers, and Sundowners, Mitchell now added Pushs.

Sydney is infested in most of her districts with gangs of young men ... Each gang, which is called a 'Push', is named after the district it infests ... and the police seem to be quite unable to cope with the trouble, and very often get the worst in encounters with the rascals. The name Larrikin given to this class of rowdies is said to have been derived from a member of one of these gangs who was on trial for nearly killing a fellow subject. When asked by the magistrate why he had done such a deed, he replied that he was only 'larking'. Being of Irish descent, he pronounced it 'larriking', and the term first used for the offence subsequently became applied to this class of ruffians, who throughout the colonies now go by the name of 'Larrikins'... The judges are now beginning to 'flog' these rascals more frequently, and with very good effect, also, instead of keeping the culprit in gaol until their backs have healed up after a flogging, they have adopted the method of flogging them when their sentence expires, so that the members of their 'Push' may have the benefit of seeing the effects of the 'cat' before the wounds are healed.

At Yarralumla, within sight of the Australian Alps, they took part in a hare hunt with mounted beaters cracking whips.

The bag at the end of the day numbering 276 hares and eight Wallaby... As the N.S. Wales Government pays 2d per head for every hare killed, the beaters scalped all the hares, strung the scalps on to their saddles, and took them home as perquisites... The kangaroo is easily killed by a blow on the head from a whip stock, but when an old man kangaroo is brought to bay, he will place his back against a tree and fight with his hind feet, the centre claw of which is a formidable weapon... Wanting to get a good specimen, we took out a rifle one day. A moderate specimen came along, and was shot through the root of the tail. The kangaroo deprived of its balance by the broken tail could only make two or three jumps before it fell over on its head, when righting itself again it would repeat the same process; this showing the great use these animals make of the tail in keeping their balance. This specimen was procured and forwarded home.

Nothing, it appears, was safe from the tourists' or settlers' guns. Not even the harmless and rare duck-billed platypus. Bullough does not appear to have shot any himself, though that was probably through lack of opportunity, but, as the *Gazette* reporter observed, he returned with 'a rug of the fur of the duck-billed platypus [which] attests the marksmanship of Australia: to avoid injuring the skin, which has a curious wiry and very handsome texture, it is imperative to shoot the platypus through the head. This particular rug represents eighteen months' marksmanship.'

Concluding their Australian itinerary – and summarising Britain's dismal environmental record there – was this account of the notorious rabbit problem.

> It has been stated on the highest authority that a male and female rabbit, will, in the course of two years produce over a million rabbits providing they are put down on ground suitable to them ... Shooting proved ineffective, dogs soon tired of endless killing ... the most effective solution was this: A paddock was chosen, and at a very considerable expense was wire-netted all round, so that rabbits could neither get in or out. This being done, about twenty thousand sheep were turned in and allowed to remain until they had eaten up almost every blade of grass. The water tank in the middle of the paddock was next fenced round with wire netting. The sheep having been driven out, poisoned water was put into troughs ranged round the fenced water tank, and phosphorised wheat put in the paddock for food. The grass having been eaten by the sheep there was nothing left for bunny but to eat the poisoned wheat and drink the poisoned water. During the course of a week no less than fifty thousand rabbits were killed in one paddock alone by this means. Hundreds of tons of rabbits were killed on this estate, and for miles along the fence sides the dead carcases lay two feet deep, and emitted such an effluvia that passengers going by rail past one part of the estate complained of the nuisance.

SOUTH AFRICA

'On account of the financial depression existing in the Australian Colonies there was at this time a great rush to Africa, which was then "booming".' The travellers' luck with ships and pleasant passages ran out here, and the ss *Port Pirie*, which they boarded for Cape Town, turned out to be a dirty overloaded tramp with an incompetent captain. Shortly before the vessel's early morning departure, five stowaways were discovered and hustled ashore.

At about 4pm the first day, one of the men employed in the engine-room came up on deck, bid good-bye to one of his mates – and deliberately jumped overboard. A cry of 'Man overboard' was at once raised, and a scene of great excitement followed. Life buoys were thrown out, the ship stopped, and a boat quickly lowered, into which the second officer (by far the best officer on board the ship) and some of the stewards and crew scrambled . . . The sea was so rough that the boat ran a great risk of being swamped. It however got away safely, and the captain climbing up to the main yard, yelled himself hoarse in trying to direct the boat. The unhappy suicide had seized one of the life buoys, and held on to it until the boat was within a few yards of him, when he threw up his arms and went down. Having gathered in the life buoys the boat returned and after a considerable time, during which it was nearly swamped at the ship's side, was safely hauled up, and the voyage continued.

The weather got worse, and next day was so bad that we were treated to a thoroughly rollicking dinner. The rolling boat made it almost impossible for anyone to walk about, and the stewards had the greatest difficulty in serving; soup, potatoes, tureens, dishes and plates went sliding off the tables into people's laps with a persistency which made the scene extremely comic – but very inconvenient . . . We were five days off [Cape Leeuwin] in one of the worst gales we have ever experienced. For three days the ship made practically no progress – going up on deck was out of the question – and there we were imprisoned in a small dining saloon full of seasick humanity, and fed on food which a convict would have shuddered at.

The captain, in our opinion, was much more fitted to carry round the collection box at a country tea fight than navigate a ship, and had it not been for the second officer and chief engineer it is doubtful whether we should ever have reached Africa.

The ship had taken on poor-quality coal and the stokers were on the point of mutiny.

Once when a huge wave dashed over the ship and flooded the firemen to such an extent that they had to work knee deep in water, they rushed up in a body determined to give up. A stiff glass of rum, however, and some kind but firm tactics on the part of Mr Morton, the engineer, tided over the difficulty.

A few days after the suicide there was a birth on board, and had it not been for the kindly offices of a first saloon lady passenger – none of the second class women passengers would lift a hand to help the poor unfortunate woman – the child and mother would have had a bad time indeed.

The doctor of the ship was one of those men who was much too fond of liquor, and was working his passage to England and back to try and recuperate a system which had been shattered by drink. The captain and agents had made no provision whatever for medicines ... The only bottle that contained any medicine was one which was filled with a purgative, known as 'black draught'. This medicine diluted to various strengths had to serve as a panacea for all ailments, from a woman in confinement to a man with a smashed finger. A good case this for a Board of Trade inquiry ...

So badly did the stewards behave in the second class saloon that the whole of the passengers mutinied, and obliged the captain to put the dirty waiters before the mast, the passengers undertaking to work in parties to serve at table and clean up their saloon themselves ... Long before the voyage was nearly over every particle of fruit, wine, beer and spirits was finished, and we were reduced to a state of 'roughing' it. Not content with this, the captain, who had robbed the ship of its smoking room by turning it into a four-berthed cabin, forbade smoking in the saloon at any time ... the smokers suffered great deprivation; until at last, losing patience, they forced the captain to allow them to smoke in the saloon after 9pm – the ladies' permission having been first obtained.

Badly knocked about and bruised, they reached Table Bay on 16 August 1893, the ship suffering a fifteen-degree list to port. They pitied the other passengers continuing on to London.

We found comfortable lodging at Pooles' Hotel, which is situated quite close to the Houses of Parliament, and is much frequented by members of the Legislature at lunch time, especially Mr Cecil Rhodes, whom we saw there nearly every day ... The proceedings in the Cape Parliament are conducted in Dutch and English, so that a member of Parliament needs to know both languages ... A speech in Dutch by a Boer member

was made during our visit to the house ... The purport of the
speech [translated by a friend] ran as follows: ... he said that
the Almighty sends rinderpest and all such diseases amongst the
cattle to punish owners for their sins, and to appoint inspectors
in the various districts to try and stamp out the plagues which
the Almighty has sent amongst them was not only wasting
money in useless salaries, but was going against the Divine Will,
and further – if this bill were passed and inspectors appointed –
the wrath of God would assuredly fall on the community, and
some dire calamity happen to them ... The above may be taken
as a sample of the dislike of the Boer to change and progress,
and of the deeply religious, though bigoted, feelings which are
characteristic of him.

After eight days of touring the city they took the ss *Arab* along
the coast, watching hysterical lady passengers being transferred
to steam tugs by means of a basket dangling from pulley blocks.
In Port Natal they were again fascinated by the coaling of the
vessel, undertaken this time by Zulus: 'Perfectly naked, with the
exception of a very small rag wrapped round their middle, of a
very fine physique, with black, oily looking skins and teeth as
white as snow, these merry Zulu boys laugh, dance, shout, and
sing in such a hearty manner whilst doing their work that they
give one the idea of being the happiest mortals in creation.'
They found the Zulus made excellent 'Rickshaw boys' in
Durban but they

and other natives are not allowed by law to walk about the
streets unless decently clad. The native policeman in Durban
is distinctly characteristic. He usually wears helmet, coat, and
knickerbocker trousers, but no shoes or stockings. He carries a
formidable truncheon, known as a knob-kerry. This is a stout
stick, about two feet long, with a rounded head about the size of
a large orange. These policemen are only allowed to run natives
in, and this work they do with great gusto, and don't forget to
use the knob-kerry on the heads of their prisoners should they
happen to get obstreperous. We saw some most amusing scenes
between the native policemen and their prisoners.

The railway line from Maritzburg to Charlestown is very steep in places, and zigzags about in such a manner that it necessitates two reversing stations. After passing over a grand and wild district, the line before it reaches Charlestown runs through Laing's Nek, and along the foot of Amajuba Hill (called in this country Majuba Hill), two places the mere mention of whose names makes the fighting blood of every true Englishman tingle in his veins, for it was at these two places the English troops suffered such terrible defeats at the hands of the Boers ... Travelling through the district makes the blush of shame rise to the face of most Englishmen, especially when they have to submit to the incivilities of the Boer officials, who, should any remonstrance be made, point the finger of scorn towards Majuba and Laing's Nek.

Mitchell castigates Gladstone's surrender as 'the vilest cowardice which has ever disgraced our arms ... The war which Mr Gladstone might have terminated in about a month with honour to England and a pacification of South African affairs, has ... caused endless trouble, and if recent events point to anything, they point to the likelihood of ... lots of bloodshed.' His words were to prove prophetic. Six years later, almost to the day, the Boer War started, and Bullough and Mitchell would return to Cape Town to play their part in it.

The railway from Charlestown to Johannesburg had yet to be extended so they were forced to travel by coach: 'We bumped along the road at a fairly rapid rate, and changed horses at the end of every stage, which was from six to eight miles. The teams were composed of horses and mules mixed up in any proportion, each team having ten to twelve animals (i.e. five or six pairs).'

Johannesburg was a phenomenon, an instant city.

In this out of the way place, one thousand miles from Cape Town, in the short space of seven years, a city had been built which could boast of having some of the best buildings in South Africa. Churches, theatres, splendid shops, and streets with tramway accommodation, together with all the luxuries which can be claimed by towns of 50 years' construction ... all dragged

there by bullock wagons ... The population of Johannesburg is
over sixty thousand souls, and is increasing very rapidly every
week. Hospital, clubs, racecourse, tennis and cricket grounds,
with pretty suburban villas, have all grown with the town, and the
district which once looked so treeless, cheerless and uninviting,
can now boast of millions of trees which have been planted, and
which grow here with marvellous rapidity ... The only nuisance
of any note being the dust ... a quarter of an hour's walk in the
street was sufficient to almost smother one; eyes, ears, nose and
mouth becoming full of it.

Indifferent champagne cost a guinea a bottle, and four
shillings was the usual price for a bottle of beer. Cabbages would
vary from one shilling to half-a-crown each. Nothing but gold
and silver coins are used, and it was most amusing to see the
indignant look on a newspaper boy's face when threepence in
copper was offered him for a paper. 'Don't take that stuff here,'
was the curt reply; 'nuffing less than silver in this place.' And he
was right, too, for in Johannesburg a half-sovereign seemed to go
about as far as a shilling would do at home.

They visited the goldfields, which had tunnels tall enough
even for Bullough to walk along unstooped, but nowhere could
they long escape the endemic racism. The Uitlanders – the
British and other foreigner workers who had once been welcome
– were finding that 'Paul Kruger and his illiterate and corrupt
Government' were increasingly infringing or removing their
rights. At one protest meeting they attended, 2,000 Uitlanders
'stated that they would agitate by every constitutional means in
their power, and if those failed they would then resort to arms.
Paul Kruger's reply was: "Go back and tell your people I will
never give them anything; I shall never change my policy; and
now let the storm burst."'

The political tension increasingly consumed Mitchell's
thoughts. He found the Boer subsumed by 'laziness, dirtiness,
and slovenliness' and his language so degenerate that it fettered
him to 'his stupendous ignorance'. It's not hard to see why the
Gazette editor decided to pull the plug on the series. In the
final episode they had reached the Kimberley diamond fields

James Bullough, founder of Howard & Bullough and George's grandfather.
(Portrait in Kinloch Castle).

Early newspaper illustration of James Bullough and one of his looms.

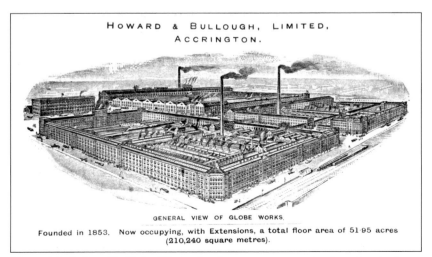

Howard & Bullough's Globe Works, Accrington, represented at its prime in the company booklet *Machinery Calculations*, 1925.

John Bullough and his first wife, Bertha Schmidlin, whose marriage produced George, Bertha and the mysterious Edward before ending in a bitter divorce. John's purchase of the Rabbeth spindle patent brought immense wealth.

George aged 16, sitting for a school portrait in 1886. (Reproduced by kind permission of the Governors and Trustees of Harrow School).

George (tallest) and beside him Robb Mitchell (holding topi). One of only two photographs showing the pair on their world tour. Amber, India, January 1893.

Crucified dacoits, Burma – a practice introduced by the British.

Public execution, China. Only a few photographs show such gruesome scenes but they reflect George's interest in methods of punishment. World tour, 1892–5.

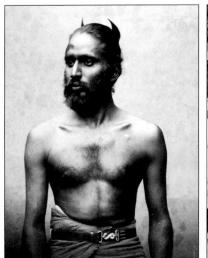

Man with a headcomb in Ceylon and a girl ('28 ½ lbs') on a lily leaf in Java. Such curiosities caught George's eye, as did all things botanical, such as giant bamboo, Peradeniya, Ceylon.

Tokyo's infamous Nectarine No. 9 brothel. The original photograph is hand-coloured.

George's half-brother, Ian (left, Archive: John Bullough) and his full or half-brother Edward, 'the forgotten son', a great linguist and polymath.

Rhouma, with its hospital quarters at the stern, in Table Bay, Cape Town, during the Boer War.

Rhouma II, still afloat and the oldest surviving steel vessel classed 100A1 at Lloyds.

Kinloch Castle circa 1910 from the south, showing the conservatory which was later removed.

No expense spared: one of Kinloch Castle's Spode WCs and revolutionary showers.

Rum, the party place: a cartoon depicting George and a guest posing by his kill.

Sir George in his Rhum tartan. His 39th birthday portrait which hangs above the Great Hall.

Above. Monica Charrington (née Ducarel), who married Sir George in 1903, here aged 40. Portrait in the Great Hall.

Right. Monica posing nude on one of the castle's tiger-skin rugs.

Monica's sitting room in part of the castle, whose dark Jacobean style she transformed into light neo-Adam.

Kinloch Castle today from the north: a unique monument to Edwardian splendour in the balance between survival and decay.

Sport Pictures 2ᵈ

No. 169. [Registered at the G.P.O. as a Newspaper.] For Week Ending SATURDAY, JUNE 24, 1922. [Phone: CITY 561.] [16 Pages.] Two Pence.

SIR G. BULLOUGH'S GOLDEN ASCOT.

Sir George's long successful interest in horse racing began as a childhood drawing on a textbook, *The Public School Latin Primer.*

Sir George in later life, perhaps in his fifties (1920s).

The majestic beauty of Harris, west Rum. The mausoleum is on the left; the groin vault was in the shadow behind it.

The final resting place of John, Sir George and Lady Monica Bullough.

and discovered a business that made Howard & Bullough look insignificant.

Mr Robert Mitchell, continuing the description of his tour with Mr Bullough, said: 'The Company known as De Beers Mining Company practically rules the diamond industry of the world . . . it pays over a million pounds a year in wages, and a 40 per cent dividend . . . The diamondiferous ground belonging to the De Beers Company is reckoned by square miles, and not by acres, and includes fields, roads, tramway systems, buildings of various kinds, and even a charming village . . . under the supervision of white officials, the diamonds are picked from amongst the other pebbles by convicts . . . De Beers employs about 7000 men, of whom about 1,400 are Europeans, the rest natives.

'The natives are engaged for periods of three months, during which time they are kept in squares called "compounds". Each compound is complete in itself, and contains stores for supplying the natives with all the necessaries of life, and is further equipped with hospital and dispensary, but NO alcoholic liquor is allowed. The compounds are lined with fine gauze netting to prevent people from getting in or out, and also to prevent diamonds being thrown out. When once a native has entered the large portals leading into the De Beers Compounds he is not allowed out into the town again until his time is expired. Before leaving he is stripped, and his body and effects most minutely searched for hidden diamonds, and for a few days before the time of departure he is treated to stiff doses of aperient medicine to enable him to leave the Company's employ "an honest man".'

MADEIRA, NEW ZEALAND

Bullough and Mitchell's journey continued for another two years. The route is now known, but dates and details are sketchy, although here and there a newspaper recorded their visit and provided some colour.

Around October 1893 Bullough and Mitchell left South Africa and travelled two-thirds of the way back to Britain, to Madeira, which in later years would become a favourite destination. Here George celebrated his twenty-fourth birthday. They stayed at least four months 'till the season suited for New Zealand', and boarded the ss *Tainui* for Port Chalmers (Dunedin). The ship called in at Hobart, where Bullough purchased some photographs from the shop of a Scottish emigrant, thirty-five-year old John W. Beattie. Some twenty years later Beattie would gain the distinction of being entrusted with Roald Amundsen's undeveloped glass plates (Hobart being his first landfall after Antarctica) and, on processing them, being the first man to view a photographic image of the South Pole.

They reached Dunedin on 5 June 1894 and stayed at the Royal Hotel, then acclaimed as the finest in the southern hemisphere. Travelling by coach and on horseback, they followed a route familiar to tourists today: Queenstown, Milford Sound, the Hermitage below Mount Cook and then north to Christchurch. Here they went fishing with a prominent lawyer, Wynn Williams (later MP – his firm still practises), and a photograph of their catch for two rods shows forty large trout.

Their route over Arthur's Pass to the West Coast, through gold and coalmining regions, touched unawares on two coincidences. At Hokitiki the incumbent laird of Rum passed within eighty miles of Lake Matheson. It was named for its white discoverer (the Maoris having known about it long before) Dougald Matheson, son of Murdo and Christine from Rum. They had left Scotland in 1875 following the tragic ravages of diphtheria on their family, and had settled at Cottesbrook Station in Otago. Bullough would have passed close to their new home too; Murdo and Christine were still alive, and though Murdo had never really adjusted to the new life, their children had. Dougald made his discovery of the lake during one of many adventurous trips into unknown territory.

The other connection concerned the Lewis Pass, just to the north of Arthur's Pass. Off this is found the Magdalene Valley, a high-country grazing once leased by two aristocratic French brothers with unwieldy names, Gerard Gustavus Ducarel, Count de la Pasture, and his brother, Henri Philippe Ducarel de la Pasture. Within a decade George Bullough would marry the count's daughter.

Shortly before they left the South Island, back in Accrington, Joe Grimshaw was writing to Mitchell to inform him that his father had died. This must have dampened the party's spirits, and quite a convivial party it had become. Somewhere along the way Bullough and Mitchell had picked up a violinist or two. The *Evening Post* of 1 August 1894 records the arrival from Nelson of the ss *Penguin*, whose passenger list included in cabin class: Misses Doyle, Mesdames Doyle, Bullough, Mitchell ... Miss Bessie Doyle is later referred to as 'a violinist of exceptional ability'. This was no transient meeting and Miss Doyle was to reappear on the scene, in Rum, some years later.

A gossip column in the *Observer* of 20 October showed they travelled together for the next eleven weeks. 'Amongst the Bessie Doyle party which journeyed overland from Taranaki to Auckland, at the expense of much horse-flesh, was a wealthy Englishman, Mr Bullough, who stands six feet four and is worth a million-and-a-half of money, or thereabouts.'

The reference to the horse-flesh is explained in another report:

> For weeks the journey in New Zealand was out of the beaten track, beyond post, roads, and civilisation. The horse Mr Bullough rode, an old racer, bore him bravely for eleven hundred miles of the roughest country, and if it had lived would have had a long holiday in an English paddock. But it died on a perfectly level road, within sixty miles of Auckland. The spurs and whip carried, and a shoe worn by the good horse form the base of the best collection of curios obtained from the Maoris by the gallant steed's help.

Their arrival in Auckland coincided with one of the worst maritime disasters in New Zealand's history. On 29 October 1894 the ss *Wairarapa*, en route from Sydney to Auckland, struck the coast just sixty miles short of her destination. Of the 206 people on board, 121 died. The captain was later charged with negligence. A few days after the accident a newspaper reported that 'The body of Mr Thos Spencer was recovered by the *Nautilus* which had been chartered by Mr Bullough, a visitor to Auckland.'

THE ORIENT, PACIFIC AND UNITED STATES

From New Zealand the travellers' route became a mad zigzag round the Orient determined either by whimsical choices of destination or the rigidity of the commercial shipping timetables. They went north-west to remote Noumea (New Caledonia) where they bought photographs of a convict band playing in the French penal colony. (Convicts were transported to Noumea until 1898, and in 1901 they numbered over 10,000, one-fifth of the total population.) Then they journeyed all the way back to Sydney in order to get a ship to Batavia (Jakarta). Here Bullough purchased a more diverse selection of photographs; lines of prisoners wearing placards and standing under guard below a gallows with eight corpses,* a child sitting on a giant water lily leaf in Buitenzorg (reputedly 'the world's best Botanical Gardens', as noted by Mitchell in Ceylon) and the brooding remains of Krakatoa.

To get from Indonesia to Singapore they made a ludicrous detour via Colombo. It was now March or April 1895, and an indication of what this trip was costing is given in a telegram from Joe Grimshaw. '$19.200 [sic] or £2,000 being forwarded to The Chartered Bank of India, Australia & China.' He asked for

---

* The Dutch were brutally suppressing uprisings against their rule around this time. The picture of the executions was actually taken in 1870 and depicts the hanging of eight men found guilty of murdering a high-ranking Dutch official.

a code word 'R-----'[indecipherable] to be used in the cabled response to indicate the funds have been received safely. £2,000 for the final four months of travel! Perhaps Bullough was aware that there were some very expensive purchases pending in Japan.

They continued to Saigon and Hong Kong, where the photograph albums record two notable events. A series of pictures show snow and icicles on the Peak Tramway, 'No Ice Having Been Known in South China for 400 Years.' These pictures were taken the previous winter, so Bullough did not personally experience this phenomenon. Neither did he witness the beheading, by British orders, of twelve pirates on a beach near the boundary of British and Chinese Kowloon, because it had taken place four years earlier, but he bought a picture of the scene anyway.

China had no reason to welcome travellers of any nationality – particularly the British who had started the Opium Wars four decades earlier – and Bullough and Mitchell's visit coincided with China's involvement in another war. Waged over the 'ownership' of Korea, the First Sino-Japanese War began on 1 August 1894 (the day the travellers landed on New Zealand's North Island with Bessie Doyle) and ended with Japan's crushing victory, which was seen as a progressive regime dominating a feudal one. The Treaty of Shimonoseki was signed on 17 April 1895, which must have been roughly when Bullough and Mitchell reached Shanghai.† Shanghai, like Hong Kong, had been declared a treaty port with an autonomous British concession, and was thus safe for the travellers to visit. The album images show the Great

† Perhaps this is partly where the myth of a peace treaty being signed on board Bullough's yacht *Rhouma* found its origin, among those believing the world tour was made in this vessel. The Treaty of Shimonoseki (or Maguan) was not signed on board any ship but in the Shunpanro Hall in Formosa. With even less justification Bullough is sometimes credited with hosting the Treaty of Portsmouth, which ended the Russo-Japanese War on 5 September 1905. This was signed in the Hotel Wentworth, Kittery, Maine, with President Roosevelt mediating. There is therefore no connection with *Rhouma* or Bullough to either treaty.

Wall of China (which they surely never saw), cotton workers in a factory, musicians, fashions, Shanghai racecourse, Chinese court trials, women being punished in stocks and a bound man kneeling before his executioner's raised sword.

In Japan they visited (or at least bought a photograph of) 'Nectarine No 9' or Shimpuro Brothel, one of the land's most famous establishments, in the Eiraku-cho district of Yokohama.

All the photographs in the Japan section are hand-coloured prints, the only ones in the entire collection. They depict Nagasaki, Kyoto, Mount Fuji, Nikko, the Great Buddha of Kamakura – again, still the most popular tourist destinations to this day – geisha girls, a collection of women's shoes and, in stark contrast, a cremation chamber. They do not show anything of what must have been one of the reasons for visiting the country and its attractions, the 4th National Industrial Exhibition in Kyoto. If Bullough did outbid the Emperor of Japan for one of the show's most valuable and exquisite exhibits, a life-sized ivory eagle – and there is no reason to doubt the veracity of the *Gazette's* confirmation that he did – then the auction must have taken place long before the exhibition ended on 31 July (having moved to Kamigyoku) because on that day Bullough arrived back in England. Perhaps he was allowed to take it with him or maybe he had to take it on trust that it would be sent on subsequently. The eagle, which will be described later, was joined by other expensive purchases (considerably more difficult to pack), including a bronze jungle cock with an immense tail of delicate feathers, and the massive monkey-eating eagle, also in bronze, which stands eight feet tall and weighs many tons.

Travelling in Japan must have involved considerable risk, for although Emperor Meiji had revolutionised the country by opening it up to foreign trade and technology, a substantial section of traditional society opposed these changes and the presence of foreigners. But without a journal to refer to, we know little of the mood they encountered or incidents of their days there. The only confirmed dates are the nights of 28 to 31

May which they spent in the Fujiya Hotel. Despite the name the famous volcano is not visible from this location.

After leaving Japan they must have kept going relentlessly, for two and a half months later they were back in England. They visited Hawaii, San Francisco, Yosemite, the drive-thru-and-under-and-along giant redwoods, and devoted an entire photograph album to Salt Lake City. Here the photographs end. No more images were bought, even though they were still far from home. They travelled by rail to Chicago, Boston and then to New York – why not a single picture of New York? – and caught a transatlantic passenger ship back to Liverpool. On 17 August 1895, almost three weeks after landing, Bullough and Mitchell were staying at the Grand Hotel, London.

After an absence of three years and ten and a half months they must have had a mountain of luggage to unpack, friends and relatives to see, personal affairs to sort out (not to mention briefing Howard & Bullough's management on how the sales drive went), but within two weeks, Joe Grimshaw was writing letters explaining that 'Mr Bullough is on holiday in Rum'. Of course, the stalking season had begun.

A month later, Mr Bullough bought a ship and instructed that it be refitted for a voyage as quickly as possible.

9

Rhouma

When the crates sent back from abroad were unpacked, Rhyddings Hall was filled with exotic mementos ranging from the exquisite to the grotesque. The Kyoto ivory eagle took pride of place. It stands on a wooden stump, neck straining forwards, eyes gazing beyond its outstretched left wing while its right curls in the act of unfolding. The tail feathers fan wide, cruel talons are open. Thirty inches high and fifty-two inches across, it appears to be one impossible piece of ivory, so meticulously have each of its components been fitted together; 'each feather a separate work of art,' one admirer remarked, 'the whole a revelation of beauty in design and skill in execution'.

The bronze jungle cock* with the four-foot tail (made by the Maruki Company, Tokyo, possibly by the legendary Narikuri Otake) and the monumental monkey-eating eagle represent relatively recent Japanese art forms. The Japanese government banned the wearing of swords in 1874 and encouraged the largely redundant metal craftsmen to turn their skills to making large sculptures for international exhibitions. These two pieces were outstanding examples, as were a pair of magnificent six-foot high *cloisonné* vases made from lacquered wire and decorated with finches and chrysanthemums. As the *Gazette* reporter

---

* The ivory eagle and the jungle cock are both on permanent display at the National Museum of Scotland, Edinburgh.

observed: 'No British example of workmanship comes within measurable distance of the indomitable spirit of the Easterners, who will devote a lifetime to a carpet, and two generations to a carving, and a score of years to a vase.'

Among other items selected for mention in the report were

> a moulding of Japanese wrestlers ... the knob kerries of Natal and the rhinoceros hide whips of the Cape ... Maori assegais and shields of hide ... In the nursery a model of a Japanese house has been put up. It is complete in every detail. All the partitions and outer walls slide ... A cannon ball from Seringapatam, a Cingalese man's comb; a model of the Taj; an opium pipe ... carved emu eggs ... a photograph of the *Wairarapa* hangs on the ship's 'blue Peter', and close by stands a portion of the fiddle which belonged to one of the stewards.

Of course there were also the unfortunate black buck, buffalo, kangaroo and the rug of however many platypuses can be killed in eighteen months ... and ' the head of an Australian black, with a hole made in it by a tomahawk'. It only remained for Bullough to send off his photograph collection to be bound into albums, and to plan his next voyage.

It is not known when the idea came to him to buy his own ship. Maybe the grim passage aboard the ss *Port Pirie* decided him, or having to board the David MacBrayne steamer in Oban to go stalking on Rum (where the lodging was squalid by comparison to Dunedin's Royal Hotel). Whatever the gestation period, the act was completed suddenly. Six weeks after his return he became the owner of the steam yacht *Maria*.

He already owned a fifty-five-foot yacht, *Mystery*, bought by his father 'with the purpose of establishing a more efficient steamboat service between the island of Rum and the mainland'. At forty-three tons she was no mean vessel, skippered by John MacAskill, a strong sullen man with eleven children, all of whom were later employed by Bullough. Clearly *Mystery* failed to meet Bullough's needs, although he took the trouble to have her registered with the Royal Clyde Yacht Club in 1893 while he was away travelling. The *Maria* was something quite different. Few vessels afloat could compete with her. She was in the elite league.

In 1863 there were only thirty registered steam yachts in the UK, but as the industrial age brought greater wealth to many, within the next twenty years this figure increased to 466. The greatest of this new breed of vessels (in 1899) was John Pierpont Morgan's 1,396-ton leviathan, *Corsair III*. The *Maria* came in at 670 tons, still easily at the top end of the market, and was 221 feet long and 28 feet wide. She had two decks, a coal-fired engine and a single propeller which enabled a comfortable cruising speed of twelve knots. Rigged as a two-masted schooner – her second (or aft) mast was the tallest and held the mainsail – she was technically still a yacht, though it is doubtful whether the sails, made by the same company that had supplied them to Nelson's HMS *Victory*, were ever used except for occasional displays of vanity. Her state rooms were sumptuous, the dining room in particular with its mahogany panelling and chairs whose feet were bolted to the floor, while the upper halves swivelled to enable ladies in voluminous evening dresses to seat themselves decorously.

Maria was just two years old. Officially numbered 102379, she had been built on the Clyde at the yard of Napier, Shanks and Bell, the company which had developed the very first steam yacht in 1820. Her first owner was Ninian B. Stewart of Keil House, Kintyre, the son of the founder of Glasgow's largest drapery business, Stewart and MacDonald. Ninian was an original member of the Royal Clyde Yacht Club and sailing was in his blood; his father had built a steam yacht and a brother owned another from which he staged extravagant fireworks displays off Rothesay. On relinquishing ownership of the *Maria* on 7 October 1895 in favour of George Bullough, Ninian promptly purchased a larger steam yacht which he again named *Maria*!

Bullough immediately changed his vessel's name to *Rhouma*, a romanticised and feminised version of Rum. His cousin Tom, the chairman of Howard & Bullough, was clearly impressed both by the vessel and the name. When his second daughter was born in August 1896 she was baptized Joan Rhouma Bullough.*

The vessel lay at the James Watt Dock, Greenock, which continued to be her base when not in use, and underwent certain modifications in preparation 'for a cruise to the West Indies'. Early in 1896 the voyage began, pioneering the 15,000-mile route that was to become a favourite, and included Bermuda, Florida, the Gulf of Mexico, the Azores and Madeira. A visitor to the ship in Cape Town some four years later mentioned in a letter that the upper deck was 'the place where they have their balls. Mr Bullough gives a ball every year at Madeira, and he generally has as guests about 60 couples.' This possibly lends credence to the story that *Rhouma* carried a twelve-piece orchestra among her complement.

Some idea of the revels aboard the vessel are given in a poem scribbled by George after a heavy drinking spree in Madeira on 31 March 1901. Entitled 'The Rhoumaging, Rumaging Rotters', it describes parties and binges, and runs for pages. Here's a small extract:

> *From the land of 'Rum' these rotters*
> *Came amidst a foreign people . . .*
> *. . . Who] said with looks amazed:*
> *'Tell us why you sleep all day,*
> *Spending all the night in laughter*
> *Sleeping daylight in the bay*
> *And why you eat and why you drink*
> *Why this brutal excursion*
> *Of your "Rotten Rummy" ways*
> *Must it always be permitted*
> *To behave in this strange manner . . .'*

* Tom's own yacht, *Waihi*, was a much more modest affair, but large enough for confusion with *Rhouma*; when the *Oban Times* of August 1898 reports that 'Mr Bullough, the popular commodore, gave a firework display from his yacht in the regatta' at Campbeltown, it is not clear if this was Tom or George. The possibility of christening his baby Joan Waihi was probably too outlandish to have been considered!]

. . . And the natives of Madeira
Often have been heard to say:
'Glory be to God – They've gone
There's peace now in the Bay!'

The last words, written in letters an inch tall, are: 'B – E – D 4am'.

On *Rhouma,* as before on the commercial steamers, cricket was played on deck. This fact is often presented as an indication of the vessel's vast size, but as Robb Mitchell pointed out in a *Gazette* article,

> Cricket on board a ship is widely different from cricket ashore. The same kind of wickets and bats are used, the wickets being fixed into a block of wood to make them stand. The ball, however, is a mass usually of string and serves its purpose very well. The sides of the ship are netted round to prevent the balls being driven overboard. The space for the pitch is so narrow that usually not more than four fielders can take part. Hits to leg, and play on the off-side, are not of much use, the great excitement being to play the ball and steal runs.

For a long voyage as many as forty crew might be employed, but for duties between the Clyde and Rum the figure was reduced to under thirty. The only crew list I have been able to unearth is for the year 1905, when no trips outside home waters were made. The Terms of Engagement stipulated that any employees

> agree to go on voyages within the limits of 70 degrees North and 70 deg South latitude, to and fro as may be required until the yacht is finally laid up and [they are] paid off in the United Kingdom. Period of engagement not to exceed twelve months. The uniform supplied for the use of the crew remains the property of the owner of the yacht. Cash and liberty allowed at the Master's discretion. Seamen, greasers and firemen to work bunker coals when required. The crew agree to work ashore for the owner when required.

In this year the Master was I. N. McDougall (32 years old) who was the only employee on an annual retainer. There were three Mates, a Boatswain, Carpenter, a Launchman/Able Seaman, a Caterer/Able Seaman, five Able Seamen, a Bugler/Ordinary seaman (the youngest at 20 years old), one Ordinary Seaman, Chief Engineer, 2nd Engineer, Greaser/Launchman, 2nd Greaser, four Firemen, Chief Steward, 2nd Steward, Mess Room Cook, Mess Room Steward and a Fo'c'sle Cook. Twenty-eight in all. Scots: 22. English: 2. Irish: 3. German: 1. The 2nd Mate and the Boatswain were the oldest at 52 years.

Under the 'Scale of Provisions' was the surprising entry, 'Crew to provide their own provisions.' The weekly wages were specified for everyone except the Master. Chief Engineer: £3 10s. 1st Mate: £2 17s 8d. Chief Steward: £2 15s. Mess Room Cook: £2. Foc'sl'e Cook: £1 10s. The average for everyone else was around £1 6s, with the Ordinary Seamen on the lowest wage of 15 shillings. The standard regulations for offences committed on board recommended the levels of fines the Master was to impose, these amounting to five shillings for every charge as follows: striking any person, bringing on board or possessing spirituous liquors, insolence or drunkenness (first offence, rising to ten shillings for a second offence). Finally, the Master was required to record any births or deaths (none), and any dismissals of which there was one, an AB 'discharged by mutual consent' in Rum, and replaced within three days.

As a base the James Watt Dock was perfect. This fourteen-acre basin was completed in 1886 and was a high-risk gamble to steal trade from the upper Clyde by providing deeper, more spacious berths at cheaper rates. However, business failed to materialise and the venture was a financial disaster, with construction costs quadrupling the projected budget. The Greenock Harbour Trust was bankrupted within a year. *Rhouma* thus found herself in a relatively peaceful and cheap haven. (Charles Rudd, a diamond magnate who owned the huge Ardnamurchan estate, intimated that the annual cost of running his steam yacht, almost identical to *Rhouma*, was greater than that of the estate.) *Rhouma*'s weekly bill averaged £2 16s 11d for harbour dues and 18s 11d for police dues. A bargain by any millionaire's standards.

10

Suitable for a Princess

George Bullough spent the last five years of the nineteenth century shooting, cruising and establishing some roots in the form of permanent homes. He entered his dogs in competitive shows in London and Birmingham, and in 1899 he was presenting cups as vice-commodore of the Royal Clyde Yacht Club. He attended the occasional meeting of Howard & Bullough, whose business was once again buoyant, but out of duty rather than interest. Each autumn he could be found stalking or – a new pastime – fishing on Rum with *Rhouma* anchored in the bay. On one occasion his 13-year-old half-brother Ian joined him. They must have been seeing more of each other, as George was still one of the guardians of Meggernie on the teenager's behalf.

Now that George was visiting Rum more frequently, the inconveniences of Kinloch House, or Tigh Mor ('big house'), built seventy years earlier, must have become increasingly intolerable. It was not particularly large, comfortable or even weather-proof, and it was infested with rats. He also owned the White House, but even with this resource, the accommodation on Rum was woefully inadequate. On his world travels he must have been thinking of what his ideal home should look like and what facilities it would contain, for shortly after his return he approached a firm of architects called Leeming & Leeming.

Given the wide field of architectural talent available, they were an unusual choice, having first blunted their pencils on, and subsequently specialised in, municipal buildings and chapels. Brothers John and Joseph Leeming had started their practice in Halifax twenty-five years earlier, but had subsequently moved to London. Most recently they had come to public attention for designing the Admiralty Buildings on Horse Guards Parade. At the time of George's extremely lucrative commission they were not known as architects of country houses and nor would they be afterwards, though later contracts for the Edinburgh municipal buildings and a new market hall for Leeds were still prestigious contracts. They were the sort of choice to be expected of the *nouveau riche* who would hire a company because it was in vogue, even if the work required was outwith its area of expertise.

The man given individual responsibility for the plan of the proposed 'Kinloch Castle' was a relatively young employee called Richard Feilding [sic] Farrer.* He eventually came up with a design for a two-storey castle built around a square with an open courtyard in the middle. Features included the obligatory crenellations, a tower block plagiarised from Balmoral and elements of the Victorian grammar schools the Leemings were more used to creating on their drawing boards. The design process ran smoothly and quickly. Tigh Mor was demolished, and on its site, greatly extended, the foundations of Kinloch Castle were laid in the latter half of 1897.

George still had no *real* home. Rhyddings Hall was rented, and besides, it was in Accrington and provided uncomfortably few excuses for avoiding involvement at the Globe Works. There were other hassles with the building too. Towards the end of the world tour (February 1895), Joe Grimshaw had to write to the landlord to complain that 'Mr Bullough has already spent some £3000 on repairs and improvements and can't be expected to outlay more'. Meggernie was not his either, even though he spent a great deal of time there.

---

* This may be a misprint for 'Fielding'.

In June 1898 the mansion house and estate of Bishopswood, Ross-on-Wye, Herefordshire was auctioned. It was owned by Colonel Harry McCalmont, CB, a renowned yachtsman, racehorse owner and friend of Edward, the Prince of Wales. The highest bid was £69,000, which was considered insufficient and the lot was withdrawn unsold. George subsequently approached the vendor and secured Bishopswood in a private deal. Included in the sale as part of the furnishings was one remarkable and historic antiquity. Around 1682 Charles II commissioned Sir Christopher Wren to create Wandsworth Manor House (often erroneously called Wandsworth Palace). Wren contracted a master wood-carver born in Holland of English parents, Grinling Gibbons, to carve something 'suitable for a princess'. Gibbons created an intricate marvel, a six-arched screen. Shortly before the Manor House was demolished, Colonel McCalmont had bought this screen, and now it passed into George's ownership. Bishopswood became his principal residence for almost three decades, supplemented by a London house at 14 Stratton Street, Piccadilly.

Around this time a New Zealand newspaper made a startling announcement. In an entertainment column entitled 'Mimes and Music', Wellington's *The Evening Post* of 18 November 1899 reported that: 'Miss Eileen O'Moore (Miss Bessie Doyle) was to have been married to Mr George Bullough, of Kinloch Castle, by Oban (Scotland), on the 10th of last month. The wedding was to take place on board Mr Bullough's yacht.'

A month later on 16 December, without a word of apology, the columnist returned to the same subject, adding a sting at the end.

The recently-announced marriage of Miss Bessie Doyle, now known professionally as Eileen O'Moore, was carried out in a somewhat romantic fashion. Miss O'Moore was married to Mr Robert Mitchell on board the yacht *Rhosima* [sic], at Loch Scresort, on 12 October, invitations for the ceremony being sent by Mr George Bullough, of Kinloch Castle. Some of these invitations reached Australian friends the other week by way of announcing the event. New Zealand has been credited as the birthplace of Miss O'Moore, who is well known as a violinist of exceptional ability, but it is pretty well known that she is the daughter of a New South Wales squatter.

The couple barely had time for a honeymoon before launching themselves into married life with a South African adventure. The day before their wedding the Boer War officially began, and two months later *Rhouma* weighed anchor and headed to Cape Town with both George Bullough and Robert Mitchell aboard. One can only assume Mrs Mitchell was with them. They were to be away for the best part of a year.*

---

* Bessie Doyle was born in 1873 and emigrated to New Zealand with her mother. At a young age she began performing in public and soon won wide acclaim. Her marriage to Robert Mitchell certainly lasted at least eight years, and may have run a full course. *The New Zealand Free Lance* of 29 June 1907, in yet another gossip column, reported that 'the fair violinist with the goo-goo eyes has just reached Sydney from Vancouver ... her sweet face and dreamy eyes made a deep impression on many a Johnny's heart ... Then she got married and there was a honeymoon trip overland through the untravelled wilds of North Island from Auckland to Wellington. [The writer has confused this 'honeymoon' with the earlier trip when they first met, and has reversed the route.] ... she has changed her name yet again and is now billed as Eileen Mitchell O'Moore.'

From 1907 for two years she taught violin at Sydney's venerable music institution, Paling's. Ominously *The Free Lance* of 2 October 1909 has dropped the 'Mitchell' from her name: 'Madame Eileen O'Moore, who was Bessie Doyle, the violinist, and will be well remembered in Wellington, has sailed from Sydney for America, where she has been appointed violin professor at the Leland-Stanford University, San Francisco.'

11

'Water Cart Passed Over Head'

Four years earlier Robb Mitchell had predicted that tensions in South Africa would lead to war, and he was proved right. Conflict over the ownership of new goldfields discovered in Witwatersrand was the flashpoint, and on 11 October 1899 the Boers declared war against the predominantly British settlers they called Uitlanders. Officially known as the Second Anglo-Boer War, it went in favour of the Boers at first, who defeated relatively inexperienced combatants and besieged several major British townships. Reinforcements sent out from Britain soon began to turn the tables, and by June 1900 the Boer leader, Paul Kruger, had fled to Europe and the British had regained control.

Many believed the war had been won, but the Boers resorted to guerrilla tactics with devastating effect. Not until Kitchener, the new Commander-in-Chief, instigated the first concentration camps and a brutal scorched-earth policy was the conflict finally brought to an end, with the signing of the Treaty of Vereeniging in May 1902.

The war took a heavy toll of lives. The British lost around 20,000, the Boers considerably less in the field – between 4,000 and 7,000 – but casualties in the concentration camps were horrendous, between 20,000 and 40,000 lives lost, owing to squalid conditions and disease. The number of indigenous people killed was not recorded.

At the outbreak of war George Bullough offered *Rhouma* to the War Office as a hospital ship. Furthermore, he undertook to pay for all travel costs, wages, provisions and every other expense for as long as her services were required. The offer was accepted, and *Rhouma* was instructed to proceed to Cape Town at the earliest opportunity.

The master for the voyage was R. L. Foxworthy, in charge of a crew of thirty-seven. Their contracts were adapted to include caring and entertaining duties under the doctor's instruction. Some reports say the ship also carried a squad of fresh recruits for the front.

Rhouma left Oban on Boxing Day 1899, diverting to Rum to pick up the owner and his secretary. The weather was atrocious and they put in to Milford Haven on the 29th to sit out gales for three days. In this somewhat frustrating and depressing situation they welcomed in the new millennium.

The weather had been unusually bad that winter. Two months earlier the troop-carrier ss *Rapidan* endured a horror that would be remembered as one of Britain's worst maritime disasters had the lives that were lost been human. Nothing of that horror is diminished by time, but the event has slipped into oblivion as yet another instance of the forgotten sufferings and cruelties of war. As the wind and seas increased that night at the end of October, the captain of the *Rapidan* was advised to turn about and seek shelter, but he refused. Off Lands End the full fury of the storm hit the vessel, which now rolled and pitched at perilous angles. A fire broke out. As well as the troops, the ship carried 500 horses in the hold. In a frenzy of terror they began breaking loose, slipping on the metal deck, running berserk and lashing out with their hooves as they fell, trampling and being trampled on until the hold was a carnage of death and mutilation. The noise of their agony was deafening. Of the men trying to look after them, one went mad, another went into a fit and others had broken bones. Before the *Rapidan* reached Liverpool the corpses of one hundred horses were thrown overboard and, a newspaper reported, 'the same number will have to be shot'.

When the weather improved, *Rhouma* headed on to Madeira, where everyone enjoyed a rest for eight days. There were other shorter breaks at Las Palmas and St Vincent, before the longest leg of 2,875 miles along the Gulf of Loanda. Averaging twelve knots and burning a ton of coal every 26.1 miles, *Rhouma* made impressive progress, her Rawsons triple-expansion engines performing faultlessly. In Loanda they recoaled, and a day later called in at Benguela where they chanced upon their first casualty. As Mitchell explained in a letter to a friend:

> We had a good passage out here and commenced our work at Benguela, for at this place we picked up a Captain Quicke, 1st Dragoon Guards, who having stayed with a party of explorers under Major Gibbs, from the Zambesi, had made his way across the continent and landed at the above place ... We despatched a runner with an invitation to the man to come aboard and go on to South Africa. The man ... worn to a shadow with fever and fatigue ... appeared next day. He was almost speechless with emotion at feeling himself really on board a British ship talking to Englishmen, and so I now have no hesitation in saying that the poor chap would have died if we had not come along. It appears he was living with some Boers. This family tried its best to prevent his coming with us, wanting to keep him so as to make money out of him, and in the event of his dying to seize his belongings. He had been sleeping in a room next to the donkey, and the vile smelling place was fast completing what the journey had begun, his dissolution. For two days on board he tried to bear up, but the fever kept devouring him, and when we arrived in Cape Town we got a doctor, who helped us to get him into a private hospital. He is still extremely weak, but the fever is getting less, and he is now able to take a little nourishment, and I firmly believe he is on the fair way to recovery.

On 11 February 1900 they dropped anchor in five fathoms, three-quarters of a mile from a pierhead in Cape Town. The ship's log read 6,958 miles from Oban, and in steaming time it had taken them 24 days, 17 hours.

On the upper deck where under other circumstances it was

customary to hold dances, they immediately set to work building a twenty-bed ward. Within ten days Mitchell was able to report:

> We have built a wooden structure on the large after-deck and have made a ward capable of holding twenty non-commissioned officers and men, with two bathrooms, a good lavatory, and wc. We are working in connection with the Portland Hospital, taking convalescents from them, and No 3 Army hospital at Rondebosch. We have now twenty men and four officers aboard, and the people say we have the best ward in the colony ... The Tommies are very delighted with their quarters, and it does one's heart good to see the poor fellows' wounds healing up quickly under the influence of good plain food, rest and fresh air. Dr Bowlby, the chief of the Portland Hospital, says the men could not have a better place to recoup in. Singularly enough, there were some wounded men from the 2nd Worcesters in our first batch who had played football with our [*Rhouma's*] men in Bermuda, and were great chums with the crew on that account ...
>
> A friend of ours – Dr Dixon – whom we knew when we were here before, has obtained leave of absence from his regular duties as chief doctor of the Loch Hospital, Cape Town, and has come to live on board and look after our patients. So I can fairly say we are complete now.
>
> I am glad we came, because now we can see the good we do for the money expended, whereas, if George [Bullough] had subscribed a big cheque to a fund, he would have had no chance of seeing the immediate effect of his gift.

The first of the war casualties came on board on 4 March, and by 13 March some had been discharged, only to be immediately replaced. The *List of Patients on Board Hospital Ship SY Rhouma, Cape Town, 1900* still exists. Officers have been excluded, but it names the men – and in one case, boy – who passed through the makeshift ward.

> Boy Tehane, Official No. 3229, King's Royal Rifles, 4th–14th March, Conjunctivitis, Bugle Boy.
> Conductor C Foles, A.S.C., Scalp wound – water cart passed over head, at Slingersfontein.

Private J Jones, Loch's Horse, Fractured ribs – injured while breaking in raw Argentine horses.

How Conductor Foles escaped with a mere scalp wound after the water cart incident would be a story worth hearing! The most common injuries were gunshot wounds to feet, knees, thighs and shoulders. Some were extreme. 'Gun-shot wound on eye and neck. Bullet entered eye, down through palate, injured vocal cords, and broke collar bone.' 'Concussion of the brain; Lost sight of left eye.' 'Shot clean through both thighs while on horseback.' Other ravages not inflicted by the enemy were dysentery, ulcers, contusions and sunstroke. A reporter from the local newspaper *Argus* concluded that 'most of the men placed on board this vessel are of the class who have just so far recovered from very severe wounds as to be removed [from hospital], and will yet require some considerable time and careful attention to reach complete recovery'.

Rhouma was not the only philanthropist's ship in the bay. The other was a three-masted steamer, *Jason*, donated by Mr Bibby of the steamship company Bibby Line. The *Jason* was larger, but there was no comparison between the two for *bon vivant* comfort, as the *Argus* and various letters testify.

In ordinary circumstances this craft is a most luxuriously equipped vessel ... Her cabins and staterooms ... are furnished and upholstered in a most luxurious and up-to-date manner ... The drawing-room and dining-room are magnificent specimens of the furnisher's art, while more comfortable staterooms have certainly never been seen in Cape waters ... The fresh breezes of the bay – let us hope for no south-easters – will have a beneficial effect on the patients, while those who are fit for recreation and amusement shall have it provided. The *Rhouma* has on her davits a beautiful steam launch, and pleasant trips round the large fleet of transports will be made, while music and other evening pastimes will not be neglected.

Another correspondent remarked: 'I spent Monday night on

board the *Rhouma* ... and they were having a concert. I never enjoyed a night better in my life.'

Perhaps this refers to the virtuoso violin-playing of Eileen Mitchell O'Moore, but undoubtedly other musicians and artistes from Cape Town were invited aboard. George took the welfare of his patients seriously, once being in charge for five weeks when Dr Dixon was sent to the front. Two members of the crew were seconded to assist at the nearby Rondebosch Hospital, while everyone else 'helped entertain the patients on board with deck games, music, stories and fishing.' Photographs show men relaxing on deck – if indeed one can relax in those stiff-upturned collars – playing charades in fancy dress and being shaved amid great hilarity. A picture of Boy Tehane shows him to be about fifteen years old. The ship was also 'thrown open to friends of the patients every Tuesday and Friday afternoon from three until five.'

One surprise visitor, mentioned in a letter, was none other than Joe Grimshaw, in what must have been his first escape from Howard & Bullough's office for decades. It is reassuring to know his job had occasional perks.

By September 1900, the numbers of casualties had dwindled, and with them went the need for a floating convalescence ward. The following month the city fathers presented the owner of *Rhouma* with a large testimonial.

In October 1900 the Corporation of the city of Cape Town do hereby place on record their appreciation of the patriotic services which have been rendered to the Empire by Mr George Bullough, Island of Rum, by Oban, Argyllshire, North Britain, in placing at the disposal of the Imperial Authorities, for a period of upwards of a year, the steam yacht *Rhouma* for use as a recruiting station for soldiers invalided from the Front and for the numerous other actions which he has taken for the alleviation of the suffering of those injured during the campaign 1899–1900.

Rhouma departed on 9 October at the end of nine months on

station. The return journey recorded 6,300 miles on the log in 23 days 1 hour 41 minutes, a faster passage than before, averaging 12.7 knots. The best day's run was 318 miles, 'a record for a steam yacht'. She consumed a total of 172 tons of coal.

The speed must have suited George, for he was looking forward to seeing his completed castle for the first time. He had been giving it considerable thought during his stay in Cape Town and decided on another remarkably benevolent gesture. As Mitchell wrote shortly after their arrival in Table Bay:

> George and I had a talk the other day, with the result that I have written to Jack Brown [the factor at Rum] to ask him to arrange and see how many convalescent officers they can put up in the new house at Rum, and also the White House. We want if possible, say, about twenty. I have told Brown to see what he can do, and then put himself in communication with the authorities. If we can handle twenty men and six officers here, and say twenty officers at Rum, we feel that we are doing our little towards the great whole.

Twenty recuperating officers did indeed travel back to Scotland on board *Rhouma*, and perhaps this is where the uncharitable rumour first started that George Bullough's hospital ship had been exclusively for officers and not for 'other ranks'. The facts could scarcely be more different. Through the floating canvas ward, fed and entertained at the owner's expense, had passed 216 men and 46 officers, without a single fatality.

Rhouma's first landfall in British waters was the Isle of Rum. On 4 November 1900 she nosed into Loch Scresort, where a monumental red castle now dominated the shoreline. Half of those on board disembarked and *Rhouma* proceeded to Oban on her way 'home' to the James Watt Dock in Greenock to be prepared for another cruise. In just five weeks she would set sail again, this time bound for the West Indies, Madeira and a tour of the Mediterranean. For five weeks George Bullough would allow himself to be distracted by an expression of excellence that had been three years in construction and had cost the equivalent of fifteen million pounds. What he had previously seen as no more than crude outlines in stone and paper was now close to completion. On that November day the castle's great door was thrown open and he stepped inside for the first time, followed by twenty limping guests.

12

A Dream in Stone, Glass and Gadgets

To BUILDERS. Tenders are invited, in one contract, for the ERECTION of a RESIDENCE, ISLE OF RUM, by Oban, West Scotland. Closing Friday 5 February. Tenders must be delivered not later than 4pm to Messers Leeming at Royal Hotel, Oban.

Advertisement in *The Scotsman*, 22 & 25 January 1897.

So enamoured was George Bullough with *Rhouma* that his initial instructions to Leeming & Leeming specified that the castle should be based on her length, that is, a square of sides 221 feet long. A site inspection of the demolished Tigh Mor supposedly showed this proposal to be impractical in the space available between two burns.* Even at the smaller size the site was predominantly a bog. The dimensions finally agreed were 150 feet.

Just as *Rhouma*'s dining room was designed for sixteen at table, the castle was intended for the same number of guests. It was therefore not a particularly large shooting lodge, for that was really its purpose, but the emphasis was to be on quality: the highest calibre of workmanship, the finest brands procurable, the very latest technologies.

---

* The 'two burns' traditionally cited as the reason for the smaller castle do not exist today and there is no obvious reason why the site could not have been enlarged as George Bullough desired.

Nothing of Leeming and Leeming's preoccupation with municipal buildings and chapels is apparent in Kinloch Castle, perhaps mercifully, but neither is there much evidence of any architectural ability at all. It is far from pretty and lacks elegance, resembling a squat pastiche of Balmoral in miniature. Its redness jars rudely in the landscape and its proportions are self-consciously awkward. The castle is a two-storey edifice liberally furnished with windows and crenellated edges. A tower stands at each corner. The main entrance is on the eastern side below an off-centre square tower on which a taller circular tower rides piggyback. The rear or western section was originally only a single-storey with a gate in the middle to allow access to the inner courtyard. Later it was increased to three storeys to provide additional accommodation for servants and guests, and the gate became a 'tunnel'. On three sides of the building guests could walk round the outside walls under a glass-roofed verandah supported by a colonnade of arches; this was the castle's most charming and unique feature. Integrated into this colonnade on the south side was a spacious conservatory – no longer in existence – with a dome like a tiered pagoda. One particularly unusual feature was the fact that the roof did not overlap the walls but ended on top of them, emptying rain into a lead-lined gutter connected to down-pipes hidden within the masonry. This feature gives the external walls a clean, uncluttered simplicity.

George apparently had not taken to the colour of the most readily available sandstone, the light pink Torridonian found on Rum, but chose instead the ruby red variety found in the Isle of Arran.† This fact is usually presented by commentators as an indicator of his money-be-damned extravagance. He *was* extravagant, but such an explanation is simplistic in the case of

---

† Corsehill Quarry at Annan, Dumfriesshire, is sometimes cited as the source, but geological analysis of the stone undertaken on behalf of Scottish Natural Heritage concludes that it came from the quarry at Corrie, Arran. Graham Bullough has corroborated this by discovering that Willie Kelso, skipper of the smack *Glen Sannox*, 'took some of the Corrie sandstone over to the Isle of Rhum for the mansion house they were building there'.

the sandstone-colour choice. The two types of sandstone are very different. The local Torridonian is full of inconsistencies and much harder to work, being well-cemented and stronger-grained. The cost of importing machinery and establishing a quarry on Rum would have been prohibitive; much greater than the transport costs of softer Arran sandstone from an existing quarry. Ironically it would have been better if he had preferred the colour of the local sandstone and applied a cost-be-damned attitude to this option, as the material might have been much more durable, a factor that is of major concern today.

The blocks were cut and dressed at Corrie and transported to Rum by sailing smacks and puffers – those stalwart, dumpy, flat-bottomed craft essential for delivering freight on Scotland's west coast. And the cargo was not just stone. Every item required to build the castle came the same way, along with 250,000 tons of Ayrshire soil for the gardens. It was a colossal undertaking and the logistics were intimidating. The railway to Mallaig had yet to be completed (1901) and the nearest serviceable port was distant Oban. There was no suitable jetty in Loch Scresort, so smacks and puffers had to strand themselves at low water and transfer their cargoes, up to 80 tonnes in the case of puffers, to a convoy of horses and carts toiling over the sand. How many tens of thousands of trips did it take? How many weeks of delays did the weather cause? Yes, it was a folly, but to have conquered such overwhelming difficulties ranks as an epic achievement.

Three hundred men worked on the castle for three years. Their camp grew up around the site, and with the addition of the ancillary staff required to cater for them, it must have seemed like a veritable gold-rush town. The main contractor was John Copeland of Uddingston, with James Reid as the Clerk of Works.* One of the Leeming brothers made occasional visits

---

* No one knew who the building contractor was until 2002, when Mary Wardle contacted the Kinloch Castle Friends Association to say that she believed her grandfather's uncle, John Copeland, had built Kinloch Castle. In *Uddingston, the Village* by David Jamieson, she found this was confirmed, and John shared out the work with other local tradesmen: the firm of Renwick & Morton

(a 'Mr Leeming' caught two one-pound brown trout on 11 June 1900), and principal architect Richard Feilding Farrer must have been there more often, but because he did not catch any fish his movements went unrecorded.

The workforce was partly local, mainly from Eigg, with a large contingent supposedly from Lancashire, but the majority must have come from around Uddingston. At the peak of construction their numbers included forty master carpenters. Scarcely a photograph of the castle being built exists, so it is not clear how prevalent the wearing of kilts was. The legend asserts that George insisted the workmen wore kilts of his specially-devised Rhum tartan, and paid them a bonus shilling a week to do so. This was not a sufficient incentive in the midge season, so a further 2d a week was paid to kilt-wearers, who smoked to create a protective smokescreen. I cannot find any evidence of this practice. It seems unlikely, considering that George was absent for the majority of the construction phase, but it cannot be entirely dismissed given his fondness for the trappings of a Highland laird, including wearing his Rhum tartan kilt for his thirty-ninth birthday portrait.

The midges were not the only curse. One Lancashire worker is reputed to have complained, 'If it in't midges, it's clegs. If it in't clegs, it's rain.'

---

supplied the masons, Morton (perhaps from the same contractor) undertook the slate work, John Williamson the painting, Hugh Binning the plumbing, and John Copeland himself was in charge of the joinery as well as the overall contract. He was born in 1841 in Auchindoir, Aberdeenshire, the son of a Master Carpenter and General Wright, and would have learned the same skills. He started his own business but had his assets sequestered in 1884 for debts that were not discharged until 1891. Mrs Wardle's grandfather invested some money in the revived business when the castle contract was awarded. Unfortunately Copeland proved far from honest in his disclosures about the project. She wrote: 'My father had one very vivid memory of old John sitting quietly in the evenings with his parrot on his shoulder both enjoying their dram – the parrot had his in an eggcup that he delicately held in one claw. When John died on 17 July 1907 he was found to be bankrupt. He had badly underestimated on Kinloch and had nothing left, all his money had gone and so had my grandfather's – he had never known John was in debt.' Perhaps for this reason Kinloch Castle was not mentioned in Copeland's obituaries.

Construction lasted from summer 1897 to some time in 1901. The castle was clearly habitable on 4 November 1900, when the owner and the Boer War invalids arrived, but some workmen remained to finish off minor details, and the place was probably minimally furnished. The 1901 census for 31 March shows that the following were still engaged at the castle: twenty-four labourers, five housekeepers, five joiners, two masons, a blacksmith, dynamo attendant, electrical engineer, engineman, upholsterer, 'oddman', 'navvy' and a 'rustic worker'. Outside, quite apart from the estate-workers and shepherds, there were no fewer than nine gardeners and six garden labourers listed, along with a coachman and two grooms. The sounds of sawing, hammering and fetching were still echoing about the place. The invalids must have longed for the peace of Table Bay. Kinloch Castle sprang up incredibly quickly, but one reason the workforce remained large right to the end was the quality of the finish. Cabinet-makers today look on the oak panelling throughout and marvel at the finesse and fit, and doubt whether such craftsmanship still exists. The most splendid and largest room lay behind the main door, the baronial Great Hall rising up the full height of the house, with an upper balcony on three sides and three tall mullioned bay windows partly decorated in stained glass. As the initial reception area it was designed to impress, and this it certainly did when filled with stags' heads and the spoils of the world tour: the multi-ton bronze monkey-eating eagle and incense-burners, the Mikado's lost ivory eagle, and numerous tigers flattened on the floor, their mouths agape like mantraps (and equally effective).

Yet what made the castle distinctive at the time were its technological innovations. A lever in the Billiard Room activated an air-conditioning system which changed the air every twenty minutes, drawing in fresh air through a grid under the table and expelling the cloud of cigar smoke on the ceiling through vents. The windows here consisted of an early form of double-glazing, or more correctly secondary glazing, being two parallel panes on a Z hinge which allowed them to open and close together. Central heating was provided through a system of radiators topped with marble, which acted as a slow-release heat store. There was an internal telephone system so rare in Scotland that possibly only a single other home could boast of having its equal (Mount Stewart on Bute, which had installed one three years earlier). George already had a telegraph link so he could catch up on the latest racing results, the ss *Monarch* having laid a cable to Rum in 1900.* Four fire hydrants – fire was one of his constant fears – were sited at each corner of the castle, with sufficient power to send a jet clean over the roof. All ground staff were trained in their use.

However, the greatest revolution in domestic life introduced to Kinloch Castle was created by the electrical engineer and the dynamo attendant, employees of G. H. Woods & Company, Blackburn, and pioneers of a new trade. England had examples of homes with private electricity supplies as early as 1880, when the first filament bulbs became available. Among them was Hatfield, the seat of Lord Salisbury who had previously owned Rum, but the technology was still experimental and one of Hatfield's gardeners was electrocuted. Such early problems had largely been overcome and it was a safer system that was installed at Kinloch Castle in 1899. Was it the first domestic supply in Scotland? No, the Berwickshire residence of Manderston had its own supply in 1897, the Peebles Hydro in 1898 and Skibo Castle the following year, but Kinloch Castle was certainly among the elite few to embrace the electric dawn. (Yet only in the castle. Electricity was not extended to the school for another fifty years.) Indeed Kinloch was a celebration of the filament lamp: over one hundred glowed in the Billiard Room alone, and the Ballroom's ceiling became a panoply of electric stars.

The system was powered by a hydro scheme which depended on a reservoir built 600 feet up in the loins of Hallival, Coire

---

* A letter in the *Oban Times* from the GPO acknowledges that 'this important telegraphic extension could never have been accomplished without the generous assistance of the proprietors of the three islands, viz – Mr Bullough of Rum, Mr Thom of Canna, and Mr Thompson of Eigg.' The cable was extended from Ardvasar on Skye.

Dubh, harnessing the Allt Slugan a' Chuillich burn. A cast-iron pipe of prodigious bore carried water to a turbine house on the edge of the castle grounds. The system was supported by a small battery house and produced 110 volts DC. It was all so well constructed that the dam and conduit are still in use today. The generator was only replaced in 1983 to upgrade to a more powerful unit that would produce AC and allow the community to use 240-volt televisions, fridges and freezers. Although none of the early lightbulbs are in use today, the original lampshades are still in service, and their survival is credited to direct current's lower wattage.

If electricity was novel, some of the plumbing was unique. Three baths were conventional at one end but incorporated a shower chamber at the other. This resembled a sentry box made of mahogany. Hidden behind were lead pipes entangled like Medusa on a bad hair day. Standing within this chamber the bather operated six taps to unleash a vertical Jacuzzi. Each tap controlled a particular effect, from giving a standard shower to allowing the user to be plunged, sprayed, waved, jetted, douched or sitzed. Douching produced a torrent from a single point above while wave was a pulsing blitz of water at neck height. Spray struck from the sides and enveloped the upper torso in sharp but delicate needles, and plunge directed a fireman's hose at the knees. Sitz was a charming inversion of a shower with the water rising up from the floor, and jet, the most dangerous, sent a single fountain up from between your feet and was once described as 'like a ramrod up your privates'. The taps could be used in any combination or simultaneously, though the effect of the latter was like sharing your sentry box with a tsunami. These marvellous inventions were built by Shanks of Barrhead, Glasgow. One exhibited at the 1888 Glasgow International Exhibition only had three taps but this was just not enough for George Bullough. And other outrageous contraptions would be added to the castle later.

Sporting facilities were given prominence in the policies close to the castle where a tennis court, bowling green, croquet lawn and even a compact golf course were laid out, and a dedicated squash court was built in isolation a short walk from the rear entrance. The only thing missing was a swimming pool, as for some reason George had balked at the cost. A letter in the castle archives dated 1899 to Messers Leeming & Leeming, Architects, reads: 'Dear Sirs, I hereby offer to do the whole work in connection with the swimming baths, Island of Rhum, for George Bullough, Esq, for the sum of £4,760. Your obedient servant, John Ross.' This was £700 cheaper than the next quote and did not seem unreasonable for excavating rock and building a miniature Crystal Palace, but John Ross's offer was declined. Bullough and guests had to make do with plunging and sitzing instead.

Gardens had been started; their full development was to take place over the next decade and culminated in ornate rockeries beside a river landscaped into ornamental pools and cascades, extensive rose beds, a Japanese garden complete with rainbow bridge and shrine, and one-and-a-half acres of walled vegetable garden. At its peak a permanent staff of twelve, sometimes fourteen, gardeners worked full time on the grounds under the first head gardener, Samuel Nash. He appears to have been the main architect of the design, probably in consultation with the owner, who had already demonstrated a particular interest in botany and its presentation. Nash had previously been employed at prestigious Alton Towers in Staffordshire so he came with impressive credentials. Rum must have represented his greatest challenge, though he was not unfamiliar with the whims of the family, having first been hired to work at Rhyddings Hall. By 1906 the Rum gardener winning prizes at shows was Thomas Young, and then came Percy Hills in 1910, so the challenge of the island's gardens obviously took its toll on staff.

Undoubtedly the showpieces of the grounds were the glasshouses on both sides of the walled garden at its north end. These were identical to the ones found at Meggernie, though it is unclear which was copied from which. Meggernie's glasshouses certainly never contained such a weird assortment of species as those on Rum. The north side was used for potting workshops but also incorporated a Mushroom House and full-sized Palm House. The south-facing sections numbered fourteen and were 110 metres in length, comprising Ferneries, a Camellia House and at least eight sections dedicated to fruit. Apart from the exotic plants and trees of Ceylon and Madeira, here grew Hamborough and muscatel grapes, figs, peaches and nectarines in an abundance that occasionally defeated the pickers. Steam-heating supplemented solar and was necessary because the Camellia House was home to around twenty free-flying humming-birds. When, eventually, the heating system failed, the birds died. In a severe test of the taxidermist's skill they were sent to be stuffed. You can see them still in the castle today, frozen in flight behind glass.

Even more bizarre than humming-birds in the Hebrides were the contents of two heated ponds in the western section of the glasshouses: one contained turtles and the other alligators. The inspiration for these pets is obvious – had black panthers been easier to find I daresay they would have ended up in Rum too. Bullough and Mitchell had taken Sunday lunch at a hotel in Ceylon's Mount Lavinia where 'Live turtles are kept on the premises, so that a fastidious eater can choose his own turtle for his soup.' And in both Jeypoor and Lahore ('see fight, see fight!') they had encountered captive alligators in tanks. Contrary to myth, neither the turtles nor alligators were ever eaten. They were kept purely as a part of a menagerie. The turtles proved more expensive than anticipated, if hearsay is to be believed. While he was leaning over the tank one day a valuable diamond ring slipped from George's hand. Despite an exhaustive search the ring was never found, and it was supposed a turtle had swallowed it.

The novelty value of these creatures lasted many years, ending shortly before the First World War. The turtles were taken some ten miles away to the far side of Canna and released into the sea. They probably died the same day, but in subsequent years an occasional turtle appeared in fishermen's nets and was assumed to be of Rum provenance. The alligators were housed in a separate tank with its surface safely below an onlooker's reach, and encircled by bars 'as thick as my thumb'. The quote came from an attendant, a Mr Macdonald of Soay, and the bars referred to must surely have been of wood rather than iron, for he complained that the captives kept gnawing their way through. When a guest met one that had escaped and suffered a severe fright, the alligators' fate was sealed. They were shot. The official reason given for their execution was for 'interfering with the comfort of the guests'.

The interior of the castle was, in terms of lay-out, décor and furnishings, very much a bachelor pad for the first two years of its existence. George's tastes appear to have leaned heavily towards the brash, vulgar and bourgeois. He shared the Victorian predeliction for dark wood and gloomy interiors, and the common man's myopia as regards domestic practicality. After his marriage the castle was to be radically altered. The cost of it at this stage had been around £250,000, still less than one year's income for him.

* * *

On 11 December 1901 King Edward VII, as an expression of the nation's gratitude for his patriotic act of bringing comfort and relief to British troops in South Africa, dipped his sword to the shoulder of Rum's owner and created him a Knight Bachelor.

The event was noted in the newspapers of the day. The *Oban Times*, which would report every one of Lady Breadalbane's tea parties but would steadfastly ignore the events of Rum, including the marriage and death of its owner, nevertheless recorded this investiture, describing Sir George as 'exceedingly popular in the West Highlands'. New Zealand's ever-vigilant *Otago Witness* of 9 April 1902 published the following article, with its light-hearted mix of bias and barbs, and some uncharacteristic grace.

THE LORD OF RHUM

Sir George Bullough, whose name heads the list of the King's Birthday Knights, is scarcely known in London Society. He is possessed of a princely fortune that his father made in business in Lancashire, and to which he succeeded when about 14. His mother speedily married again and the lad was left much to his own devices – with the usual result. His father had purchased the Island of Rhum in the Hebrides, one of the most wildly desolate of all those misty isles. It was a curious fancy to enter the head of an Accrington cotton-spinner, but the late Mr Bullough became so devotedly attached to his Highland home that he desired to be buried upon one of the mountain spurs that overlook the sullen, plunging Atlantic, miles from any human habitation. And there he lies in a tomb far more desolate and romantic than is that of Chateaubriand, off the Breton coast.

The monument above him is weird in the extreme. It is built of costly marbles, adorned by mosaics of finest Italian workmanship. Long before it was finished, and the £50,000 which it cost was paid, his widow had re-married, and people said that Rhum had seen the last of the Bulloughs. But the son, now Sir George, also felt the charm of the place. His splendid yacht, the Rhuma, or his sailing-cutter, Mystery, often carried him across the 40 miles of water that stretch between his island and Oban. But the companions he chose were not wisely chosen, and the county magnates of Argyll and Inverness began to look askance at the young laird of Rhum.

Then came the South African war. Wretched work as it has proved, it, as it were, threw a rope to George Bullough. Here was something his thousands could do – something better than providing pleasures which brought trouble in their train. So the beautiful Rhuma was fitted out as a hospital ship, and her owner took her himself to Cape Town, where he spared neither time, nor purse, nor brains to serve his country in the time of sore need. His enormous mansion house in Rhum was placed at the disposal of wounded officers: and their wives were invited to be fellow-guests.

The long range of conservatories sheltered fruits and flowers for them in winter; the pretty Mystery took them lazy cruises in calm summer days. There were grouse on the moors and deer –

Rhum is one of the finest deer forests in Scotland – for autumn sport; and salmon in the streams which come tumbling down the steep glens of Oreval and Haskaval, the giant hills of Rhum.

It was not only generosity and the lavish use of gold that Mr Bullough gave, but a rare personal devotion and self-sacrifice. Patriotism woke up all the good in the man's nature. He is a healthy, busy, happy man today, and his Majesty's birthday present comes, we believe, to one worthy to receive it, and who will worthily wear it.

The reference to his less respectable companions and catching the attention of Argyll's magnates may be the usual gossip-mongering of the press, but nevertheless it is interesting to note that rumours of the Lord of Rhum's excesses, self-confessed in Madeira, had crossed the globe.

Kinloch Castle was built as a party house, never as a permanent residence. It was only ever occupied by its owner for around six weeks each year, and it has been calculated that his total use of it amounted to less than a hundred weeks. This made it a very expensive holiday home, but that was not the point. The role of the castle was to provide privacy and pleasure. It was a house of flamboyance in which luxurious comfort could combine with a fantasy of Highland chieftainship, in which the trappings of society's highest refinements could be indulged or discarded in complete secrecy. However reprehensible this may be judged to be in terms of selfishness or immorality, it would be hypocritical to pretend that contemporary society is any different; such a dream remains the Holy Grail of the masses. Here was one man who could, and did, live that dream.

Sir George he might now be, but the wild parties were to continue. In fact, they had hardly begun.

13

Sexuality and Parties

The ballroom at Kinloch Castle was designed for privacy. The windows are disproportionately small and distinctive in being placed too high to be looked through by prying voyeurs in the courtyard. The orchestra played in a chamber recessed into the upper storey and screened from the ballroom by a heavy curtain, which remained permanently closed. That chamber was accessed by an external stairway. No servants entered the ballroom. Drinks, cigars and any other requirements were delivered behind a screen and through a dumb waiter, a hatch with a door on each side which opened only when its opposite door was shut. Whatever went on in the ballroom might be heard but not seen. And whatever was heard was of less value than a contract of employment.

In the castle library, not hidden but not on show either, there is a hand-painted cartoon of three inebriated men, perhaps dancing the Dashing White Sergeant, perhaps supporting each other at the end of a party. All three are wearing top hats, two are in long-tailed evening dress, while the huge central figure wears what can only be described as a mini-kilt. One man has a bottle stashed under his arm. The caption reads: 'These little creatures are not dangerous!!! they are only merry – (result of Friandises)'. On the back it says, 'A happy Christmas to little George', signed 'Bullough'. I assume the Bullough was one of his cousins. Little George is obviously the central figure in the kilt and the reference to friandises (sweets containing liqueurs) is a jest to divert attention from the effects of the bottle. Is there any relevance in that it only depicts men, that the kilt is extremely short and that one man could be construed to have a hand in a compromising position? Can anything of George's sexuality be extracted from a Christmas card, for goodness' sake? Well, more lurid deductions have been made out of even thinner material:

> This lavish baronial Edwardian pile was the home of gay George Bullough, a man who was responsible for turning it into, well, a pretty plush brothel that hosted the wildest of orgies. Royalty attended. Not only did Bullough, an enthusiastic writer of erotic fiction, recruit his own team of handsome young men for occasional footie, but his staff were promised a bit extra in their wages if they wore a kilt. Bullough was an expensive queen. Just imagine spending £20 million in today's money on a holiday home. He had to have the latest and the best ... The Edwardian showers were delightful, tantalisingly spraying water into every orifice. But while the silk brocades, the fabulous paintings and elaborate furniture remained intact, the S&M cage was politely returned to the family.
>
> And his parties? Well, if walls could talk ... I eagerly watched [a television guide] take viewers round, waiting for this important monument to our sexual history to be uncovered. But the nearest we got was a discreet mention of lavish dinner parties and wild soirées. In Edwardian times when the working classes were exposed and castigated for any lapse in morality, the upper classes quietly got away with murder. No change there then. Their secret was safe.

This extract from *www.scotsgay.co.uk/text/sg53a.txt* is a recent addition to the castle archives and someone has annotated it, 'Proof? Proof? Proof?' The challenge is justified. What evidence is there of Sir George's homosexuality? The reports of his world tour certainly show a bias towards admiring the physiques of men, in particular the semi-clad coalers in various ports and the almost naked Zulus. The writer found nothing attractive in the

Maharajah of Jeypoor's dancers who had been picked for their beauty. (Not much to go on here, for these observations were not made by Sir George but Robb Mitchell.) Is it significant that he shared a bedroom in a Japanese hotel with his male secretary? Well, it was a large room with twin beds, and perhaps every other room was taken? The financial inducement offered for brawny Lancashire builders to wear kilts does indeed seem perverse, but may have arisen from nothing more than a liking for the Highland image to the point of parody, an attempt to make Rum an extreme of Highlandification. And the main fuel for the rumours, the overwhelming numbers of male guests at the castle? This may indeed be the clincher, but it could equally well mean that as some of the chief attractions of the island were hunting, shooting and fishing – predominantly male pastimes – judging the sex of visitors from the signatures in the *Game Books* will inevitably produce a male bias. Yet where does a rumour of male orgies stem from? Was it a true story or was it a smear made by those forced to serve the idle rich while they revelled in potting deer and downing jeroboams of champagne night after night? And the evidence against? It is equally vacuous. George's alleged affair with his stepmother would indicate heterosexual interest. The World Tour photographs do show several semi-naked women, in particular the forty bare-breasted wives of Zulu chief Usibeppo and some of those of John Dunn.* The

---

* John Dunn was one of the legendary figures of what was Natal and Zululand. The son of Scottish emigrants who were among the first to settle in Natal, he was born there in 1833. Brought up outside the influence of the colonial power, John Dunn 'went native' and 'renounced civilisation', wanting no part of the administrative restrictions that increasingly imposed themselves on his freedom. He spoke Zulu, took forty-eight wives and fathered an estimated one hundred and seventeen children. An exceptional ability with a rifle earned him occasional employment as a hunting guide. When King Cetshwayo of the Zulu nation realised he needed white support against the encroaching colonists, he selected Dunn and they became close friends. As a 'white chief' Dunn attained considerable power and wealth, and did much to found a sugar industry in the region. Unable to remain neutral in the Anglo-Zulu War of 1879, Dunn served the British in an effort to save his Zulu subjects. After the war he retained his status as chief, but not for long, dying on 5 Aug 1895, roughly two years after Bullough's first visit.

visit to the Shimpuro Brothel is relevant, as is the fact that both Bullough and Mitchell married and, although this may have been a convenient front for their predilections, the marriages endured longer than would be expected if purely charades. The only clear evidence of homosexual tendencies would come from 'confessions' or other testimony, and none has so far come to light. Homosexuality was a crime in Britain until 1967, punishable by imprisonment. It took both conviction and courage to 'come out' in those days, and few were like Oscar Wilde who did, and suffered for it. George Bullough would have nothing to gain and everything to lose by admitting such a sexual preference. On Rum he could have exercised it, and perhaps he did. There is nothing more substantial than whispers behind any allegations of homosexuality; most indicators point to heterosexuality.

In a self-deprecating poem scrawled in the *Rum Deer Forest Book* in 1929, Sir George (calling himself 'Paul') lampoons his own fondness for women and his narcissistic habit of combing his hair – to the exasperation of his stalker, Sinclair, who walks away and leaves him to his vanity. ('Pete' is probably his great friend, Sir William Bass, the brewer.) In the second verse Sinclair† says:

> *Let's leave him there*
> *To comb his hair;*
> *I'm certain you'll find*
> *If you leave him behind*
> *He'll attract every hind*
> *From far and near.*
> *Leave his Lordship behind*
> *To deal with the hind;*

---

† Sinclair is referred to as 'that stalker bold'. He has 12 entries in the *Deer Book* for 1928 alone, and none before or after. This verse was written in 1929 when he was no longer stalking. It's curious that he was featured and not others who had longer and more distinguished service.

We'll go to yon crag
And shoot a big stag.
So Pete who was fleeter
And footed it neater
O'er hillock and crag
Went and shot a fine stag
While Paul stayed behind
Making love to the hind.

Again, how much can one read into a whimsical poem? More significant is the fact that at the time of his knighthood George was already having a long-standing affair with a married woman. She was, it is said, enjoying numerous other affairs simultaneously, most notoriously with the man who had held the sword that knighted Sir George. Yet the suggestion persists that there was something artificial and contrived about this key relationship in Sir George's life. It progressed into a marriage throughout which husband and wife kept separate bedrooms situated in different corners of the castle. Although they continued to holiday together, it soon became the gossip that they preferred to visit Kinloch Castle with their own choices of guests, that the licentious parties continued, George's with male friends and occasionally Gaiety Girls from Glasgow, conveyed north in private rail coaches and across the sea in *Rhouma*. George's half-brother, Ian, aged twenty-six, married a former Gaiety Girl called Lily Elsie in 1912. A connection therefore exists, but once again whether this shows that the rumours were fact or speculation has not yet come to light.

However many men or women came into his life, the one who claimed him was Monica Charrington.

14

Gomma and the Half-Tarpon

Monica Charrington was born as Monique Lilly Ducarel in New Zealand on 8 April 1869, making her one year older than George. Her father, Gerard Gustavus Ducarel, 4th Marquis de la Pasture*, had ended up in New Zealand after his family had fled from France during Madame Guillotine's Reign of Terror in 1791. With his brother he leased 31,000 acres of high-country sheep-grazing near the Lewis Pass, although he spent most of his time in Christchurch which was where Monique was born. She never knew her mother, Léontine ('Lilly') Standish, who did not survive the delivery.

Shortly after this, the count left New Zealand and settled at Somerford Manor in Cheshire. Monique switched between using the French version of her name and Monica, depending on the language she was using at the time. Her religion is never mentioned, though her first marriage took place in the Church of the Sacred Heart, Hove, which suggests she was a Catholic. Catholicism certainly played no further part in her life, nor did any other formal doctrine. She owned a copy of *The Scottish Hymnal* ('Kinloch Castle, Not To Be Removed From This Pew') which marks two favourite hymns, *Rock of Ages* and *Oh God Our Help in Ages Past*.

---

* The emphasis is on *lá*, and the 's' of Pasture is not pronounced – delápature.

At the age of twenty, in 1889, Monica married a man ten years her senior, Charles E. N. Charrington. A member of the wealthy brewing family, he was a partner in the firm and a talented pianist and amateur composer. The couple lived at Frensham Hall in Surrey, and their daughter, Dorothea Elizabeth, was born a year later. They also had a London house in Pont Street, and each residence would eventually prove useful to husband and wife as a refuge from the company of the other.

Monica's unfaithfulness hit the papers in 1896, when she was named as the 'intervener' in Lord Cowley's divorce case. Their affair had begun in 1892 and continued for four years, with trysts in hotels as far afield as Holland. Both denied the charges under oath, and the case dragged on for weeks, with so much evidence emerging that it finally went undefended. Charles Charrington was aware of his wife's infidelity by 1895, when the couple separated. Monica was given an extraordinary allowance of £2,000 p.a. Denied custody of her daughter and apparently abandoning her, she subsequently moved between residences in London and Paris, and continued to enjoy life as a society belle.

Her beauty was such that it would have been nigh on impossible for her to have avoided the countless affairs she is said to have had. Whether she can be counted as one of the Prince of Wales' mistresses has not been proved. Her name does not appear in any of the published works on the subject, but it would not be surprising – in the same league as John Dunn for womanising, his favours were bestowed on a considerable proportion of his female subjects. It is therefore not beyond credibility that Sir George received his knighthood at least in part for a service beyond those rendered during the Boer War, but the possibility remains slight. Why should he have merited such a reward when, for example, Emma Hartmann's husband did not, under identical circumstances?*

---

* When Edward VII made his 'coronation cruise' in the late summer of 1902 there was great speculation in the press about his destination after leaving the

Gomma and the Half-Tarpon

Monica's thirteen-year charade of marriage to Charles Charrington ended in the Divorce Court, London. The case was heard on 18 November 1902 with 'Sir George Bullough – Knight' cited as her co-respondent. *The Times* announced the details: ' . . . by reason of her misconduct with Sir George Bullough. The suit was undefended . . . Counsel explained that Sir George was a great yachting man. Earlier this year Mr Charrington's wife went out to Madeira where Sir George's yacht then was. She travelled with him in his yacht. Decree nisi, with costs, was granted.' (In fact she joined *Rhouma* at Tangiers and went on to Madeira and the West Indies.) The divorce was finalised on 25 May 1903. Within a month Monica and Sir George were married.

They had met at least six years earlier. A copy of *Anna Karenina* in the castle library has the following inscription in George's writing: 'To Monica – 1898 in memory of our first year of friendship from Zuzu'. To be signing himself 'Zuzu' (she would become 'Gomma' both to George and friends) hints at a relationship that was already intimate. Certain pages from this era have been torn from a family photograph album in the castle but others show Monica on a cruise whose itinerary appears similar to the one cited in the divorce proceedings, only it took place a year earlier in celebration of George's thirty-first birthday early in 1901. She is pictured with a half-tarpon she had caught, most probably off Florida. Tarpon are a coastal species of fish found in warm Atlantic waters, and popular with anglers because of their size and fighting qualities. Known as 'silver kings', they grow over six feet in length, weigh up to 350 pounds and have the unusual ability to take in oxygen from the air when their gills fail to find enough in water. George's poem 'The Rhoumaging, Rumaging, Rotters' written in Madeira on that trip reveals their next destination, 'To the land of stars and stripes, Where the

---

Sound of Mull. Rum was cited as a strong contender. Why Rum out of all the places where other stately homes or aristocracy might be found? Might it be because of a previous 'connection' to the owner's wife? In the end the royal vessel passed between Rum and Canna and headed round the top of Skye.

Tarpon glides and plunges'. The tarpon caught were preserved and sent back to grace the walls of Kinloch Castle, where they can still be seen. One is labelled, 'Weight: 150 lbs, Length: 7 feet. Girth: 39 inches'. Monica's fish was whole when she hooked it, but a shark bit off the lower half before it could be landed. In a loving gesture, or perhaps as a joke, George had it stuffed and mounted too, and the half-tarpon hangs without explanation alongside the others.

In August 1902 Monica's first official visit to Rum is recorded (as Mrs Charrington) along with her father, who spent two months stalking, making four kills, the largest a magnificent stag weighing 17 stone. He can only have been elated at his daughter's choice of companion. As an imminent divorcee, and doubtlessly long considered a predatory flirt in respectable society, Monica would have been judged harshly by the strict moral code of the period. To become Lady Bullough with an instant fortune at her disposal must have seemed a dream-like reversal of fate, enabling the restoration of both her and her father's reputations.

The wedding took place at Kinloch Castle on 24 June 1903. The bride was thirty-four years old, the groom thirty-three. If he was exceptionally tall, she appeared tiny, at five feet five inches a good foot below his hairline. He was tanned, for he had only just returned from another voyage (to Nice) and *Rhouma* was anchored in the bay, gleaming in her role as a floating hotel for the guests. It was reported to be 'a glittering ceremony'. The service itself was held in the White House, the island's 'church' being the cramped school and wholly unsuitable, and was conducted by the Reverend John Sinclair, the incumbent minister of the Small Isles.*

George must have been slightly nervous, because he got confused while signing the register. Under 'Rank or Profession, whether single or widowed', he wrote 'Single', crossed it out and added 'Gentleman Bachelor'. His usual residence was given as

---

* Several months later he emigrated to Nova Scotia where he died after only a few years.

'Rum'. (The spelling at this stage is significant.) Monica's entries were: 'Divorced' and 'Paris and London'. The best man was Major Hugh Tristram, and one of the witnesses was Charles Costeker, George's lawyer from Darwen in Lancashire.

With the world at their disposal, how interesting that they chose Papadil for their honeymoon! At least this is what a newspaper reported, though the *Rum Fishing Book* shows Lady Monica fishing far from Papadil the day after the wedding and not visiting the spot until October. Perhaps it was a delayed honeymoon. They would have been landed nearby by boat for otherwise Papadil lay at the end of an extremely rugged six-mile walk towards the southern tip of the island. Here was a small 'lodge' – more a bothy, really – panelled in pitch pine and with white cane furniture.† Under perfect conditions it's an idyllic spot with its lochan on the edge of cliffs and its neck-craning view up the muscular thighs of mountains, but in June they would have suffered from voracious midges.

Their only child, a daughter called Hermione, was born in their Piccadilly home three years later on 5 November 1906. She was a 'sickly child' (but would live to an admirable old age). She can scarcely have had a particularly loving childhood because Monica had little maternal instinct or interest. Never having had a mother herself must have put Monica at a disadvantage here. She had taken scant interest in Dorothea Elizabeth, her daughter from her first marriage, and had abandoned her along with Charles Charrington, probably both of them years before the divorce. In some ways, it seems, she was still a child herself.

In the castle archives there is a red notebook, bound and embossed in gilt, with the title 'Monica's Lie Book'. This is not what it seems, but a light-hearted fiction composed by Monica after some witty exchange with friends. The writing and sketches look like the work of a young teenager, but apparently

---

† I remember peering through the windows on my first visit. The lodge has gone now, allegedly burned down by walkers who broke in and were careless with fire.

they were penned by Monica when she was almost forty. As one commentator remarked, 'it contains a degree of self-mockery and makes much use of pseudo-Cockney and Edwardian slang. There are clear echoes of Pygmalion.' The stories take the form of letters to a 'belovedest aunt';

> This is Nenette, here's a picture of her from my friend 'the Prattler'. How I hate her! Horrid little skimpy witch, no hair all fluffed up as my picture shows, she flirts horribly and drops h's and raises h's at the wrong time, so vulgar, see her signature – 'Yours crawlingly'! . . . 'Belovedish aunt', writes Nenette, 'not a penny have poor little me, do you wonder! I've been betting with 'orrid young Male . . . etc,'

and;

> Just a line to say that I lost all the old allow' on a brute of a horse who wouldn't win! Ain't I too unlucky for words, it was all jolly skipper's fault – he said the wretch must win – it was fourth, 'orrid take-on, I call it...by the way, I went with 'alf a doz' or so young males...to Cadzow's ball after 'din' – did enjoy it too... and saw Goit with Topsy Drawler – Topsy said she'd take me off to her house at Milan for a bit next week – but I had to go off with Johnie Smuik to races, Newmarket . . .

Perhaps in context these jottings are amusing, but lacking one, they seem faintly disturbing.

* * *

Monica had strong views, and was not one to shy away from expressing them. If she had hinted that Kinloch's design and décor were not to her taste before the marriage, she certainly made it clear afterwards. She commandeered the ground floor rooms on the sunny south side, shunted George's study and library from the prime spot to a room at the rear, and had a wall taken down to create a spacious sitting room. The heavy, gloomy oak panelling was ripped out from this sector and decorative mouldings, pastel paints and silk brocades were added; a complete make-over from neo-Jacobean to neo-Adams, from masculine to feminine. It was filled with delicate-legged Parisian furniture in glazed chintz, Louis XVIth this and that, and many a curiosity such as the grandmother clock whose face contains a single hand – it was said that ladies need concern themselves only with hours, not minutes. A grand fireplace in an inglenook provided a perfect theatre for gossip. The adjacent room was made into her 'Empire Room' for private entertainments.

Like many French aristocrats, Monica claimed vague descent from Napoleon and a portrait of him hung on a wall. The other pictures in the room, and there are many, have a common theme, all mildly titillating etchings of seduction and fondling. The subject seemed close to her heart. Beside one of the Indian tiger rugs in the Great Hall she drank tea while posing nude for the artist Galliac. This portrait hangs outside her bedroom on the first floor. If the Empire Room was a seduction closet then it entailed some risk, for it opened into the pagoda-conservatory, through which someone might spy from outside, albeit with a view hampered by the potted jungle which was installed whenever the Bulloughs were in residence.

One early flaw that Monica spotted in George's bachelor pad was the lack of adequate laundry facilities. Not wishing to have her washing aired within sight of either the castle or the community, so it is said, Lady Bullough had a dedicated laundry built six miles away at Kilmory. A corrugated iron shack was erected and equipped with coal-fired coppers, mangles, a stove and flat irons. Crude accommodation was included and washing lines were strung out in what soon became known as Kilmory Greens. Here two laundry maids lived and worked for up to four months each year in an isolation that must have tested companionship to the utmost and ranks as one of the strangest and severest hardship postings in the British Isles. For company they had one shepherd and his family, and the weekly man who arrived by pony and cart to exchange wicker baskets of dirty laundry for their neatly pressed and starched replacements. He was their only link to the world and its news. How slowly time must have passed with only the sounds of curlew and oystercatchers wheeling round the nearby graveyard in which so many of the Mathesons' children were buried! Their only consolation was the magnificent beach of Samhnan Insir a short walk away (later a favourite picnic spot of Queen Elizabeth when holidaying aboard *Britannia*), and perhaps the drier climate. This possibly was the main reason for siting the laundry here, though at a saving of only sixteen inches of rain over the annual figure for the castle, it must have represented an invisible bonus.*

The castle was now much more homely as a result of Monica's intervention. Not that George had done badly on his own. Three valuable seventeenth-century Flemish tapestries that appear to have belonged to his father and once adorned Meggernie were stylishly presented in the Great Hall. There were magnificent watercolours of George's favourite scenes in Rum painted under his patronage by Manchester-born artist Byron Cooper. The Grinling Gibbons carved screen from Charles I's time was taken from Bishopswood and fitted in one of the bedrooms in the new three-storey section that completed the castle's quadrangle.

Having Walter Shoolbred as a fellow member of one of his yacht clubs, the Royal Thames, may have influenced George at the outset to have the castle furnished from London's most fashionable and expensive supplier, James Shoolbred & Company in Tottenham Court Road. In an article in *Country Life* (1984) Clive Aslet wrote: 'The interior furnishings in particular were done to a compellingly high standard, and Kinloch shows with near total completeness the seductively easy, at times sumptuous,

---

* Average annual rainfalls for Rum are: sixteen feet on the mountain tops, 87 inches at the castle, 120 inches just three-quarters of a mile up the glen, 71 inches at Kilmory and 50 at Harris. By this reckoning Harris should have been the chosen spot, but hanging undies around John Bullough's mausoleum was clearly unacceptable.

look that top-quality London decorators would create for a country house – opulent, informal and richly coloured.' With so much ormolu, gilt, silver, brass, ivory, cloisonné, crystal, lacquer, silk and feather about – there were even Spode lavatory bowls – there was nothing ordinary about the place, and George kept adding to it.

He spotted a Steinway grand piano in a London shop window and immediately bought it. It predates the manufacturer's numbering system and is thus among the earliest ever made. Monica was a pianist, and judging by the complexity of the music she collected, she must have been reasonably accomplished. As for the story of the scratch on the piano's lid being incised by a Gaiety Girl dancing in stilettos, sadly, this is not true. Girls may have can-can-ed there, but the scratch was part of more substantial damage caused in the 1980s when one of the ponderous incense-burners toppled over and struck the piano. New Steinways today cost in the region of £90,000.

It has long been said that there used to be two Steinways at the castle and that one was taken away by the friend who was the most regular visitor to Rum, Sir William Bass. ('Only at Kinloch Castle,' a tour guide quipped, 'could you lose a Steinway.')

And there was the fabulous Orchestrion, purchased in 1906. By the crudest analogy this rare instrument was the Ritz of fairground organs, though it worked on a different system and produced a more sophisticated sound. Special scrolls of paper punched with holes were unwound by an electric motor and passed under a battery of levers. These 'read' the music and directed air from bellows to an astonishing array of musical instruments, both standard instruments and simulated ones. Drums, cymbals, trumpets, horns, flutes, fiddles and a host of others found voice in the Orchestrion, which serenaded, cat-gutted, rat-tat-tat-ed, crashed and chimed for twenty minutes, at which time the piece ended and the scroll had to be rewound or another one inserted. The Orchestrion could take the place of a forty-piece orchestra. With no form of volume control it could be something of a loose cannon; the *William Tell Overture* exercised its artillery to the full and shook the corridors and stairs. It cost £2000 at the time it was bought (circa £100,000 today) and much more besides to install. The technicians given the task wanted to put it in the ballroom, but Sir George insisted it went underneath the stairs off the Great Hall. The space was too cramped for it, so the uppermost organ pipes and trumpets had to be sent away to be bent through ninety degrees. Despite all this effort and expense, Sir George never really liked the sound of what has been called the 'king of instruments', and it was only used occasionally, mainly as a dinner gong summoning guests to eat.

Orchestrions were made by a German company, Imhof & Mukle, who had their factory in Vöhrenbach, Baden, and remained in business until 1930. Bullough's instrument was said to have been ordered by Queen Victoria, who died before it could be delivered, but this is incorrect. She did order one, thus justifying Imhof & Mukle in advertising themselves 'By Appointment to the late Queen Victoria' but that particular example is today in the Deutsches Musikautomaten Museum, Bruchsal, Baden-Württemberg. Several thousand Orchestrions with different features were made, but only two examples of the type found on Rum are known to have survived in working order. Kinloch Castle's is in the best condition and has the greatest selection of music: forty rolls.

* * *

Adding and improving were not restricted to the confines of the castle, and one particular change around this time shows that Sir George was still haunted by a spectre. The only plausible explanation of him suddenly changing his mind about his father's last resting place – designed in such detail and constructed at considerable cost – and blowing it to smithereens, is the oft-related anecdote about the remark made by a tactless friend. The latter was being shown the vault and let slip the opinion that it resembled a public lavatory. Horrified as he was by the comparison, Sir George must nevertheless have recognised the similarity, for he had the sarcophagus removed and the vault dynamited. Today, over a century later, you can still find tiles and mosaics scattered around part of the rear wall which remains intact.

Nearby he built a new mausoleum which could be confused with nothing but a Greek temple. The sarcophagus rests on a bed of sandstone slabs, surrounded by eighteen Doric columns supporting a stone roof with a cross on the apex of each gable. It is a stately building, particularly when compared to a Victorian public lavatory, but no less incongruous on a Hebridean shore. This must have been constructed in the first decade of the century, but sources as far apart as Argyll and Otago remain mute on the subject.

Following his father's admirable but largely unsuccessful tree-planting policy, Sir George experimented with no less than 120 different species, 80,000 trees in total, and planted twenty-eight hectares around Loch Scresort. Fifty species survived, and the tree desert Byron Cooper painted at the beginning of last century is almost unrecognisable under the woods of today.

A furious burst of roadmaking and mending began, so that the owner and his friends could drive various sports cars across the island to Harris, and their maintenance in the harsh climate ensured permanent employment for two men, with occasional support from up to a dozen others.

He imported deer, game birds, trout, hares, wild goats and even frogs. Few of the game birds apart from grouse survived for long, and neither did the hares. Goats were an odd choice. Sir George had shot the species on Desertas, an island off Madeira, which probably accounted for this foible. He imported specimens first from Perthshire and later from Sunart in Argyll. These augmented a small indigenous flock which had survived on the island over the centuries. They can have provided little sport except for mountaineering practice and were largely left alone.*

The frogs were another experiment. For amphibians Rum has only palmate newts, so frog spawn was introduced to ponds and bogs. However it seems the water is unusually acidic and there are still no frogs on Rum.

Dogs were another of Sir George's passions. Among the great camp retinue which accompanied the Bulloughs on their annual trips to Kinloch Castle were a pack of fox hounds and several pedigree English setters. Three weeks before his return from the Boer War at the end of 1900, some of his dogs were winning prizes at Crufts. The 45th Kennel Club Show at Crystal Palace awarded '1st prize to Mr George Bullough's team of black and tan setters'. Rhum May, Rhum Beauty and Rhum Meg each picked up various seconds and thirds. In 1903, Sir George was elected president of the Scottish Kennel Club. In July 1912, the housekeeper at the castle sent off an order to 'Messers Harrods: 2 enamel bowls (puppies)'. Nothing but the best for them, it seems.

Highland cattle too were a favoured species, and the *Rum Private Herd Book* lists 'Rhouma Og of Rhum, colour red, January 1901, bred by Sir George Bullough of Rhum'. He was buying stock from such sources as 'the Late Earl of South Esk', which produced Princess Iris – so not every creature on the island was Rhumified.

However it was to the island's distinctive breed of Highland garrons that most of his attention was given. Rum's ponies were believed to be descended from horses which swam ashore from a wrecked ship of the Spanish Armada. As every other odd characteristic found on the western seaboard, from olive skin

---

* When it was suggested that goat's milk might be beneficial to Hermione's precarious health, a domesticated nanny was sent to Rum. After its milk failed to bring about any improvement, it was turned out to join the wild herd, but died soon afterwards.

to Fair Isle dyeing, is attributed to this source, it must be taken with a pinch of salt. In fact the Rum ponies' black 'eel-stripe' along the spine and dark bracelets above the fetlock appear to be throwbacks to the *fjordhest* of Viking Norway, and show up in variations among many regional breeds in Britain.

The bloodline in Rum was dying out until John Bullough re-established a stud, and he deserves credit for doing so. Sir George continued the expansion, sending mares to the mainland to be served by the last traceable remnants of the Rum stock owned by Lord Arthur Cecil. The breed attracted interest at national shows and from at least one geneticist interested in hereditary characteristics, as shown by *The Times* of 26 August 1897: 'Professor Erwart of Edinburgh University reports that having "crossed a male zebra with an Island of Rum mare, he obtained a finely-marked zebra-like foal"'! Sir George conducted some experimentation himself and imported a white pure-bred Arab to introduce fresh blood, winning prizes at Highland Shows with Claymore and Rory o' the Hills. Of course the more common names were Rhum Laddie, Rhum Kinloch, Rhum Star, Rhum Pride, Rhum Princess, Rhum . . .

The prevalence of these names highlights the resolution, in Sir George's mind, of an inconsistency in the spelling of Rum. Where did the 'h' come from? Neither Gaelic nor Norse aspirate a leading 'r', so there is no philological precedence for the insertion of the 'h'. When John Bullough first set foot on the island it was known as Rum. It remained Rum for roughly fifteen years under Sir George's tenure until 1905, when he demanded that the Post Office recognise the new spelling of 'Rhum', which it did in June by issuing a new date stamp and changing the lettering on the mail bags. For the next three-quarters of a century this spelling remained in use.

Why did he do this? One answer frequently given is that it was an act of late Victorian prudishness to disassociate the island from the vice of alcohol, and thus avoid having to send 'postcards from Rum'. In Sir George's case this carries little conviction. Given his propensity for consuming the stuff, he was more likely to revel in the connection. Yet it may be that he tired of the clichéd quips every time he had to give the address. More likely he found 'Rhum' more romantic. He was certainly not the first to use the spelling.

The origin of the name is obscure, but it appears to have existed in some form before the Norse version of 'Romoy'. Timothy Pont's description of the island *c.*1677 begins, 'Rhum is one big island ...' The somewhat fearsome and inquisitorial document *NOTES ON THE NUMBER OF EXAMINABLE PERSONS AND NUMBER OF CATHOLICS ON RHUM* (*c.*1741) uses one spelling in the title and another in the opening sentence, 'Roum an isle in argyleshire ...' Rum becomes the name used almost exclusively thereafter, the sole exception being a gravestone in Kilmory which bears the epitaph: 'Sacred to the memory of Catherine Henderson who departed this life upon the 5 day of May 1843, aged 49. This stone erect here by hir belovied husband Walter Cowan, manager Rhum.' As the mason's spelling was none too competent this may account for the isolated reappearance of the 'h'.*

With the castle remodelled, the gardens well under way, the roads repaired and the 'h' nicely installed in the name, the island entered a Golden Age. Never before or since did life come so close to perfection. Smooth efficiency supplied a seemingly effortless profusion of all good things, and on and on they flowed. Here the world was at peace. If it was enjoyed to the full then it had to be. Whether the Bullough circle recognised it or not, the manipulation of resources that created Rhum could not be extended to the wider world. The island's clock could be stopped, but the illusion that it was a sanctuary against change could not long be preserved against the force of new events. The Golden Age would not endure, but how bright it was for a while!

---

* In 1992 the island's name was officially changed back to Rum, more correctly written as 'Rùm'. This renders the pronounciation 'room', though this is never heard in common parlance! In this book I have used 'Rum' by preference but 'Rhum' where quotes are from material that uses that spelling.

15

The Golden Age

The arrival of the *Rhouma* was the highlight of the year. The mechanics and chauffeurs would be there with the two highly polished Albions. The deer ponies would have been broken in ready for the moors. Fishing lines and creels would be in first class order for the supplying of the daily fresh fish and lobsters. Roads would be freshly resurfaced and the boats delivered to the various hill lochs by horse-drawn sledges. The four gamekeepers and ghillies would be dressed in their new issues of Rum Tweed and the whole island would feel alive.

Archie Cameron, *The Scots Magazine*, December 1978.

Loch Scresort has a hazardous reef close to its southern shore, but the entrance is wide and otherwise clear. The loch's generous proportions on the surface conceal a rapidly shoaling bottom, and *Rhouma*, with a draft of 17.2 feet, was forced to moor in five fathoms a long way from the shore (roughly opposite the modern slipway). Sir George had sold his father's sixty-foot cutter *Mystery* by this time and replaced her with the eighteen-ton 'tender' *Kinloch*, which was a more practical workhorse. Yet Lord Salisbury's old pier was tidal and the tender could only come alongside at above half-tide, so sometimes the landing party had to wait. No such convenience attended those who arrived by MacBraynes' ferry, and if the tide was low, they would be transferred to rowing boats which were stranded on the beach. Estate workers would then wade in and carry passengers ashore on their backs, occasionally losing their footing in the process. In winter the ferry could be cancelled for weeks.

In the early days the housekeeper was a Miss Campbell, who was related to George's stepmother and may well have been poached from Ian's Meggernie Castle. The factor was Jack Brown, followed in September 1911 by R. Wallace Brebner, who remained in the post for around twenty years before being dismissed. Rum gardener Archie Cameron was to hold nothing but contempt for Brebner in particular, and factors in general: 'the curse of the Highlands was midges and factors, and the worst was the factor.'

Twenty years was a long time to hold such a post, but the Bulloughs did seem to attract an uncommon degree of loyalty among key staff. John Hookey Ashworth was head keeper for over twenty years, and his successor, Duncan Macnaughton, served in excess of thirty before his son took over. At Hermione's coming-of-age party (6 September 1928), a presentation was made 'by John Macaskill, the oldest retainer with 52 years service in the family.' Mr Brebner made a speech in which he mentioned that six employees present at the celebration 'aggregate 217 years' service, an average of 36 years each.' The Bulloughs must have been tolerable employers at the very least. For an enterprise of this nature to function at such a distance from the owner, these key staff were vital and partly autonomous until the Bullough cavalcade appeared over the horizon.

The Bulloughs would arrive with about a dozen personal house staff, including at least one French chef, a butler, footman, valet, lady's maid and several kitchen maids. Any vacancies would have been filled well in advance through advertisements, such as this one in the *Scotsman* (14 June 1905): 'Chef (first-class French) or exceptionally good woman cook wanted for large establishment in remote Western Highlands. Must have highest credentials as to character & ability . . .'

In addition to this invading force, seasonal workers were

brought in, mainly from Skye, between April and October. Rum's off-season population at this time was around ninety, including children, but the number of workers almost doubled during the stalking season, when at least one hundred and twenty-five pairs of hands were directly or indirectly available to serve the Bulloughs and their guests. The bustle of activity must have been a marvel to behold, and with the numbers of guests usually restricted to around sixteen in the castle (though *Rhouma* was used to accommodate more), the degree of personal service was second to none.

The day started at eight o'clock with a piper walking round the castle playing 'Johnnie Cope'. The first to do this was Neil Shaw, a steward on *Rhouma*, who was rowed ashore each morning. When he moved on to greater things – he founded the Highlander Association which led on to the National Mod – the versatile keeper Duncan Macnaughton assumed the mantle. He also stood atop the castle tower and piped a welcome to *Rhouma* at the start of each season. From here the views were splendid and rolled unhindered to the Aird of Sleat, the mountains of Knoydart and Loch Nevis and, by night, the comforting flicker of Mallaig's lights.

Each day offered the opportunity to shoot, fish, walk or take sightseeing excursions on land or water. For most men the chief attraction was stalking red deer. Novices had to prove their worth before the head keeper by practising on a wooden target. Those who passed had a strenuous day, as the terrain was rough and the ponies were used exclusively for bringing back the kills. Other days could be spent walking the policies with shotgun in hand. As many as twenty-four gun-dogs were available for nosing out game, though the opportunities never justified such a pack. Sir George's favourites would be chauffeured in a Trojan van to his chosen patch. Grouse were still plentiful, and these were the second most popular quarry after deer. Sea trout and brown trout could be caught in the river bordering the policies, but they were seldom of notable size. Better specimens inhabited the dozens of stocked hill lochs. As Lord Salisbury had discovered, and failed to rectify, Rum was never a salmon beat. The adventurous might base their sporting trips in the bothies of Guirdil or Papadil, being delivered as close as possible by boat and with a few servants sent ahead to light fires and prepare food.

There were always the turtles, alligators and humming-birds to provide interest on short walks from the castle, but transport was provided for longer excursions. John Love* recorded that the Bulloughs kept on the island

> two luxurious four-wheeled, horse-drawn carriages with deep blue upholstery and their personal monogram on the doors. They could rarely be used, however, since a pair of horses had difficulty pulling them up the hilly road ... [In addition] two Albion cars could transport guests on picnics to Kilmory. On special occasions the local children were bundled aboard with two carts following behind to transport hampers of strawberries, melons, grapes and other treats. The Albions rarely clocked up more than a hundred miles each year. Sir George preferred to walk while Lady Bullough had her own palomino called Pebbles which could pull a trap, always referred to as 'the machine'.

In addition Lady Bullough kept an Austin 7 for her personal use, while her husband had 'a bigger vehicle', possibly a Rolls Royce. Sir George was the only known person to have a road accident on Rum, leaving the road near the Kilmory junction while driving too fast. The vehicle was dragged back to the workshop for repair on an improvised wooden sledge. Despite the roads being in excellent condition, they were narrow and twisty, and the fabled races across the island at 60 mph never took place. The engines of the time were not capable of such speeds.

Guests could play bowls, croquet, tennis, golf or squash. Lady Bullough was not overly fond of the outdoor life. She shot

---

* In *Rum: A Landscape Without Figures*.

her first stag on 7 September 1904, an eight-pointer weighing fourteen stone, and that satisfied her for the next fifteen years. She was more partial to casting a fly, having spent the first day of her honeymoon in this pursuit, and though her entries in the *Game Book* are not regular or prolonged they indicate more than a perfunctory interest. She preferred playing bridge for money. A scorebook from a later period (1938) survives and one entry shows an accumulated stake of 193 shillings.

For quieter times there was the castle library. As a result of Lady Bullough's alterations this was compressed into a small room in one of the castle's turreted corners. Among 2,000 books stood Sir George's desk with his initials tooled in gilt on red Morocco accessories, overlooked by a Rum golden eagle holding in its talons an even rarer Rum white hare. Derek Cooper, in *Hebridean Connection* (1977), dismissed the library's contents as worthless: 'none of the books reveal even the remotest preoccupation with culture . . . the kind of ephemera that would have passed a mindless rainy afternoon for the kind of people who assembled in country houses in that carefree time.' A more careful examination reveals a far-ranging breadth of interests, from European politics to medieval myths. The collection contains many specialist works analysing military history – particularly the Boer War and colonial power – as well as literary classics, though many of the latter appear to have been bought by the yard and never opened. It was certainly a haphazard accumulation, with guests dumping their 'penny-dreadfuls' to mingle with the complete works of Tolstoy, Dumas and Scott. Lady Bullough added some novels in French and histories of Napoleon to offset her husband's bound copies of *The Brigade of Guards Magazine* and an almost complete set of *Baily's Magazine of Sports and Pastimes*. Other titles reflect Sir George's interest in natural history and country pursuits (*The Grouse in Health and in Disease*) and his choices from *The Times* Book Club to which he subscribed – *Court of Philip IV: Spain in Decadence* and *Rolf in the Woods: the Adventures of a Boy Scout with Indian*

Quonab and Little Dog Skookum. Perhaps he ordered the latter for Hermione, but it is interesting to discover that such clubs were well established even then.

One set of books bound in blue with gilt-edged pages is striking for its overwhelming abundance. They weigh down shelves everywhere, are stacked as bookends and double as insulation against damp. They are *John Bullough's 'Speeches'* in three volumes, the third extended to include poetry that should have been blown up with his tomb.

Bridget Paterson, a member of the Kinloch Castle Friends Association (KCFA), undertook a detailed study of Kinloch Castle's books, and counted 220 sets of the speeches just in the library. The gunroom contained at least as many again. She found token acknowledgements of the past, *Bits o' Broad Lancashire* (1888, William Baron) and *Lancashire Songs*, (1881, Edwin Waugh), noting that 'the family may have gone up in the world but the roots are still there.' In other books there were more personal discoveries in which 'the very ordinariness of the Bulloughs came through. One of Monica's bookmarks is a bill for shirts for £1 9s 6d from midsummer 1904. It was delivered to her in London and then redirected to the Park Hotel, Preston.' And an inscription at the front of *Poems*, collected by W. E. Henley, 1910, made me wonder what on earth had gone on to lead to an inscription like this. It has a certain tone:

> *To MB from HWB*
> *To my mind there is no crime so*
> *Atrocious, no voice so petty that*
> *cannot be ascribed to the influence*
> *of the three most virulent pests*
> *of human nature – meanness,*
> *vulgarity and narrow-mindedness.*

Of Sir George's fabled pornography collection, nothing remains. Either it was removed, stolen or, most likely, never existed in the first place. The only contender for that genre, *Ladies Fair and Frail, The Gilded Beauties of the Second Empire* would not have been out of place in a nursery.

At the end of the day's activities the Orchestrion would leap into life, summoning guests to dinner with waltzes by Strauss, *Madame Butterfly, Ma Blushin' Rosie, Geisha* or perhaps the *Pirates of Penzance* and *HMS Pinafore*. After the meal the ladies would retire to a sitting-room, while the men crossed the corridor into the Billiard Room for port and cigars. It is easy to conjure up a picture of the smoke layering the air above the full-sized Eureka table with its 'Extra Low Fast Cushion', the best, bought from Burroughs & Watts of Soho Square, London. This, of course, was before the ventilation system replaced the stale air every twenty minutes. Here they would have dissected the day's stalking or fishing, and the qualities of the absented ladies – just as their qualities, or lack of them, would be being discussed by their counterparts while they played mah-jong, cards or roulette.

Most evenings there would be dancing in the ballroom, the twelve-piece orchestra being rowed ashore from their quarters aboard *Rhouma*. In their absence, from the butler's pantry a 'Simplex Piano Player' could be wheeled in for any of the guests to play simply by working two foot pedals. Like the Orchestrion this worked with rolls of punched paper, and when it was carefully lined up before a piano, thirty-seven arms depressed the keys. The choice of music included: *The Wine, Women and Song Waltz, 'Neath My Lattice through the Night, Scotch Reel,* Sousa's *The Man behind the Gun March, An Alabama Blossom, March and Two-Step* and even – if they had completely overdone things – *Nearer My God to Thee*. Sometimes, primarily for the ladies, musical soirées would be arranged with artistes specially transported to Rum. They might be singers, or piano or violin players. On one occasion it was a man named McNally who was the country's leading dulcimer player, and who later, in old age, could still be found entertaining Glasgow folk going 'doon the water' on holiday steamers.

Who exactly were the favoured guests of the Bulloughs? Again, the game books provide the fullest record of names, and the gradual increase in those with titles reflects the Bulloughs' rise from the ranks of 'new money' to social respectability. Money of course still spoke loudest of all, and it had to because there were still those bad slips on social banana skins that were not readily forgotten: John Bullough had divorced, George had married a divorcee and was co-respondent in adultery, and his half-brother Ian twice married actresses. These were unconventional acts in a taboo-riddled era. But the fact of being enormously wealthy, even if it was new money, *and* having a knighthood, overcame most prejudices eventually. At first the guests were predominantly cavalry officers, Horse Guards, businessmen and occasionally their wives. Then, into the mix more and more, came the odd politician, knight, general, admiral, earl and count.

Francis Cadogan (later Commander), grandson of the 5th Earl of Cadogan, first visited Rum as a fourteen-year-old in 1899, and years later he recalled three of the 'regulars'. 'The house party consisted of Cole (a stockbroker), Costeker (solicitor), J. Homfray (in Welsh coal) and others, and were known as "the Rum Brigade"'. The young Cadogan was not privy to any wild parties as he slept aboard *Rhouma*. He returned many times over the next decade, sometimes with his uncle, Captain the Hon. Gerald Oakley Cadogan, and sometimes with his father, who suffered the misfortune of dropping dead on Rum in 1901. His widow promptly remarried a Harry Hinton – the Cadogans, Hinton and George Bullough had all become friends at the Madeira balls – and among this group of slightly confused relationships the young Francis continued to visit Rum with his stepfather. Harry Hinton left a better impression of his fellow guests during George's bachelor days:

> I met a house full of about ten sportsmen – none of whom I cared for very much except for Hermon-Hodge – all the others spent their time sucking up to our host. The dinners were a very tedious matter and we sat round the table drinking until two

in the morning. I did this for two nights and then got up and went to bed as soon as dinner was over. I never met such a set of sportsmen and they rarely killed anything. I had never seen a red deer but after the shooting of wild goats on the Desertas [Madeira] for many years, a stag looked like a haystack to me.*

Hinton left his mark elsewhere too. In mirror script on the blotting paper used by Lady Bullough on her sitting room desk, the words, 'must post this now, yours Harry Hinton', are still legible over a century later.

One of the men Hinton refers to was Sir Robert Trotter Hermon-Hodge, former Conservative MP for the Accrington area. Other great names were the Cholmondleys, 1st Baron Wyfold, Sir Humphrey Edmund de Trafford (a relation of Camilla, the Duchess of Cornwall) and the redoubtable regulars who came to know the staff as if they were family: Colonel Duff, Major General Gregson-Ellis and Sir William Bass. Some of these names span decades, some persist long after the ink on Sir George's signature dried for the last time.

So we are left with conflicting reports. At one extreme are the parties of sheer boredom, at the other the cherished rumours of the wildest of orgies. Which way a party went must have depended on the company and the occasion. It's tempting to wonder whether any opium was used after the declared fondness for the substance when Bullough and Mitchell were travelling in

---

* In fact Hinton got so bored he made a bet with the others that he could get round the island on foot in under eight hours. Shepherds advised it would take twelve. He lost his way in mist and had to pay out five pounds. When he recovered he bet he could do it in under four hours. He picked better weather and 'reached home in under four hours and won some hundred and twenty pounds. 'The laugh that night was on the other side although my legs suffered for a day or two! ... I forgot to say that the castle was being built then and there must have been a hundred workmen there. Most of them had bets on the result and I was met with great cheers when I got home.' [This can not have been a true coastal route, more likely a circuit taking in Papadil and Harris, but was still a great achievement. The head keeper, John MacAskill, later beat Hinton's record and won a gold watch and a handsome purse!]

India. (Carbisdale Castle in Caithness reputedly had an opium den around this time.) What appears to have been consistent, however, is that a great deal of alcohol was involved. In 1927 David Sandeman & Son and J. Carlow & Son Ltd, Export Wine Merchants, London & Glasgow, wrote the following letter to Sir George:

> Dear Sir, In accordance with your kind instructions our head cellarman went to Kinloch Castle ... and examined all the Sandeman vintage 1896 Port by taking off all the old wax and examining the top of the cork ... The quantities are as follows: 61 dozen Sandemans 1896, recorked ... 13 and 9/12th dozen Sandemans 1896, resealed ... 44.6/12th dozen various Madeira... About four dozen bottles of both Port and Madeira were found empty and useless and this was pointed out to Mr Brebner ... Assuring you of our best services at all times, we are, Dear Sir, your obedt. servants., David Sandeman and Carlow.

1927 was long after the peak party era and the Bullough fortunes were at their lowest. Yet the depleted cellars still contained 921 bottles of vintage Port and 558 bottles of Madeira.

16

Bare Feet and Tackety Boots

The only published account of life on the island during the
Bullough period, written by an estate employee, is Archie
Cameron's delightful *Bare Feet and Tackety Boots – A Boyhood
on Rhum.** Scattered amongst his recollections of an unusual
upbringing and mischievous adventures are fascinating insights
into the Bulloughs and their lifestyle.

Archie's father Dugald was from Acharacle in Moidart, and
had first worked as a galley boy aboard a ship and then as a cattle
drover. He came to work in Rum when he was nineteen. Here
he met and married his wife Annie, from Tolsta in Lewis. Archie
was born in 1903, the third of their seven children (three girls,
four boys) but the eldest son. 'My mother had come to Rhum
as a maid in the White House, where the gentry lived before
the castle was built. She was the cook there when she met my
father . . . He had a very interesting and satisfying forty-six years
on the island, in the position of ghillie, boatman, alligator and
turtle keeper, with a little surreptitious poaching on the side . . .
Latterly he was George Bullough's personal ghillie.'

He was also required to row many miles to the fishing
banks in the Sound of Rum and secure fresh fish and lobsters
for the castle. He used hand lines and took a bottle of cold tea

---

* Luath Press Ltd, 1988.

for sustenance, as thermos flasks – invented in 1892 – were not yet available. In the 'off-season', he and another ghillie, Angus Thwaite, were employed in the never-ending and back-breaking work of 'knapping' rocks for the maintenance of the island's roads, often basing themselves at Harris and getting home only at weekends. The Camerons also derived some income from providing food and lodging for tradesmen visiting the castle, one of the regulars being a piano tuner who came twice a year.

'My father's wage was never more than twenty-five shillings a week ... [but] ... there was a free house ... free meat, fish, milk and five tons of coal a year.' The meat was mainly venison, distributed fresh in the shooting season after the castle had taken the best cuts, and any excess being dried or salted for the winter. Being nine in all and the largest family on the island, the Camerons received the greatest share of the handouts.

Fish was another staple, supplemented by the odd sheep found dead of the lung infection braxy. Although Archie never witnessed it, the test for determining whether a carcase was fresh enough for human consumption was to swing it by the hind legs, and if it held together for six revolutions, it was suitable for the table! Despite such 'wholesome fairin' the children seldom satisfied their hunger, and would risk confrontations with the farm manager by raiding the troughs where tups were fed 'sweet locust beans' in winter. Chocolate was unknown to them – Archie first discovered it in his twenties when he left Rum, and for months it became an addiction on which he spent all his wages – and sweets were so rare that they sucked cod's eyeballs instead and regarded them as chewing gum. At Christmas the most dreamed-of present was a barrel of apples – each – and to be allowed to eat them in a single sitting. It never happened. 'On special occasions we were given one orange ... divided among the seven of us. One wee segment each, which we made last a very long time.'

Basic provisions such as bread and sea-biscuits were sold at the Post Office, but other supplies had to be ordered from the mainland. *The Oban Times* was hoarded and rationed out as toilet paper. Alcohol was not available on the island, and Archie's father saved his precious stock of whisky for special occasions and medicinal purposes: toothache was treated with either a clove or a wad of cotton-wool soaked in whisky pressed into the cavity. The cure for bleeding cuts was even more novel; the wound was wrapped in the largest cobweb that could be found, including 'dry bluebottles, old spiders, butterfly wings and a good mixing of plain muck', which invariably stopped the bleeding immediately.

'In Kinloch there were nine houses as well as the "Yard", and the Farm Manager's house was at the Yard together with the garages for the Albion cars, the chauffeurs' rooms, the byres and horse boxes and such things as tack and harness rooms.' The contrast between life in the castle and life in the nine houses was the extreme between the 'haves' and the 'have-nots', but in an interesting moral dynamic, some of the latter's deprivations were voluntary. While playing cards was a fundamental mainstay of entertainment among the gentry, in the Cameron home, 'cards were very much frowned upon as being the "Devil's Bible" and were not played in our house.' Later, when aged eleven, Archie began poaching the odd trout, he returned to the same theme: 'My parents, being very religious and Sabbath-minded, looked on Sunday fishing as a sure way to eternal damnation.' If proof were needed, it came on a Monday when one of his young siblings unwittingly revealed that the trout they had just eaten, which Archie had lied about and said he'd caught that day, had been caught on the Sabbath. His father immediately tried to vomit up the devil's bounty.

For many years there was a mandatory ban on islanders keeping cats or dogs, though this was later relaxed to allow ownership of small dogs. Archie recalled the Bulloughs' 'large pack of "Black and Tan"' dogs which terrified him as a small child and which he always encountered being exercised on his way to school.* Yet his dread of the dogs was nothing compared to his suffering at the hand of the teacher. Teachers enjoyed an elevated status in society and their methods were not to be questioned. Lessons were conducted exclusively in English, whereas Archie was one of six children who spoke Gaelic. His classroom beatings were not for misbehaviour but for being considered 'stupid'. 'It is surprising we were not seriously injured by those assaults', he recalled. The other children came from non-Gaelic parts of the mainland or from England. No one at the time ever questioned why Gaelic was ostracised.

> I cherish many happy memories of life on Rhum, both indoors and out. The annual staff picnic to Kilmory, for example, in the shining Albions, always seemed to take place on sunny days. Two horse drawn carts went ahead, laden with the necessary food produced by the castle kitchens and carrying all the spare produce of the castle gardens and greenhouses – grapes, nectarines, peaches, green figs and strawberries I remember – all the exotic things of which we had hardly heard before, and certainly never tasted.

Archie and his pals always yearned to sneak into the garden and steal their fill of the fruits but they never succeeded. Probably it was just as well, for had he been caught he suspected that his entire family would have been dismissed from the island. However, on the day of the picnic, for once he was able to satiate his appetite. 'We were loaded into the gleaming Albions and carried away in real Gentry style over the miles to Kilmory, miles that we often trudged but rarely rode. I still remember the smell of the exhaust of those Albion engines. It seemed very fragrant, and far removed from the stink of petrol today . . .' As wonderful as he found the experience, he reflected, it must have been

---

* There's no evidence to suggest the dogs' kennels were heated at a time when the servants' quarters in the castle were not. In fact neither had such comfort! Although the servants' rooms had open fires, the system of radiators was not extended to their section on the third floor until 1920. The kennels were never heated.

euphoric for the two laundry maids to have their monotonous isolation of months interrupted by such a party.

Among the estate workers certain sports were keenly contested. The crew of *Rhouma* lived aboard the vessel, but came ashore occasionally to play football, there being no fewer than three teams on the island! And each summer there was a Sports Day held in the castle grounds. 'There were all the events associated with traditional Highland games, with some of the guests taking part. There were three tug-of-war teams, one from the *Rhouma*, one from the gardeners and the third composed mostly of farm-workers, gamekeepers and ghillies. The last team always won.'

The castle order books for July 1914 show the housekeeper ordering from Kennedy of Oban: '20 lbs currant cake, 20 lbs seed, 20 lbs sultana cake, 6 doz currant buns, 4 plain gingerbread cakes @ 1/6d each (for grown-ups sports).' Archie and his friends weren't the least bit interested in the sports. They had other trophies in mind. Creeping into the tent which emptied during each event, they finished off everything they could find on bar and table.

They got up to other mischief too, and one alarming incident shows that *Rhouma* brought back some dangerous souvenirs from the Boer War. Archie's friend Angus entered a small gazebo built into a wall at the front of the grounds. Among a collection of weapons stored there he found a four-inch shell, which he proudly carried home. Hoping to examine its contents, with his sister watching by his side, Angus hit the shell with a hammer. 'It exploded, making a large crater and showering them both with gravel but miraculously they emerged unhurt.'

The island children took particular interest in Rum's animals, both wild and domestic. The place was infested with rats, and they set traps baited with herring, Archie once catching twenty-three in a single night. The arrival of new farm stock was always eagerly awaited, as the animals were usually 'unceremoniously pushed over the side of the steamer, and allowed to make their own arrangements about swimming ashore.' Pedigree bulls and stallions suffered the same fate, but were towed to land behind a dingy. Replacement stalking ponies were procured from the island's wild herd, and each year a selection were sent to the sales in Oban. The castle also kept pigs, which enjoyed the leftover French cuisine.

The French and Scottish worlds did not always cohabit easily:

> Dingley was the farm manager . . . it was his job to find out, from the French chef, what meat was required each day for the gentry in the castle. I listened to one of those confrontations, and it was just as confusing to me, who was not concerned, as it was to poor Dingley. He could speak no French, and the chef could speak very little English . . . Those chefs were highly mercurial, their tempers strained to breaking point, working in front of the huge open range, among the steaming and rattling pots and pans. I was one day almost run down by a fleeing kitchen girl, pursued by an infuriated chef waving a large kitchen knife.'

When the Bulloughs were in residence the 'natives' had little time for leisure pursuits and were denied access to much of the island. Thinking back to the time when Sir George and Lady Bullough (she was never referred to as Lady Monica) reigned on the Island of Rhum, it now amazes me to realise what little contact we had with them. By 'we' I mean the common herd. The Gentry had their personal servants and attendants, of course, but they lived a life as exclusive as that of their employers, and seldom left the policies to mingle with the natives.

Sometimes Archie would spot them when off-duty, strolling in the garden, feverishly swatting clouds of midges and pausing before the policy gates which were shut to keep the islanders out, looking dreamily at the world beyond. 'It was all a bit like some great beehive within that barrier, with the Queen Bee and her attendants sacrosanct within, with the attendants humming and buzzing about, serving Her Majesty, while we workers ensured that the inner sanctum was secure and well-provided for.'

Sir George was frequently spotted either visiting the steading to inspect the ponies or else heading for the hill with his head keeper and a ghillie in charge of the pony they all hoped would return laden with a stag. Other guests were seldom seen and

> if any of them did venture out, we, the workers, were expected, even obliged, to scurry into whatever refuge we could find until the entourage had passed. If we were not smart enough and an unexpected encounter did happen ... Sir George was always quite friendly, and would pass the time of day, but he had the rather austere air which he thought appropriate to the Highland laird, a role he tried hard to play to the full.

Lady Bullough, however, was relaxed and friendly, without any airs and always enjoyed 'a bit of chit-chat and gossip. Her first call on arriving at the island was invariably at our house. My mother had been in the service of the Bulloughs for many years, and the two of them could gabble away all afternoon enquiring about each other's friends.' She was generally accompanied by her daughter, Hermione, and Archie observed the latter's disconcerting habit of aping her mother's mannerisms and repeating her every word. Her Ladyship would speak, then came the echo! Archie was told this was part of her training for her future social life. Hermione was 'tall, willowy and delicate-looking' and one day at the farm Archie fell in love with her. She'd come to visit the nanny goat whose milk was part of her special diet. However his crush came to nothing, as she was always chaperoned and he had to secretly admire her from afar. The only direct contact between the likes of Archie and the gentry came on special days such as school prize-giving and the annual sports. The white gates were swung open to all and these were 'days to be treasured and talked about for a long time, but when the day was over, we all reverted to our proper stations. Certainly we did not resent this, at the time, and simply and unquestioningly accepted them as Superior Beings.'

During the stalking season it was the custom for a guest making his, or her, first kill to be 'bloodied' – having a fistful of blood smeared across the face. Archie remarked that the ritual took many by surprise, the ladies being less concerned over the physical contact with blood but greatly alarmed in case their new hunting clothes should get stained. He added that they had nothing to fear

> for deer blood, if allowed to dry, will rub off like powder. Having recovered from this they were all delighted and full of bravado, striding home behind the loaded ponies.
>
> The arrival of the ponies carrying the carcases was a welcome sight to us, who hung around, savouring the smell of hot leather, sweating horses and the smell of the deer themselves, which of course meant venison, our main food in the stalking season.' [Archie admits that he and other 'Rhoumarions' did occasionally poach a deer despite the dire consequences if caught, for it was considered the most heinous crime on the island.] When the carcases had been dressed ... the ghillies and gamekeepers would make their way to the gunroom at the castle, to enjoy a drink and a crack. There was plenty of real beer on tap there, and it was free, and they could regale each other with tales of other days, of other stalks, of points and weights.

Lady Bullough seldom participated in the stalking. She might chase a ball round the golf course [enabling Archie to hunt for lost balls from which he extracted the elastic for catapults] but her favourite occupation was socialising. Whatever the day's entertainment, all the guests would gather in the evening for pre-dinner drinks, anticipating not just the meal ahead but also its presentation; '... the head gardener and myself, after I had left school and become a gardening apprentice, would be decorating the dining table with some sort of exotic and flowery lay-out. Percy Hills* was master at this, and some of his creations

---

* By April 1910 Percy Hills was head gardener and his wife Agnes was housekeeper at the castle. They had four children. A distant relative recalled that Hermione often came to play with the older Hills children, and the eldest, a girl called Ross, would go for walks with the Bullough family. One day she fell in a bog and the only person she would allow to change her sodden clothes was Sir George. That the gardener's children enjoyed the trust and companionship of the laird shows a different side to the somewhat austere man described by Archie Cameron. Percy Hills and his family left Rum around 1920 to start a market garden in Coventry. He died of quinsy

were really beautiful.' The floral arrangements were set in peat and the mess they made on the tablecloths caused considerable hard work and resentment among the other staff.

> We changed all the designs each day, so perhaps the complaints were justified. But they were lovely displays, and we thought so, anyway, when we received effusive thanks from her Ladyship.
>
> After the port and cigars had gone their rounds and the day's activities embellished upon, the gentlemen would join the ladies, and all would make their way to the ballroom, to dance through the night, under the heavenly blue ceiling, with its starry decorations shining through, to the music of that amazing contraption, the electric organ.

* * *

Throughout this Golden Age Sir George, possibly from an autocratic need to control, took an active part in the administration of the island, and Archie Cameron's hated school is an example of this. A school had opened on Rum around 1850, funded by Lord Salisbury, but it had folded by 1872 when the Education Act (Scotland) introduced compulsory schooling for children aged between five and thirteen. Despite the Act it took another seventeen years to re-establish a school on Rum. The job of teacher was never an easy post to fill. Miss Janet Cameron was appointed in May 1897, but soon a petition to have her removed was raised, the School Board subsequently admitting that she was 'not conducive to progress or harmony' and was indeed 'obnoxious to the majority'. Yet she continued in the post for two more years. She agreed to leave if another position on the mainland was found for her, but eventually had to be removed by solicitor's letters after refusing to yield up the

---

within eighteen months. Mrs Hills would have faced destitution but Lady Bullough heard of her plight and offered her the job of housekeeper at Down House, Redmarley, and later at Warren Hill. None of the Hills family would ever hear a word spoken against the Bulloughs.

school log-book and register, or to vacate the schoolhouse for fifteen weeks after the new incumbent had arrived. She left in March 1903. John Love's research revealed the sad conclusion to the affair. 'In August they discovered that "Miss Janet Cameron, late teacher of the school at Rum, is now an inmate of an asylum owing to insanity".'

When the next teacher resigned within the year, Sir George decided to take the school 'under his full control' and deal directly with the Education Department. He built a new premises, and his first appointee as teacher was the short-tempered and violent Mr Peter Jopp who terrorised Archie Cameron. After Jopp was dismissed there was a period of grace with two kind and dedicated women teachers, followed by several alcoholics. Then came one of the best, a Mr John Johnston, but he (like Archie Cameron) was driven off the island by the irascible and dictatorial factor, R. Wallace Brebner. A remarkable development took place in 1918, when the education authorities recognised that there were some children in rural areas who lived too far from a school to walk there and back in a day (on Rum, in cottages at Kilmory, Papadil and Harris) and were not receiving any education at all. They introduced the ingenious expediency of 'side schools'; the most senior scholars from the nearest school would be sent out to lodge with remote families for a week at a time and tutor their children.

Such were the problems of schooling in places like Rum that by October 1915, Sir George conceded that he had done no better than the previous School Board and handed back control, which was accepted with no enthusiasm whatsoever.

* * *

Rum's permanent population in 1901 was ninety, and peaked at ninety-four in 1911. This was a period of relative prosperity and easy employment for the islanders. Down south in Accrington things were going less well for the 3,500 employed at the Globe Works. The belt was being tightened, and such trips as the all-expenses-paid train and hotel excursion for thirty foremen to visit the Rouen and Paris Exhibitions (1896) were luxuries of the past. Cousin Tom Bullough had resigned the chairmanship in 1904 and was succeeded in an age of industrial disputes by a nephew. In 1906 the company introduced an employee profit-sharing scheme which was heralded as 'Sir George's greatest achievement', but by 1909 the *Accrington Observer* reported the trade unions' grievances against him, most notably that the workers had no representation either to him or the firm. As the owner was, if anything, spending even less time on management affairs, he was probably unaware of the ill-feeling and certainly did nothing to address it.

The factory was still extremely profitable, but perhaps Sir George felt uneasy about the future because that year, 'owing to the burden of taxation', he declined to donate money to the council, who had bought the home he had formerly leased, Rhyddings Hall, as a community amenity. That same year he accepted the nomination as parliamentary candidate for the Accrington District Conservative Party, only to withdraw suddenly a few months later 'due to work commitments'.

In 1912 the Globe Works was deeply affected by coal strikes and this resulted in lay-offs, shorter working weeks and even occasional closures of the plant. Five hundred members of an engineering union began a three-month strike in July 1914, resulting in Howard & Bullough locking out the remaining 4,000 workers and closing the factory until the company's terms were accepted in late October. By then Britain was at war and many workers were so disillusioned with the inconsistent hours or uncertain work prospects at the factory that they signed up for the ill-fated 'Accrington Pals', and were despatched to the Front. Most of them would have been called up anyway, but the majority of these early enlisters were slaughtered in the opening minutes of the Somme. Their families held Howard & Bullough to blame, and even today that resentment against the company is remembered.

Other members of the Bullough family achieved pre-war milestones. Ian Bullough signed up as a Captain with the Coldstream Guards shortly before he came of age on 13 February 1907. On that day he claimed his inheritance of Meggernie (see Appendix B) with a week of celebrations. The following year he raced a 44.5 horsepower 'Junior' at Brooklands, the world's first purpose-built car-racing circuit in Surrey, and, finding this more to his liking, promptly resigned from the Guards. Devilishly handsome, he married an actress, Maudi Darrell, two years later. Within a fortnight she contracted blood poisoning from which she never fully recovered, despite eight operations, dying eighteen months later aged twenty-eight.

Around this time Ian had a connection with an Irish residence, Oakgrove in County Cork, and became Master of the Muskerry Foxhounds. In January 1912, he married a second actress, Lily Elsie. She had made her name as 'The Merry Widow' (Ian must have hoped this was not prophetic) in 1907, and was described as 'the full moon among stars of the theatrical firmament.' In a worrying similarity to her predecessor she too fell ill before their wedding and her doctor advised her to recuperate in the sun. The couple decided to bring their wedding forward and go to the sun together on honeymoon, motoring in the south of France. Accordingly they surprised their friends with a sudden Registry Office wedding at Paddington. The *People's Journal for Perthshire* on 11 November 1911 reported that 'The wedding was semi-private, only about 150 persons being present . . . Miss Elsie despises superstition, unlike most actresses, and had several of her costumes made with thirteen buttons. Also, she broke two mirrors shortly before the ceremony.' Perhaps her disregard for superstition paid off, or cost her belatedly – the couple were married for eighteen years before divorcing as a result of Ian's adultery in 1929. They continued to spend time at Meggernie, where Sir George and Lady Bullough were frequent guests.

At one shooting party in 1913 they met the Honourable Denys Finch-Hatton, who would go on to become a big game hunter and the lover of Isak Dinesen of *Out of Africa* fame.

Around this time the ostracised Edward Bullough was marrying Enrichetta M. Checchi, daughter of the Italian actress Eleonora Duse – the Bullough sons must have been sensitive to theatrical pheromones.

George's half-sister, Gladys, came of age in December 1909, and immediately went to court to resolve the terms of inheritance in her father's odd and convoluted will. John had stipulated that on her twenty-first birthday she could have £20,000 in cash and the life rent on the remaining £30,000 to be held in trust. She argued for the right to the full amount, and won.

Of George's two cousins, the younger, William – who had called his house in Accrington 'Kinloch' and subsequently moved to live in Deeside – died, after a lengthy illness, in the Palace Hotel, Aberdeen, in 1913, aged just forty-nine.

But his brother Tom was the real hero of the family. Since 1896 when he began renting properties around Oban, he had been spending increasing amounts of time in Scotland. In 1901 he purchased a Highland estate of his own called Fasnacloich at the head of Loch Creran, north of Oban. Here he entered a phase of exceptional philanthropy. He too was clearly wealthy, but his fortune must have been small compared to that of his cousins, George and Ian. In memory of his grandfather, James, he donated the 50-acre Bullough Park, a large sports ground on a hill overlooking the town, to the citizens of Accrington. He presented his first residence, Benvillin House and grounds, on the edge of town by the sea, to the citizens of Oban. In July of the same year, 1909, Oban's Country Chest Hospital opened (Sir George brought *Rhouma* into the bay for the occasion), partly built and entirely equipped from the £12,000 Tom had gifted anonymously for the purpose. It was said he had lost a child to tuberculosis, though the family tree does not support this claim. Each year he took children from the Fasnacloich estate for a day out aboard his yacht *Waihi*, which involved sports, games, a ramble, pipers and dancing.

On a more modest scale Lady Bullough displayed a sensitive social conscience similar to that of Tom. A photograph in the Billiard Room shows a gathering of local worthies, all men with sabre-toothed moustaches, below the words: 'Lady Bullough's Accrington Relief Committee, 8 December 1905 – 2 February 1906: Distribution of 3401 lbs English Beef, 5352 lbs Bread, 50 Pheasants. Assisting 3805 Poor, Sick and Needy Persons, besides 450 Children's Christmas Presents.'

Sir George had of course funded a hospital ship, was about to chip in £1,000 to the National Relief Fund and may have supported charities apart from his various social duties and activities. In 1905 he held a season ticket for Accrington Cricket Club. He was elected a Fellow of the Zoological Society of London in 1906. In 1908 he became Master of the Ledbury Hunt, close to Bishopswood at Ross-on-Wye, a post he held until 1921. In 1908 he also signed up as a Captain with the Scottish Horse Imperial Yeomanry, serving for three years, though only in peaceful capacities.

Sometime over the years he may have acquired another couple of residences – Down House, Redmarley D'Abitot, Gloucester, where he allegedly kept eighteen horses and 110 dogs, and High Coombe, Kingston Hills, Surrey – *Burke's Peerage* of 1923 lists the latter, but few other sources mention it. (Sir George's residences seem a bit like Steinways – so hard to keep track of how many you have.) In 1908 he sold the tender *Kinloch* and replaced her with a Lowestoft fishing boat which, at 80 feet and 64 tons, was twice the length and four times the weight of her predecessor. She was named, with masterly imagination, *Kinloch II*. Despite the tax burden which precluded donations to good causes, his fleet was expanding.

It was about to change again, and in an unforeseeable manner. First, though, in 1909 he and Monica sat for their fortieth-birthday portraits, which were painted by Hugh Riviere.

In fact George was only thirty-nine, but if they had waited until 1910 Monica would have been forty-one and the result might have been less flattering. These are the larger than life portraits hanging in the Great Hall today. Given their schedule, it's a wonder they found any time to stalk and party at Rum.

The devastating change, made without explanation, came on 26 June 1912, when Sir George sold his beloved *Rhouma*. In May 1898 the *Oban Times* had reported that *Rhouma* was about to be sold to the American navy while on a cruise to Florida. This proved unfounded, but it exhibits a curious resonance with the genuine event of 1912. The bill of sale showed the new owner to be 'Charles Arthur William Gilbert of the Sports Club, St James Square, London, Gentleman'. Whether Gilbert was a speculator or a stooge, he had no personal interest in the vessel, and nine days later comes the entry: 'Registry Closed this 5 July 1912 on advice received from the owner that he has sold the vessel to an Italian subject. Certificate of Registry delivered up and cancelled.' The Italian subject was none other than the Italian navy. We don't know what Sir George paid for *Rhouma*, but *The Scotsman* revealed a relatively paltry return: 'The Italian government bought three yachts over the last few months, *Capercailzie* (£13,000), *Evona* (£15,000) and *Rhouma* (£10,000).'

It seems likely Sir George knew who the eventual buyer was, for he had *Rhouma* stripped of her valuables before the sale. The beautiful mahogany panelling from the dining room, along with the novel chairs with their swivelling upper halves, were reinstalled in the dining room at Kinloch Castle, where they still remain. *Rhouma* was turned into an 'armed yacht', with so much reinforcement that her weight increased by a third to 934 tons, and her engines devoured 180 tons of coal per day. Renamed the *Giuliana* and fitted with four six-pounder guns and a crew of forty-six, she saw active service in the Italo-Turkish war and served until decommissioned in October 1928. Her eventual fate is not known, but it can be assumed she was scrapped.

The most likely reason for the sale of *Rhouma* was that

George's use of such a large vessel had declined and the maintenance costs were disproportionately expensive. He still had no intention of forsaking the steam yacht fraternity, though, and in 1913 he purchased the *Triton*, which had come on the market following the death of the previous owner, the Paisley cotton magnate, James Coats, Junior. Built of steel by the Ailsa Ship Building Company in 1902, she also was a magnificent vessel with twin decks, the upper one in teak, but considerably smaller. *Triton*'s overall length was 147 feet (against *Rhouma*'s 221), her width 22 feet (28) and her gross weight 290 tons (670). With similar engine power she would have been slightly faster. While not quite as graceful in proportions as her larger sister – and sister she became with a new name, *Rhouma II* – she was still an eye-catcher.

It was not a good time to be buying pleasure-yachts. The Bulloughs had less than a year in which to enjoy her.

17

Poppies and Turf – The War Years

The end began, as did so many other ends, in nineteen-fourteen. There was no more rattling of pots and pans, no more anguished shrieks from the chef, no more of those tantalising smells. Gone was the delicious roast beef dripping we collected every week and spread thick on home-made oatcakes. There was no butter like that!

Everything was replaced by preparations for war. The Albions and the carriages were packed away for the last time in their dust sheets. All the young men, including the fourteen gardeners who maintained those glorious policies, were mustered. The riding ponies were assembled with all the harness – some of it quite unused.

Those gardeners were made into cavalrymen, although most of them had hardly touched, let alone ridden, a horse. They were hoisted up and in turns walked and trotted and cantered round the castle until they were considered capable of hanging on. They then disappeared like a cloud of midges in a breeze of wind to display in the mud of Flanders what they had learned in a quick canter around the castle on the island of Rhum. Mostly they are still in Flanders.

There were only the boys left, of which I was one, to maintain the gardens and the greenhouses, and gradually the grapes, the peaches and the orchids vanished, gradually sliding into the wilderness of weeds and broken glass that marks their position today.

Archie Cameron's words eloquently summarise the decline of the estate, but it was not 'the end' literally. Sir George would continue to use the castle over the next twenty-five years, and his wife for another forty-three. Yet it was the end of the heyday of lavish parties, of an excess of staff to keep every aspect of the estate working and beautiful. The grounds were largely neglected, and invader species conquered and concealed the once-manicured gardens. Kinloch Castle's household was reduced to the minimum, a minimum that still allowed considerable comfort, but it was a pale shade of what had gone before.

The factor Brebner remained in control of the island during the war, and he received a letter in August 1916 from the Venison Supply Committee in London urging him to do all he could to increase the meat supply by way of 'gifts to hospitals and other institutions, supplies to the troops or sales on private account.' On Rum there was no one left to contribute to the scheme. The men had gone to war. For almost five years between December 1914 and August 1919 the name Bullough is absent from the *Game Books*, and not once did Sir George set foot on Rum.

He spent some of the time serving as a superintendent of the Remount Department, whose remit was to procure horses for the army – a task he must have enjoyed to the full – and was accorded the rank of major. *Rhouma II* was requisitioned by the navy in October 1914 and not returned until April 1919, working as a minesweeper with the modest armament of a single six-pound cannon and the same size of anti-aircraft gun. Howard & Bullough too was commandeered for the war effort, and adapted for the production of 'shells, hand grenades, mine sinkers, fuses, bombs, exploder containers, Handley Page wing fittings and other forgings and stampings'. For four years the factory worked day and night, employing 5,000 people, 3,000 of them now being women and girls for the first time in the company's history.

Sir George responded to the 'Victory Loan' campaign and lent the government an interest-free £50,000, and was rewarded on 21 January 1916 with a baronetcy; created 'of Down House, County of Worcester'. Any sense of jubilation in the Bullough household was short-lived, for the honour came exactly one week before the news that Monica's father, the old Marquis de la Pasture, had died aged seventy-eight at his home in Wales. By this time Sir George seemed to have tired of the war. He served on various textile and engineering committees, but resigned from his Remount duties and quietly retired to his stud of racing horses.

Over a thirty-year commitment to the turf, Sir George owned more than 150 racehorses. Initially his interest lay in steeplechasing, and all twenty-nine horses of note that he owned were trained by a man whose name alone was a testing course, the Honourable Aubrey Craven Theophilus Robin Hood Hastings. Research by George Randall shows that they achieved a win in every six races entered.

The year 1917 brought the first of Sir George's most famous successes. The Grand National was held only once during the First World War, not at its traditional Aintree home but on this occasion just outside London at Gatwick, now the site of a runway. Bullough entered two horses, Denis Auburn and ten-year-old Ballymacad, the latter ridden by Edmund Driscoll, who had only been on the horse twice before. Neither horse was ranked as a serious contender, Ballymacad's odds starting at 100–9, but a short snowstorm before the race made the going greasy and opened the field. Denis Auburn suffered an early fall and Ballymacad tailed the field, but gradually advanced. One of the favourites, Limerock, cleared the last hurdle well ahead of the others and only had to keep going to win, but a few strides after landing the horse went down. Ballymacad came through to win just ahead of Chang. The *Daily Sketch* of 23 March described the result as 'beginner's luck' and Ballymacad as 'winning only by a stroke of fortune'. Limerock's fall, widely reported as occurring 'a matter of yards from the finishing post', went down as one of the great 'disasters' in the Grand National's history.

Remarkably, Sir George was not there to witness his triumph. *The Scotsman* reporter recorded some of his interviews that day, the first with Aubrey Hastings: 'Sir George is controlling some big munitions works, and wrote to me that as the munitions workers could not get away to see the National, he would not come himself. It would be a big disappointment to him, because he is so fond of his horses; but it shows what a sportsman he is.'

The reporter continued:

I also had a conversation with W J Smith, the rider of Limerock, and in view of what is likely to appear in the press concerning Limerock it is interesting.

Smith said: – 'The race was over after I leaped the last fence. I had won easily. My horse was full of running. He could have gone round again. He jumped the fence all right, went other two [sic] strides, and twisted his feet and fell on the flat.'

'You say Limerock only went two strides after leading? We thought from the stands he went twenty yards.'

'It was only two strides; it was the second stride he twisted and went.'

My last interview was with Edmund Driscoll, the rider of the winner.

He said: – 'It is nonsense what they all say about Limerock winning in a canter if he had not fallen. I had Limerock well beaten. He struck his hind legs into the last fence, and that is what brought him down. They blame Smith. It was not Smith's fault at all. He was riding a tired horse, but he does not know he was. I had always got Limerock whacked.'

Regardless of the bickering, Ballymacad was the hero of the day, and the 'War National' (it was never officially classed as a 'Grand National') would forever be Sir George's triumph. In recognition of the times he donated the 'value of the stake', nearly £1,000, to St Dunstan's Home for Blinded Soldiers.

18

Rum Revisited – The Post-War Era

The Bulloughs returned to Rum in August 1919, Sir George resuming the sporting life and being joined on the hill one September day by Lady Bullough, who shot her second-ever stag. Fishing and hunting might have felt like a return to the old world and perhaps even as a palliative against the forces of destruction which had run amok for half a decade, but irreversible changes had taken place and there were few remaining illusions of stability. According to official figures, the 8.7 million men who served in the British Army suffered 2,272,999 wounds and 956,703 deaths. Such slaughter devastated families, communities and workforces, and naturally it changed attitudes. The future was suddenly uncertain, rights and responsibilities assumed greater importance and frivolous lifestyles could no longer be conscientiously justified when the freedom to indulge in them was now measured in so much death and grief.

The Bulloughs too had suffered. Monica's eldest half-brother was the first to fall, dying of wounds at Flanders during the first October of the war. Her other half-brother was wounded in 1917. Within the space of a year George's stepmother, Alexandra, lost her husband (in war service in Lincolnshire) and a son killed in action. His sister Gladys married in July 1915 and was a widow within two months. Tom Bullough's eldest son fell at Loos (although Tom never knew it, as he himself had died a year earlier.) Fortune smiled only on Ian Bullough, who fought through the war unscathed and was awarded an M.C. for 'heroic conduct'.

Of the former male staff at Kinloch Castle, it is said that fourteen gardeners and estate workers trooped off to the trenches and only two returned. Catherine Duckworth is suspicious of this assertion, pointing out that Sir George was a driving force behind war memorials in Baxenden and Oswaldtwistle, and he officially unveiled the one in Accrington. Given this degree of commitment, she asks, surely he would have paid for a memorial for such a large proportion of his former employees in Rum? This is a compelling argument and must cast doubt on the authenticity of the figures traditionally given. Whatever the true level, the number of employees on Rum dropped drastically, either through death or because the estate had been mothballed for so long. What is certain is that among those who did return safely from the war, was the much-respected piping stalker, Duncan Macnaughton.

The alligators had been shot, the turtles released, the humming-birds chilled to death, the grounds were overgrown and the magnificent glasshouses in complete disrepair. Gradually the broken panes were replaced, the woodwork painted and the grounds brought back into some degree of order, though at a vastly reduced level of maintenance. No longer was the atmosphere characterised by exuberance and extravagance; now everything was sober and calculated. *Rhouma II* was returned to Sir George in April 1919 and sold the same year.* Despite

---

* Her subsequent life is extraordinary. Sir George sold her to a Vincent Grech of London who had her lengthened by 9 feet 2 inches. He sold her in 1924 and the new owner renamed her *Osprey*. She subsequently changed hands at least another eleven times, and names five times: she became *Rhouma* (again), *Hiniesta*, *President Roberts*, *Hiniesta* again and *Madiz*. Her owners have included Iranians, Greeks and, during WW2, His Majesty's Government. Popular opinion reports that she was broken up for scrap in 1975, probably because she disappeared from Lloyd's *Register of Yachts* around this time. In fact she survives to this day as the *Madiz* under the flag of Cyprus. Her

making such a sizeable investment, he had had no more than thirty months in which to enjoy her over seven years. His heart had gone out of luxury cruises, Madeira balls and exotic travel.

He was now a reasonably well-known figure in a world that was less keen to respect position and wealth but more ready to exploit it, as was demonstrated by a curious case of fraud that not only hit the papers but created a legal precedent.

The King's Bench Division sat on the hearing of *Phillips* v *Brooks* on 1 May 1919. 'A man entered the plaintiff's shop and asked to see some pearls and some rings. He selected pearls at the price of £2550 and a ring at the price of £450. He produced a cheque book and wrote out a cheque for £3000. In signing it, he said: "You see who I am, I am Sir George Bullough," and he gave an address in St. James's Square. The plaintiff knew that there was such a person as Sir George Bullough, and finding on reference to a directory that Sir George lived at the address mentioned, he said, "Would you like to take the articles with you?" to which the man replied: "You had better have the cheque cleared first, but I should like to take the ring as it is my wife's birthday tomorrow," whereupon the plaintiff let him have the ring. The cheque was dishonoured, the person who gave it being in fact a fraudulent person named Roger North ... In the meantime, North, in the name of Firth, had pledged the ring with the defendants who, bona fide and without notice, advanced £350 upon it.'

There was no doubt about the fraudster's crime – although there was some honour in having selected the item of lesser value! – but Judge Horridge's dilemma was which of the injured parties should suffer the loss: the plaintiff who parted with the ring in the first place, or the defendants who bought it. In a long-winded summary he sided with the defendants and awarded costs. He determined that the original seller had formed a contract with the man in their shop, albeit under a false

---

owners, the Keletsekis family (presumably of Greece), gave her an extensive refit in 2003 which took three years to complete. At 110 years old (in 2012) she is the oldest surviving steel vessel still to be classed 100A1 at Lloyd's.

name, which made the contract 'voidable but not void', and thus the property had passed to him, making his subsequent sale to the defendant a legitimate transaction. Roger North (a nephew of the Earl of Guildford!) was sentenced to nine months and thereafter became an habitual offender. Remarkable as it seems, this was the first case of its kind. Sir George would have read about it in the papers but without much interest or surprise. It was a time of great change. What could possibly shock him now? Racing results, mainly.

Suddenly in 1920 Sir George abandoned steeplechasing, sold off his stock of jumpers and devoted the rest of his life to flatracing. In Glenlyon, Ian Bullough sold Meggernie after it had been in the family for thirty-seven years.* In Rum, Archie Cameron, now aged seventeen, was dismissed.

'When the Laird and his gracious Lady had returned to their winter residence in the south, we were left to the merciless and villainous factor, and with no redress against his wicked decisions. The one I remember as the most virulent was, after many years of villainy, instantly dismissed on one occasion when Sir George returned to the island. That evil being [Wallace Brebner] was last heard of trying to sell books to his erstwhile friends in Mallaig.' Archie and a friend, Willie, went fishing in one of the estate's boats without permission. At a time when their wages were ten shillings a week, Brebner fined each of them one pound. Archie threatened to take the matter to Sir George and was promptly given one month's notice to leave the island and the only life he had known. His last act was to walk up the Harris road with a friend and carve his name on a rock at the junction with the Kilmory road. (*Archie Cameron, July 14th*

---

* The asking price was £160,000, but the best offer was £120,000. Meggernie was bought by Sir Ernest Wills, of the Wills Tobacco Company, who had been a frequent sporting guest of Ian. The change of ownership reversed their roles, and the former host now became a frequent guest of Sir Ernest. Ian moved to Redmarley where he and Sir George were neighbours. At the time of his death Ian was living at Inverawe, Taynuilt.

1920 is still legible today.) Before leaving he managed to secure a job as a 'delver' – digger – in the gardens of Inverlochy Castle, near Fort William, and thus was introduced to the delights of chocolate and the wonder of frogs.

Sir George's delights around this time centred on cerise vests with purple sleeves, as worn by his jockeys. In 1919 he had purchased a yearling called Golden Myth for 1,400 guineas, one of his more modest purchases. In the forty-eight hours of 24–25 June 1922 Golden Myth clinched both the Ascot Gold Cup and Gold Vase, an unprecedented feat. This time the papers did not mention flukes or luck, but christened the event 'Sir George Bullough's Golden Ascot'. Two weeks later he won the Eclipse Stakes. Over the years Golden Myth earned over £15,000 in stake money alone. He proved less successful as a stud in the stables which were founded on the strength of his reputation by Sir George in conjunction with 'Jack' Jarvis, in the early stages of his rise to fame. In later years Campanula was their most successful horse.

Having been Master of the Ledbury Hunt for thirteen years, Sir George stepped down in 1921 (and was succeeded by half-brother Ian in 1924). A pamphlet from the time recorded that Sir George 'ran the hunt on a lavish scale, buying, in his second season, some hounds at the sale of Mr Frank Bibby's North Shropshire Hounds for £250 a couple. Many members had second horses out and I have often seen over twenty men out, including six from the Hunt, all dressed in pink.' Sir George was an accomplished horseman and his tall figure bursting through the bushes in bright pink must have been a striking sight to fox and spectator alike.

Now he joined the Jockey Club and was a member for his remaining seventeen years.

* * *

And every year until his death Sir George continued to visit Rum, often accompanied by his wife and daughter. Now that *Rhouma*s *I* and *II* had been sold, they usually arrived with their modest entourage on the mail boat, even though a new tender, *Golden Myth,* had been purchased. Compared to the previous vessels she was a minnow, a compromise between the old *Kinloch II* and nothing. One of Duncan Macnaughton's sons, Stuart, recalled that, 'during the stalking season, when Sir George and his guests were on the island, it made two crossings per week to Mallaig for groceries. It rolled terribly.'

Around this time Monica and Hermione began winning prizes at dog shows with their preferred breed, the Alsatian. Hermione is remembered by one distant relative as being notable only for her lack of character. At sixteen she was plain-looking, incredibly tall and thin, her hair plaited in pigtails which reached her hips. She does, however, appear to have inherited her father's propensity to drink, or attracted friends of that disposition, if her drinks order for a party she threw at the castle in August 1926 is anything to go by: 169 bottles of champagne (Krug, Cordon Rouge, Coulet), twenty-six of wine (list incomplete), sixteen of brandy (mostly 1818 vintage), three of fifty-year-old port, and unspecified numbers of Corona Brillante and Habana Hoyo de Monterrey cigars. That doesn't sound like the catering of wispy wallflowers.

And three years later, aged twenty-three, she has certainly shed her weak image. 'Miss Bullough' is recorded as shooting her first stag on 2 September 1929. She goes on to make another two kills within the fortnight, one being annotated in the *Game Book,* 'Shot against a bright sun'. Whether this was written in genuine admiration or intended to encourage is not important – Sir George was so delighted he devoted a nook in the Great Hall to the display of this particular head, along with the finest procured by himself and Monica. Had anyone else been invited to contribute to the trophies, the honour would have fallen to Sir William Bass. The millionaire brewer and fellow racehorse-owner was one of Sir George's closest friends, and easily the most frequent guest to the island. If the behaviour at parties had mellowed, the numbers of guests over this period show scant sign of having diminished.

Occasional improvements continued to be introduced, though on a scale that was minuscule compared to orchestrions and steam yachts. The first refrigerator was purchased in 1928, presumably replacing the subterranean ice house, though doubt exists as to whether the latter was ever used. Heating was extended to all parts of the castle and a new telephone system installed. Each year Sir George imported up to a dozen red deer and tens of thousands of trout. In the light of events that were about to unfold, this apparent display of commitment to his sporting estate begs the question as to whom these improvements were intended to benefit?

The Great Depression struck during the 1920s, a deepening shadow at first until Britain was overwhelmed in the second half of the decade. Howard & Bullough were the largest employer in Accrington by this time and the Globe Works dominated the valley. A long history of robust management had enabled it to develop into an extraordinary phenomenon of specialisation. At its peak of peacetime production in the early 1900s, the factory utilised no less than 5,000 machine tools which were arranged in sequential order. Each speed frame contained hundreds of fliers and spindles, and the manufacture of each flier-spindle set involved 250 operations, each one performed by a different man. For speed and efficiency, the idea was to turn every operator into a specialist. The policy worked; H&B remained the world's largest producer of ring spinning frames and would hold the supremacy till after Sir George's death. Each year, as far back as memory could recall, the company had declared dividends equal to or in excess of ten per cent.

The downside was that such factories were truly filthy places to work. Machinery manufacture involves large quantities of grease and iron filings, and H&B's workforce were largely indistinguishable in appearance from miners. No smoking breaks were allowed. Yet it was work, and as the depression deepened, the company regained some respect among the workforce, despite redundancies and slumped profits, because it survived.

Conditions scarcely improved in the run-up to the Second World War. In 1931, Sir George decided to amalgamate his company (he was still nominally Chairman) with those of his five principal rivals, to form an alliance called 'Textile Machinery Manufacturers'. He was appointed Chairman of the consortium, but the move came too late, and within a year four of the six had gone into liquidation. H&B fought on, but the market was shrinking and the cheap labour of foreign competitors was decimating the home market. Sir George's income was radically reduced.

Yet it was all relative. Whereas before he had been fabulously wealthy, now he was plain wealthy. His lifestyle remained the same. In these 'lean' years he still commissioned a new home to be built at Newmarket, close to the racecourse. Set in 150 acres, Warren Hill was an immense mansion of imposing stateliness, designed by Thomas Tyrwhitt. With a frontage of forty windows on three storeys and with an adjoining lodge on each wing, the house was a striking picture of symmetry. He also established a second stud nearby, Longholes, and his horses continued to tour the racing circuit.

Given these massive outlays and this new source of interest in the south, Rum naturally retreated into the background. The castle correspondence shows that around this time Sir George's annual visits were probably perfunctory. In early May 1930 the following advertisement appeared in *The Times*:

Deer Stalking, sea loch and burn fishing in the Isle of Rhum off the west coast of Scotland to be let for the season. Kinloch Castle and deer forest which have never been let before, affording some of the finest stalking in Scotland. The Castle stands amidst magnificent scenery in lovely pleasure grounds and gardens, and contains four reception rooms, billiard room, saloon with organ,

21 principal and secondary bedrooms, 11 servants' bedrooms, six bathrooms and simple domestic accommodation. Electric light and central heating etc, the whole being in excellent order. Garage, squash racquet court, motor boat. The stalking is over the whole island, extending to about 25000 acres.

For further particulars apply RW Brebner Esq, Estate Office, Isle of Rhum

Agents in Edinburgh and London were also given the task of finding a tenant for an annual rent of £3,000. One of them, Watson, Lyall of Piccadilly, responded: 'Can you let us have a record of salmon and sea trout caught in recent years?' Might this have been the reason for Sir George's restocking programme? It is possible, but a more likely explanation is that the Stock Market crash of 1929–32 caused him a momentary loss of confidence in his affairs and he determined to recoup some income from the money drain of Rum. This proved unusually difficult. One potential tenant tried to haggle over the rent, but Sir George refused to negotiate and Rum went unlet. Watson, Lyall wrote apologetically that, 'It has been a very bad letting season and a great many forests are without tenants.' So the Bulloughs went stalking themselves instead. The castle Order Book for September 1930 requests delivery of 'three doz bottles of Challoner's "Discovery" whisky'. Some consolation!

The process was repeated the following year, at first with the rent unchanged, until it was acknowledged as unrealistic: 'We thank you for your letter and have noted on our particulars that the rent of the above has been reduced to £2000 for the season and that now only two stalkers are retained.' Still there were no takers for the 1931 season. Brebner even wrote to the Inland Revenue asking for a reduction in the rates, but the outcome of this is unknown. Then the first inklings of desperation appear in the correspondence.

August, 1931, from Watson, Lyall: 'We've had an enquiry as to whether the island of Rhum is for sale. Will you kindly reply.'

Brebner did so on 1 September:

Dear Sirs, I received your letter of 27th last night and placed your enquiry before Sir George Bullough. He says that as he has no intention of selling, he is not able to mention a price and does not want the island placed on your books as for sale. On this understanding, however, he would be prepared to give favourable consideration to any genuine, bona fide offer to purchase. If therefore any client of yours definitely wishes to purchase, it would be best to submit an offer which I could place before Sir George. Yours faithfully ...

Either no offer was forthcoming or it was rejected. This remains the sole instance of Sir George ever considering selling Rum. The only other proposal put to him, also in the 1930s, was one by the naturalist Frank Fraser Darling, who requested permission to use the island for a deer research project. This was also refused, though the idea did not die.

* * *

1931 was the year of a happier event, however, the marriage of the Bulloughs' only child, Hermione. On 4 March at St Mark's Church, North Audley Street, London, she walked down the aisle in her father's arm carrying a posy of 'real orange flowers and buds, wearing a deep cream satin wedding gown with a long train and a tulle bridal veil six yards in length.' In one respect the wedding was a close parallel of her grandfather's to his second wife, for she was twenty-five and the groom was forty-six. He was a widower, successful racehorse owner and well-known patron of the turf, John Frederick Lambton, 5th Earl of Durham.* Thus

---

* By his first wife, who had died seven years earlier, he had two sons. The eldest died 'in a shooting accident', also reported as suicide, aged twenty. The other son was Antony Lambton (1922–2006) who was Parliamentary Under-Secretary of State for Defence (RAF) in Edward Heath's government in 1970. That same year he succeeded to his father's title and briefly was the 6th Earl of Durham, before disclaiming the title 'for life' in order to remain in the House of Commons. Despite this, he insisted on being called Viscount

Hermione became the Countess of Durham, and moved to the family seat of Lambton Castle, Wooler.

Sir George celebrated his sixty-first birthday in 1931. His health appeared to be sound. He and Lady Bullough had moved into Warren Hill as their main residence. The annual visits to Rum now held more the status of pilgrimage. The castle was in good repair, but the grounds were woefully neglected. By 1936 the island's population had contracted to thirty-six. In this year Ian Bullough, aged fifty, underwent a minor operation and died suddenly while recuperating in an Edinburgh nursing home. Two years earlier he had fathered twin sons (his only progeny) by his third wife. Sir George was a pallbearer at the funeral.

Hermione produced a son the year after her marriage, but this did not end her association with Rum. She continued to make occasional sojourns to the island, accompanied by her husband and the infant John George Lambton. The visit of 1938 was special. John George was six years old and better able to appreciate the world around him. Sir George was therefore able to share with his grandson some of the magic of the place, both natural and of his own creation. For a spell Sir George shot a stag every other day, the last being a seven-pointer weighing fifteen stone and twelve pounds, shot on the North Side with Duncan Macnaughton by his shoulder. He did not know it, but this was to be his last entry in the *Game Books*.

Lambton, which caused a heated and unresolved controversy. In 1973 photographs of him in bed smoking cannabis with two prostitutes hit the headlines and forced his resignation. (Lord Jellicoe was exposed in the same scandal and resigned the following day.) 'Lord Lambton' took up gardening in Italy. The 7th Earl of Durham is his son, Ned Lambton, former lead singer of the band The Frozen Turkeys. One of Ned's sisters is Lucinda Lambton, author and TV presenter.

19

Deer, Fish and Fowl – Notes from the Records

Red deer had been hunted to extinction on Rum by 1787. The Marquis of Salisbury reintroduced them from English parks during his twenty-year ownership from 1845, at the time of the failed experiment in fallow deer. By the time John Bullough bought the island in 1886, red deer numbers were estimated to be about 600, subsequently increasing to 800 by 1895, with an annual cull of forty. The average weight of a gralloched carcase around this time was eleven or twelve stone. No hinds were killed, it seems, or else they were never recorded. The favourite rifle had the comparatively large calibre of .450, but other calibres were .360, .303, .256 and only Sir Hermon-Hodge used 6.5mm.*

After 1900, with the .303 now the most popular calibre, the average weights of kills increased to sixteen stone. Not just trophy beasts were targeted, as later entries in the *Rum Deer Forest Book* show: 'All marked bad heads are specially picked as "weedy" stags'; or 'Selected for the good of the forest'. As a result of this policy the 1908 average dropped to 14 stone. On 24 September 1910, a thirteen-pointer shot by Sir George tipped the scales at 19 stone 6 lbs and was described as the 'Finest head killed at Rhum'. There are oddities recorded too: hummels (stags

---

* Contemporary stalkers use .308, .270 or .243, which is the smallest legal calibre for killing deer.

without antlers); a single instance in 1900 of an 'Austrian stag';†
one with 'Three antlers'; many marked 'switch' (antlers with no
tines); one with 17 points; a 'blind in both eyes'; a 'lame stag';
one which 'fell over the cliff into the sea', and one bagged by
Hermione in 1930 with the affectionate observation, 'Old Sandy'.

Annual kills topped fifty for the first time in 1925. Over the
next five years Sir George imported deer from Warnham Park
in Sussex, whose stags were renowned for having very large,
multi-pointed heads. The numbers were not large – over a three-
year period, for example, 19 stags and 21 hinds were released
– but given the difficulty in transportation this was no light
undertaking. 1929 and 1930 witnessed two unusual events: the
heaviest stag on record weighing in at 21 stone 6 lbs, and the
first known defection from the island, when a young stag was
watched by a missionary, John Campbell, arriving exhausted in
Eigg having swum five miles from Rum.

The deer population had risen to between 1700 and 1800 by
1934, which made possible Sir George's ambition to take the cull
into triple figures. The weather favoured the stalkers, and by 10
October he was able to enter in the record: 'Hundredth stag of
the season; 87 stags average 14 stone 1 lb. 13 other weedy stags
were killed but not weighed. 100 stags killed, weight of heaviest
18 st 8 lbs'. A new telescope was presented to head stalker
Duncan Macnaughton to honour the occasion.

* * *

Of the three records, the *Isle of Rum Game Book* provides the
most dramatic revelations about the changes in species and
the 'health' of the sporting estate. Neither John nor George
Bullough were particularly fond of shooting small game, but,

---

† Austrian red deer are the same species and were imported into Britain
because they tended to be larger, heavier animals. If this stag was indeed
Austrian it must have been imported via an English park. For some reason its
weight and points were not recorded.

as previously mentioned, John had made some attempts to introduce new species. Some blackcock were released but promptly starved. Partridges dug in around Kilmory, but they too were out of their element and one of the last of their ghetto bravely battled with a hawk but died of its wounds. Mallards were said to have been too successful for their own good, and their ravaging of crops resulted in their eradication as vermin, not even worthy of mention in the records. Being roosting birds, pheasants naturally had a hard time of it, but John Bullough observed: 'It is interesting to see the pheasants adapting to their new conditions. They have no trees; there is no proper covert and yet they flourish. They roost on the ground in the heather and seem quite at home there.' They certainly never flourished sufficiently to appear in the *Game Book*, other than as ones or twos, and even this small death-toll was too much for them to maintain their delicate balance. Rum has no pheasants today. Red grouse survive as a low fraction of their former abundance, though they were almost wiped out in the 1930s. Woodcock and snipe remain common.

The shooting was let in 1890 when the tenant, Mr Blakey, shot 318 grouse in six days. He must have been an exceptional shot, for 63 of that total is annotated 'In 6 hrs with 62 carts'. While George was away travelling in 1893, his cousins Tom and William bagged 381 brace of grouse, 68 snipe and one duck in twenty days. On George's return in 1895 he took up his shotgun enthusiastically at first, bagging 405 grouse in September, and the following year fifty brace in a single day. One 1895 woodcock weighed 16 ounces.

After this year boredom appears to have set in, and despite the high yields continuing, most fell to the guns of guests or keepers. The reason may be that the newly knighted George had found richer pickings on the estates of friends. In 1903 he shot on the Redlynch Estate near Bruton, Somerset, which belonged to Henry Strangway, Earl of Ilchester. The bag for five guns over two days was 294 rabbits, 476 pheasants and one woodcock (total kill 771). He returned to Redlynch the following year for the whole of January, and shot 1,706 rabbits, 8 woodcock, 1,098 pheasants, three partridges and eight hares (total kill 2,223). He nevertheless took part in bagging 209 grouse on Rum in the same year. It seems that as the grouse on Rum declined, either woodcock and snipe increased or they were now the popular species to shoot. The following is a summary of the three principal game birds shot over five-year periods.

	Grouse	Woodcock	Snipe
1894–1898	2513	184	129
1899–1903	2155	198	152
1904–1908	2102	197	204
1909–1913	616	153	259
1919–1923	386	417	157
1924–1928	182	598	504
1929–1933 [ends]	141	201	76

The last two hares entered the book in 1908, the last partridge in 1909 and the final pheasant in 1914. It seemed an ignominious end to their struggles. Several dozen plovers and curlews were shot over the years, an occasional pigeon and at least twenty now-protected 'landrails' (corncrakes), the last being shot as recently as 1951. The rasping echoes of corncrakes are no longer heard on Rum. The only increase is in greylag geese: today they are abundant visitors, but only two are mentioned over a sixty-year span a century ago.

After the war Sir George was mainly interested in stags and fishing. He potted game only in 1923 and 1926. For the remaining thirteen years till his death, under the heading 'Name of gun', the *Game Book* is filled exclusively with 'Keepers'.

* * *

After the Marquis of Salisbury's expensive failure to establish a salmon run, fishing on the estate was confined to sea trout and brown trout. The first entry is for cousins Tom and William Bullough in 1893, who caught 485 sea trout and 712 brown trout. These total 420 lbs for the season, with individual weights not being given. The totals drop over the next few years, but bounce back at the start of the new century. Lady Bullough, as Mrs Charrington, first appears in August 1902, fishing with Sir George and catching forty sea trout to his five. By 1904 the seasonal totals are 107 sea trout and 925 brown trout. Yet these impressive statistics are misleading. The average brown trout weighed three ounces – these are minnows, and the only reasons for keeping them are to flatter novices (which must have been the case with a relative of Monica's, Miss M. de la Pasture, who recorded '2 totalling 6 oz') or to clear the lochs of small fry to leave more food for the others. Over the decades the catches of sea trout drop to several dozen annually, while hundreds of miniature brown trout continue to be taken. Brown trout were obviously considered light entertainment, although a splendid record for the island came out of Loch Mitchell in 1903, weighing 4 lbs 4 ozs. (Robb Mitchell's loch is frequently fished successfully, but the other two bodies of water, named in honour of Sir George's most esteemed companions, Loch Monica and Ashworth's Model Loch, are never mentioned.) Generally the largest specimen each decade weighed around 2 lbs. Sea trout were considered serious sport, and Sir George imported large numbers of eggs in the twenties. The largest sea trout fell to a rod in 1925 and weighed 8 lbs 2 ozs. The single comment of note in the book appears under 14 May 1926 when Sir George caught a 4lb 2 oz sea trout in the river: 'This fish was hooked at 10.20am and landed at 12.15pm.'

20

A Selection from the Castle's Correspondence

16 April, 1909
From Queen Street Iron Works, Peterborough, in response to Brebner's letter expressing dissatisfaction with the road roller he purchased.

> We are bound to say at once that we are sure that the motor roller will do good service on the island, provided the ordinary road-making methods are used. Seeing that our motor roller only weighs four tons and is of the tandem pattern it will cost much less to make the foundations good for its use than if any other roller was employed. Our engineer says he was three hours getting up the first hill which was of course far too long but it was pointed out to you by Mr Keen that it will be necessary to take some of the projecting stones off the surface of this hill, and if this had been done, the roller would have climbed the hill, we are sure, without this stoppage.
>
> Our position now is that if the roller is returned we shall be put to a very heavy expense and must of course suffer some loss in reputation. We do not admit that there is anything the matter with the roller and we do not think we ought to suffer in this way.' [The roller was returned.]

7 November 1910
From General Post Office, London, in response to a letter of protest about unannounced visits to the island:

I am directed by the Postmaster General to say that notice
will, as far as possible, be given whenever it is necessary for a
servant of the department to visit the island of Rhum on official
business, and it is probable that in most instances notice can
be given but there may be occasions when this course will not
be feasible and the Postmaster General assumes that in such
emergencies there will be no objection to his officers landing on
the island without prior notice, or to their being accommodated
for such a time as may be necessary by such of the islanders as
may have accommodation available. [Another letter hints at
closing the post office, pointing out that the telegraph extension
to the Small Isles cost over £5,000 to lay in 1900 and 'telegraph
[use] at Rhum has steadily and heavily declined since 1902.']

FROM THE KITCHEN ORDER BOOKS: 1912–1914

Please despatch the following goods to the order of Sir George
Bullough, Isle of Rhum, by Oban, N.B.

1912

28/6 Messers Harrods: 2 doz Bridge scoring block, 14 lager &
beer.

1/7 Messers Harrods: mustard 6 tins, blk peppercorns 1/2 lb,
Anchovy & Worcester Sauce, black polish, 1 roll of fine emery, 2
doz pen holders, 1/2 doz packets playing cards, 3 doz meat plates,
3 doz pudding plates, 2 soup tureens, 6 saucer bowls.

3/7 Messers Black: half a sheep, half a lamb, joint of sirloin
15 lbs, 12 lbs stock meat, half doz sheep's kidneys, 2 lbs beef suet

12 Feb 1913

[Sir George must be considering installing log-effect electric
fires in the castle.] From the Prometheus Company Ltd, Sole
Manufacturers and Patentees for Great Britain and Northern
Ireland of the Prometheus System of Electric Cooking and
Heating:

We thank you for your favour and for your benefit we would state that our standard pattern log fires are made in seven different sizes. We note, however, that you would like the logs reduced in height but in this respect we would state that it is impossible for us to alter the existing measurements of any of the sizes as the moulds are made and cannot therefore be reconstructed or altered.

February 1914

Duncan Macnaughton applied for a job with this letter, a model of succinctness, which is reproduced as originally written:

Dear Sirs
seeing you are advertising for a GameKeeper Stalker in Sats Scotsman I apply for same. I am 27 Years old Married one in family I may say I thoroughly understand Pheasant rearing Grouse and Partridge Driving the breaking and working of mostly all sporting dogs Eleven Years experience in dogs and the management of a Grouse Moor nine of which I had experience in Deer stalking and Driving on the strathgartney Deer forest and Grouse Moor where they killed annualy 20 stags.

I am strictly sober (and good piper)

You can have my character by writing to Mr John Paterson Brinachoile Lodge Trossachs Callendar and another one A S Macnaughton at Balquidder Perthshire ... I am yours obediently Duncan Macnaughton.

[He was appointed keeper/stalker at a wage of '23/- per week, with free house, £5 value per annum in coal and 4d. cash in lieu of paraffin. Wages to be paid every four weeks.' He was still employed on Rum when the Bullough connection ended in 1957.]

22 June 1920

Mackenzie and Moncur Ltd, estimate for painting hothouses: £468.

10 Dec 1921

From the Cornwallis Kennel of Gun Dogs, Grange, Banffshire

Dear Sir, I have to thank you for yours of the 7th instant regarding pointers and setters, and can offer you the following: Grouse and Bruce, black and white, and lemon and white English setter dogs, third and first season dogs respectively, excellent workers on all game, pedigree of the best working strain and heavily shot over to date and all season ... You can have Hughie and Shot, black and white ...

31 Dec 1921

If you want to keep Hughie only I cannot accept less than twenty-five guineas for him as this is a definite offer I have for him waiting. Shot you can have for fifteen guineas or as already stated the brace at thirty-five guineas.

1926

Brebner orders a stonebreaker

One 8 by 6 Blake Crusher mounted on road wheels and complete with screen ... one pitman, a dragbar ... [The rusted remains of this Crusher still stand beside the road to Harris.]

21 Feb 1926.

Lucas (of Horsham in Sussex) writes:

have booked with pleasure Sir George Bullough's six stags and two hinds, delivery next September. As you know the price of three-year-old stags is £15 each and of hinds, £13 10s. But my father and I will be pleased to supply Sir George with the six stags and two hinds for the sum of £96 and I will see that he has good strong and promising young beasts. They will consist of two five-year-old beasts, three four-year-old beasts and three three-year-old beasts. [He is not selling any two-year-olds because he assumes Sir George would want the hinds to calve next year.]

6 April 1926
From Brebner to Royal Insurance:

> There would appear to be two "Trojans" an "Albion" and a motor lorry. One Trojan is covered by a new item on page one for £150 and the lorry by item number 48, but we do not find an item for the remaining Trojan and Albion. Will you please insert these and also if necessary the amount on the racquets court, item 30, which is not now covered.

10 Sep 1926
Telegram from Brebner, Rhum:

> Can Sweethome take delivery 14 live deer in crates arriving 6 train Wed evening or same train Sat evening next week and convey immediately to Rhum? If so please quote and will wire again definitely which day arriving.

1929
Awaiting overdue spare parts from Stockholm for the Magneto Wall Telephones.

23 Jan 1929
From The Solway Fishery:

> I am arranging to send you ten hatching boxes and 25,000 sea trout ova ... [by train from Dumfries to Mallaig, via Glasgow St Enoch]. The eggs will be packed with ice and will need no attention until they are unpacked when the temperature should be raised gradually before they are placed in the hatching boxes [known as Kashmir boxes] as described later. The boxes are to be moored in the stream by stakes which may either be driven into the bank or the bed of the stream itself. Enough rope should be given them to float when not weighted. After the eggs are put in a stone or stones large enough to sink them to the bottom should be placed on the lids.

26 April 1929

I am very sorry to hear that the salmon did not do better. The symptoms which you describe are like those which follow when eggs due to hatch have been checked and delayed in hatching by a cold spell. I do not think it likely that any disease could have been present.

7 Aug 1930
From A. S. Bowlby, Knoydart, Mallaig:

I came over yesterday on behalf of a friend of mine who wants a shoot but he is anxious to have a place where there are grouse and that is what brought me over. I remember the excellent sport we had in 1891 and 1892 in Rhum and I am sorry to have heard that grouse have now almost disappeared. Your grieve told me this so that I did not wait . . . I think also the castle would be too large for him. Yours faithfully . . .

12 Sep 1930
[Unfavourable train connections are causing problems with the delivery of large cans containing 1,000 Loch Leven yearling trout]:

The alternative is to send them by motor to Mallaig which would entail considerable expense. We can arrange for 9d per mile on the round trip. Or another way would be to motor to Glasgow for the early train. [£3 10s to motor them to Glasgow, plus railway carriage to Mallaig at £7 19s 10d.] I cannot quote steamer charge but I think it will be about 3/- per hundredweight.

23 Dec 1930
Letter from accountants Ryder, Heaton, Meredith & Mills about Sir George's Schedule A income tax return for the year 1928/29. The annual values assessed are:

Kinloch Castle and offices £250, garden and vineries £30, garage £6, electrical plant and waterworks £20, house & farm £500, shootings & deer forest £450, small houses, cottages etc £115. Total: £1371. Less allowance for repairs, land £123 2/-, houses £74, net amount charged with tax £825 12/-.

12 Oct 1931
From accountants Ryder, Heaton, Meredith & Mills, Lincoln's Inn, London:

The number of wireless valves purchased seem to us rather a lot but we have no doubt they were all necessary. Also there was no receipt for £2 15/- paid to Macleod for eggs. Yours faithfully . . .

21 Oct 1931
From Brebner to Sir George's solicitors in Newmarket, concerning a compensation claim:

As desired I enclose for you a copy of my letter to Mr Francis Laing of 19th. Originally I had written expressing regret that circumstances had rendered cancelling his engagement necessary and enclosing a cheque for £12 to compensate him and in lieu of notice, covering also his expenses meeting me in Inverness for an interview which expenses were to be paid him on arrival here. This letter however was never sent, Sir George Bullough objecting to making any offer and telling me not to send it. I was allowing £10 as a month's wages and perquisites and £2 to cover the said expenses. I trust this will enable you to get the matter settled. Yours faithfully Wallace Brebner.

Oct 1931
Royal Insurance are wanting a premium of £86 16s od for fire insurance and are intending to send an assessor to Rum at Sir George's expense. He telegrams Brebner to say:

Definitely refuse to pay expenses for assessors visit. You must make that clear.

26 Oct 1931
Brebner writes to the Royal Insurance:

Meantime, if I am to expect a visit from your representative next Monday, at your expense, please wire me. We have only a weekly mail on Mondays so that after tonight I cannot hear from you by post till after arrival of steamer on Monday next.

This was R. Wallace Brebner's last communication. Shortly afterwards he must have been dismissed, according to Archie Cameron. Whatever his faults, some pity may be due to him for the massive correspondence he had to maintain on the infinite details of running the estate. His successor's correspondence is missing.

21

Death at Château de Courcet

Sir George Bullough, Baronet, of Rhum, suffered a fatal heart-attack while playing golf and died at the Château de Courcet, Pas de Calais, near Boulogne. The date was 26 July 1939. He was sixty-nine years old. His body was repatriated and the funeral held at Moulton near Newmarket. Among the many mourners were his widow, the Earl and Countess of Durham, Mrs Bertha Young (Sir George's sister), the Marquis de la Pasture (Lady Bullough's brother) and Sir William Bass. The *Accrington Observer* recorded that its prodigal son, who had left and largely failed to return to its precincts, had nevertheless still been President of Accrington Conservative Club and Vice President of Accrington Cricket Club at the time of his death. It also reported his failure to make himself destitute, his estate being valued at £710,037 gross, with a net personalty of £661,079.* His wife was left £25,000 and a scattering of valuable peripherals, including his horses, studs, farming stock, motor cars, yachts, boats, furniture and household and personal effects. His houses, castle, island and residual investments were to be held in trust for her for life, 'with the remainder to his daughter Hermione, Countess of Durham, with remainder to her husband and children as she may appoint, or to her children in equal shares.'

---

* Some sources give the gross figure of £714,639, but any quibble is pedantic at that scale of wealth.

He saved himself the responsibility of other bequests, 'feeling sure but without creating any Trust in the matter, that she [Monica] will carry out any wishes informally expressed to him with regard to friends and servants.'

His body was transported to Rum and laid to rest in a granite sarcophagus alongside that of his father in the mausoleum at Harris. Its inscription reads:

SIR GEORGE BULLOUGH
BARONET
OF RHUM
JULY 26 – 1939

22

The Forbidden Island

After his death Lady Bullough continued to reside at Warren Hill and added to her holding by buying the adjacent 152-acre Ashley Heath Stud (the vendors being none other than the 5th Earl of Durham and her daughter Hermione). She made occasional and irregular visits to Kinloch Castle, though probably not during the new hostilities sweeping Europe, for not even Rum was safe, as *The Times* (8 November 1940) reported: 'German Attacks on Shipping – In an attack on the harbour of Kinloch Castle, on the Scottish coast, a large merchant ship received two heavy direct hits. Warehouses were set on fire.'

Following the custom of Victorian widows she changed her private bedroom from the sunny south-east corner to the gloomy Oak Bedroom No. 4 at the back – quite why she did this is not clear, as her husband appears to have had little association with her original bedroom for decades. To the surprise of many, her interest in the affairs of the estate intensified and she took personal responsibility for making decisions. One of the first came as a result of the war.

In 1940 the Agriculture Executive Committee, whose remit was to increase wartime food production, pressed Lady Bullough to advertise for a tenant farmer to restock Rum with sheep. John Bullough had acquired a sizeable flock with his purchase of the island in 1888, but over the years numbers were reduced to about 1,000 ewes, concentrated around the laundry at Kilmory. The flock was finally cleared in 1926 and shepherding came to an end, despite local proposals to maintain smaller private flocks. A wartime tenant was found, Donald Cameron, who later wrote about his experiences in *Where Wild Geese Fly*:

> There were several empty houses at Kinloch, the landing place, and the huge castle with its disused walled garden, a derelict bathing pool [an incorrect observation] and aquarium. The castle itself had been kept in good condition ... There were some 15 of a population, being two stalkers, a cowman, a boatman, the castle housekeeper and their families, plus a teacher ... I learned that permission to land was required and often refused unless it was someone – fishing boat crews etc – wanting to send messages from the little post office which had the only telephone on the island. The lady owner would be really annoyed that I was about to break the spell and could not be expected to welcome my sheep, my shepherds or myself.

And she did not. She refused to allow Cameron use of the estate boat to transport his stock, but in fairness to Lady Bullough this might have proved an expensive favour, since he was secretly keeping almost 7,000 head of sheep on the island when the agreement stipulated a maximum of 2,000. Another sheep and cattle farmer, Major Walter Mundell, took up a ten-year lease in November 1947. Neither ventures were notably successful, but were sustainable. High mortality rates and low lambing figures were attributed to excessive grazing by the deer, and Cameron quit in 1956. He was unable to sell the tenancy as a going concern and his stock was cleared. Mundell did want to renew his lease but by then the island was under new ownership and he was refused. When he left, Rum ceased to be a producer of food for the first time in millennia.

Over the twentieth century Rum acquired the reputation and sobriquet of 'The Forbidden Island'. Wallace Brebner's correspondence with the General Post Office proves this was a sensitive issue as far back as 1910. Stories of visitors being turned away at gunpoint by keepers are unsubstantiated, but it is clear that casual visitors were not encouraged. This attitude was prevalent among all landowners at the time, and it is curious that Rum alone was singled out as an example of autocratic exclusion. Had this been a 30,000-acre site on the mainland with a 'Private' sign at the entrance it would probably have attracted less attention, but islands have always been special cases. While the Forbidden Island assumed the impregnability of Colditz in the minds of the masses, the experiences of those who dared test the hypothesis presented a different picture.

As a young journalist, Alastair Dunnett (later editor of *The Scotsman*) canoed with a friend to Rum in 1934 to exercise their right to roam over Scottish land. The pair set up their tent in full view of the castle and were politely asked to camp elsewhere. When they refused they were bidden to the castle where Lady Bullough received them over tea, said they were welcome to camp where they were and presented them with a haunch of venison. In an 'oppressed worker's' house they were treated to a 'sumptuous supper' and provided with a packed lunch for the paddle home. As Dunnett recalled in *The Canoe Boys*, 'it was a tricky run, a large lump of venison being awkward cargo for a one-man canoe.'

A 1946 edition of *Guide to the Island of Rhum*, published by the Junior Mountaineering Club of Yorkshire, advises: 'MacBraynes's steamer calls three times a week as a general rule. Landing from it will not be allowed unless permission has been obtained from the owner, Lady Bullough, Warren Hill, Newmarket, but this permission is unlikely to be granted.'

One visitor attempted to use this deterrent to his advantage. John Harrison, a professor of botany at Newcastle University, was frequently given permission to take students on field trips to Rum where he invariably discovered new species, some unique to the Canary Islands, which supported his theory that Rum had escaped the last Ice Age. Unfortunately another botanist was given permission to land to check his claims, and his fraud was discovered. He was secretly importing the plants to the island. The full story is told in Karl Sabbagh's *A Rum Affair – A True Story of Botanical Fraud*, which shows that Rum was easily accessible to those who observed the courtesy of asking beforehand.

Hermione also returned to Rum from time to time. She always brought her son, John George, and it is said he was sometimes left on the island with Duncan Macnaughton, in the hope he would become as passionate about the land and sporting life as his grandfather had been, but it was not to be. He did however return on 10 June 1953 to set the castle ablaze in celebration of his twenty-first birthday. Lady Bullough spent her later days at Warren Hill, returning to Rum for the last time in 1954, aged 84, when her old Austin was cranked into action and she drove herself over the hills to Harris to visit her husband's grave.

That Lady Bullough held Rum in deep affection is beyond doubt, and the bond seems to have strengthened with time. In old age she suffered considerable anxiety over what to do with the island. The obvious solution would have been to leave it to Hermione. In a letter dated 18 March 1966 – dictated to a friend, as she was too blind to write, and sent to Edward Max Nicholson, Director General of the Nature Conservancy – she confided that 'the probability was that her husband's heir (the Earl of Durham) would have been tempted to sell it on for a vast sum to some American millionaire'.* To suspect that the island might end up belonging to someone who might desecrate the image she and her late husband held of it seemed beyond contemplation.

The Nature Conservancy desperately wanted the property and entered negotiations. Edward Max Nicholson undertook the task. He was a man of considerable charm, and established

---

* Sir George's heir was of course Hermione, but Lady Bullough was saying that in effect Hermione's husband, the 5th Earl of Durham, would be the one to make the decision.

a friendship with Lady Bullough which endured beyond the settlement of Rum's future. On 28 February 1957 – the very day on which Sir George would have been eighty-seven – she signed the Minute of Sale transferring ownership of the island and castle to the Nature Conservancy for £23,000. The price was but a token, £12,000 less than John Bullough had paid for the island in 1888 and a fraction of its market value; it was a noble gesture of generosity. The contents of the castle alone were valued at £142,691.50.

The Scotsman of 5 April 1957 reported that 'heavy taxation had obliged Lady Bullough to make her decision. Her one fear, she confided to her factor, was that the Government would take over Rum for a rocket range or other scheme. She wanted it to remain unspoiled for all time.'

She lived for another ten years, dying at Warren Hill on 22 May 1967 at the venerable age of ninety-eight. The Nature Conservancy sent a bouquet of her favourite flower, Lily of the Valley. The 'funeral undertakers' were reported in the papers as being Anthony Bampfylde and Roger Delappature. (The reporter must have meant the principal pallbearers, as the latter name is the phonetic rendering of her father's title, de la Pasture, and the former was Monica's nephew.) A train carried her coffin to Mallaig, and after the ship transferred it to Rum, on a stormy day which soaked the mourners, a landrover completed the last leg to Harris, bucking ferociously on the road that Blake's 8X6 Stonebreaker and Barford & Perkins' roller had given up trying to tame. Her sarcophagus must have been prepared in advance, waiting only for the final date to be chiselled in place:

MONICA LILLY
WIFE OF SIR GEORGE BULLOUGH OF RHUM
BORN APRIL 8 1869, DIED MAY 22 1967

Archie Cameron had watched the funeral train pass through Fort William where he was living at the time.

I stood on the hillside at Corpach as the train went by carrying the mortal remains of a most gracious lady to her last resting place, beside her husband, the late Laird of Rhum, on the stormy shore of Harris.

I raised my hat and held it there until the sound of the train died away, and ended an era to which we can never return.

23

On Trust, in Trust

Rum now belonged to the nation, under the stewardship of the Nature Conservancy (NC), the government agency in charge of protecting the natural heritage and advocating policy for it. The NC 'agreed that it would (unless prevented from doing so by circumstances over which it had no control) use the island for the purpose of a Nature Reserve in perpetuity, and maintain Kinloch Castle and the adjacent premises thereon (so far as it might be practicable to do so in the circumstances)'.

Five weeks after the transfer, Rum was declared Scotland's second National Nature Reserve. The principal attraction of this particular parcel of land was its inaccessibility. On an island reserve the NC could conduct its work in isolation and exert maximum control over human intervention. The declared purpose was 'safeguarding and perpetuating the natural assemblages of plants and animals which they [the reserves] now contain, plant and animal assemblages which might settle there under more favourable conditions, and special features of geological interest'.

Of course this excluded any farming practices. Major Mundell's request to renew his lease in 1957 was refused. His cattle and sheep were removed in September. This and the official restrictions on access to Rum unleashed widespread public protests and caused a furore in the press. A motion entitled 'Twentieth Century Highland Clearance' was tabled in Parliament. The NC sought to reassure the country of its commitment to maintaining a community on Rum and allowing access to *bona fide* interest groups, but this was a flimsy cover for its real position. The NC's preference was unequivocally expressed in a letter written by its head, Edward Max Nicholson, to Wm. Mackay, of Messrs Innes and Mackay, Inverness (Agents for the Bullough Trustees) on 22 March 1957. His final sentence read: 'Perhaps we should consider other ways too of making Rum a model Hebridean Community (without Hebrideans).' Had that communication been leaked to the press, the reverberations would have rocked the NC.

Lady Bullough handed over the castle exactly as she had left it on her last visit three years earlier. Her personal belongings and certain requested items (including thirty-five cases of Madeira from the cellars) were returned to her. Otherwise the castle was a time-warp of the Edwardian days. Sir George's outsized boots still stood by his bed (and remain there to this day). Seventeen bottles of port were declared 'of no commercial value' by Sandemans. When Max Nicholson heard about this he sent a memo – and the note is still in the archives – ordering the cellar to be locked and no one to be allowed in until his next visit. There is no mention of the port in subsequent inventories.

Max Nicholson had won Lady Bullough's trust and she had relinquished island and castle in good faith that both would be conserved. The Nature Conservancy was solicitous in its attempts to assure her this would happen, but can have had no serious intention of honouring the commitment in the case of the castle. Its vision was exclusively limited to land and wildlife. It had no expertise or interest in buildings and, most crucially, no budget for them either. The NC wanted the island and unfortunately a castle came with it. At first it was a jolly and exotic place for NC executives to stay while contemplating their acquisition, but soon it became a millstone round the NC's neck.

Serious attempts were made to offload the responsibility onto another organisation, but these came to nothing. There were proposals to turn the castle into a conference centre, an alternative to Balmoral for the Royal family, an open detention centre run by the prison service and, one which did come to fruition for a few years, a hotel administered by the National Trust for Scotland. Yet the season was too short and the running costs too high. The project was abandoned. A recurring solution was to raze the castle to the ground. In the Report of the Rum Working Party, March 1975, Section 65, it was suggested that 'Kinloch Castle and the houses could be allowed to decay and become ruinous. If this is implemented, early demolition of the castle [is recommended] as this would cause less of an uproar than allowing this Grade A listed-building to slowly deteriorate'.

The NC had undertaken to 'maintain Kinloch Castle and the adjacent premises thereon (*so far as it might be practicable to do so in the circumstances*)'. This last qualification appeared to annul any obligation. Legal opinion was sought as to whether a shortage of funds would be valid grounds for allowing the castle to fall down. Lawyers agreed that the NC would be within its rights to take such a course of action. One consultant added that the contents of the castle could be sold, while another's interpretation was that the requirement to retain the contents was not legally binding but was 'a moral obligation'. Any of these options would have been too controversial and were not pursued. Instead the dilemma remained, the status quo of the castle being used as a bunk-house for workers continued, as did the slow deterioration underneath a veneer of maintenance.

In 1992 the island's name was officially changed from the Bulloughs' 'Rhum' back to 'Rum'. The Nature Conservancy was given the same treatment and subsequently had its identity changed three times, ending up as Scottish Natural Heritage (SNH), with its remit unaltered and the problem of the castle unresolved.

In 1976 the United Kingdom Atomic Energy Authority

identified Rum as an ideal place to bury its nuclear waste. Fortunately this idea was instantly dismissed, as were the enquiries in 1981 by a member of the Saudi Arabian royal family, who was desperately keen to purchase the entire package. The island continued to be used for research, and a change of policy opened the island to all visitors.

So what has this government agency achieved in a little over fifty years? In his incisive book, *Isles of the West*, Ian Mitchell put this question to the warden, and concluded that the answer was astonishingly little, at an annual cost of roughly £250,000. One-and-a-quarter million trees had been planted. Sea eagles, or white-tailed eagles, had been reintroduced from Norway to Rum – the first return of the species to Scotland – but had all promptly made their homes elsewhere. The flora and fauna had been surveyed in detail. A research project on red deer had been put in place, which still continues and is claimed to be the longest-running continuous study of a large mammal in the world, but this is largely funded and entirely conducted by Cambridge University. Some critics say there is now less diversity of wildlife on Rum than under the Bulloughs' ownership, and part of the reason is the absence of farming. (SNH undertook to continue Lady Bullough's provision of free milk for the islanders and did so until 1976, when they declared it too costly and removed the dairy herd.)

If tangible evidence of the benefit of such a massive expenditure is hard to come by, ironically it could be argued that probably SNH's greatest achievement has been to maintain a community on the island. Rum's population remains at between twenty and thirty. It has not been easy. Such is the artificiality of society here, with every house owned by SNH and everyone except the teacher and post deliverer employed by SNH, that individual relationships are further complicated by living cheek by jowl and confined within a hierarchy of power and salary differentials. Staff turnover is high, in many instances less than two years, and this is another destabilising factor in the community. This was recognised in an internal letter dated 30 October 1975: 'In view of extra-special circumstances for staff on the Isle of Rhum, selection and recruitment ought to be tightened up considerably. The circumstances of living on Rhum may be compared with those of the British Antarctic Survey where a psychologist is invited to be present during interviews and to comment once the various candidates have left.'

The proposal to include passive psychoanalysis in SNH interviews was not adopted, but it shows the seriousness of the problem. From the community's point of view, a leading bone of contention was the rule that if any employees lost their jobs, they had to leave the island. Without the option of living on Rum and conducting business there the islanders had no security, and there was no chance of establishing a core community independent of SNH. The matter was finally addressed in 2009, when the Isle of Rum Community Trust was allowed to assume ownership, in stages, of the houses, the community hall and the land within the village. Three new crofts will be formed, with a possibility of more in the future. It is a radical experiment which will hopefully prove successful, despite considerable challenges.

Today Rum welcomes visitors, and the castle is divided into two. Half is a hostel which sleeps up to fifty-five, with a choice of a self-catering kitchen or an excellent bistro. The other half is locked off as a Bullough Time Capsule and opened for guided tours and special events. The castle is in a desperate state. Rot, damp and leaks have weakened or destroyed considerable portions of the building. Mould clings to walls, ceilings, pictures and books. Wallpaper bubbles and peels. As yet the general appearance looks 'not too bad' to the superficial visitor, whereas to the specialist the castle teeters on the brink of being beyond saving. Damp has penetrated the walls to corrode the steel frame.*

---

* George Randall's research into the sandstone deposits at Corsehill Quarry produced the following extract from the company's Technical Data Sheet: '... tests indicate limited resistance to salt damage under normal conditions

In 1996 two individuals, George Randall and Ewan Macdonald, started the 'Kinloch Castle Friends Association'. Without this group pricking the (formidably defended) conscience of SNH and drawing attention to the castle's dire state of decline, little might have changed. In 2003 Kinloch Castle was a finalist in the BBC 'Restoration' programme. It brought wide attention to the castle's plight but, alas, no money. Prince Charles lent his support to the campaign, and there is hope that the Prince's Regeneration Trust may come up with funds to save the castle, but at the time of writing the flight path of angels avoids Rum. The castle's future hangs in the balance.

Like its predecessors, SNH has largely ignored the castle's welfare. While this originally stemmed from the organisation's traditional lack of interest in buildings, attitudes today within the administration have changed, but the overwhelming problem is money. Their huge budget is ring-fenced for land and wildlife. Some major repairs are being undertaken, but the fundamental flaw is that the government of the time undertook to maintain a historic building, placed it in the hands of the wrong administrative body and has turned a blind eye ever since. Kinloch Castle is a problem too big for SNH. Why does this nation's government continue to ignore its undertakings and shirk its responsibility?

* * *

Kinloch Castle excites passion, not all of it favourable:

> a nightmare of an edifice. Into it Sir George and Lady Bullough crammed the most ponderous and pompous articles of furniture they could find ... In the plenishing of Kinloch nothing of

---

and the high weight loss in the harsh saturated sodium sulphate test indicates susceptibility to salt damage in harsh environments, for example in coastal locations.' Corrie sandstone would have a similar rating today. It would not be considered suitable for building a castle on Rum.

Edwardian ostentation, bad taste and sheer vulgarity was overlooked

Alasdair Alpin MacGregor, *An Island Here and There*, 1972

an undisturbed example of pre-1914 opulence. Whatever people may think of the taste of their grandparents, at Kinloch Castle will be found nothing plastic or jimcrack. Good money was paid for good workmanship ... There will be few examples surviving in Great Britain of Edwardian splendour equal to the interior of Kinloch Castle ... In time to come the castle will be a place of pilgrimage for all those who want to see how people lived in good King Edward's days, that is, if Kinloch Castle survives.

Sir John Betjeman in an article for *Scotland's Magazine*, 1959

Sometimes it is said, usually by those who have never been there, that Kinloch Castle was built on the immoral earnings of industrial exploitation, that it is an alien feature on the landscape and deserves to be demolished or allowed to crumble. In response it can be said, firstly, the Bulloughs were no worse than any other employer of the day – indeed if anything they were more progressive than their rivals in providing better working hours, wages and conditions for their workers. Secondly, if this argument is applied to all man-made monuments, as it would only be logical to do, would any survive? The Great Wall of China is also known as the 'world's longest graveyard'. The builder of the Taj Mahal was imprisoned for squandering public money to the cost of everyone's welfare. Do such critics really believe Edinburgh Castle, Scotland's number one visitor attraction, was built in accordance with the International Charter of Human Rights and trade union agreements? The argument is specious. Kinloch Castle deserves no less than equal treatment to these other monuments. In architectural terms Kinloch Castle is not an august creation. Where it is superlative is in its completeness as an icon of the period.

Rum's natural beauty and unique geology will always attract visitors, but that alone will not be enough. With a castle that sleeps fifty-five and is itself an edifice of exceptional historical value the community has a hope of a bright future. I would argue that Kinloch Castle is Rum's greatest asset in its potential for providing a financial basis for a sustainable future, and that without it the island's economy is moribund. And for as long as records and memory exist, to lose it would stand as a benchmark of shortsightedness, administrative incompetence and national shame.

24

Loose Ends

Howard & Bullough was once again requisitioned for the wartime manufacture of munitions and plane parts in 1939, employing 6,000 at its peak. After the war the slow process of decline began, as demand for British textile machinery contracted. In 1970 the name Howard & Bullough disappeared, and the company was taken over by Platt International. The factory endured a change of name by Platt, going bust and being sold again to an American magnate, until finally, in 1992, the Globe Works fell silent for the first time since 1853. The majority of the buildings which once covered fifty-two acres have been demolished, but a corner remains, converted into a hotel, restaurant and business complex called the Globe Centre.

Under the terms of Sir George's will, Warren Hill was sold after Lady Bullough's death along with the Ashley Heath Stud. Warren Hill is still lived in today, and is classed as one of Newmarket's most prestigious properties. In 1988 both house and stud went on the market, described as being 'in impeccable condition', at an asking price of around £10 million.

Sir George's half-sister Gladys died in 1975, aged eighty-seven. Hermione Bullough, Countess of Durham, died in 1992, aged eighty-six. Her son, the Honourable John George Lambton, is the only surviving direct descendant and the end of the line. One acquaintance who knew him as a young man found him 'rather strange, very withdrawn and unable to get on with anyone except the elderly'. He never married. He lives in Surrey and still owns his grandfather's Longholes Stud.

* * *

> I don't intend to get involved in discussion about the rights and wrongs of big estates. Really, that is quite pointless, since there are so few of them left. But this I know: the estate of Rhum employed about a hundred people, and they were better off there than they would have been almost anywhere else. Of course it was a patriarchal and even tyrannical society in which we grew up, but I would rather have grown up there, with all the freedom and beauty of the island, than in some Gorbals slum.
>
> Archie Cameron, *Bare Feet and Tackety Boots*

Rum and Sir George were indeed closed entities, and secrecy turned the reputations of both into monuments of exaggeration. Is there any basis for speculation about the legend built up around the Bulloughs in the fact that 'Rhouma' is phonetically indistinguishable from 'rumour', and that other favourite family names were Mystery and Golden Myth? Was there something contrived about the way Sir George wished to be remembered, or was it born of a genuine desire for privacy? The latter, I now think. For all the external extravagance, the inner man, I believe, was reserved and introverted.

One of the more valuable items removed from the castle to the custody of the National Museum of Scotland (as it is now) was an 1835 jug bearing the following inscription: 'When this you see remember me, And bear me in your mind, Let all the world say what they will, Speak of me as you find.'

I began this biography with a suspicion that I would not like Sir George Bullough, that he represented most things that are the antithesis of my nature. He is an extraordinarily difficult man to know, but my respect for him has deepened. I feel he has suffered a bad press for too long. When we are dead, what is left of any of us? Memories, reputation, some writings maybe, some tangible legacies in objects or institutions created. He seems to have left behind no writings and no institutions. Memories have been lost to time and should not be confused with hearsay. I prefer to judge him on the legacy of the Isle of Rum and, in particular, Kinloch Castle. Each year between 8,000 and 9,000 people visit that castle, and not one ever forgets the experience. It has been a source of wonder and enjoyment for visitors who, hopefully, one day, will become millions. I consider that no mean achievement.

Sir George's was a life of extraordinary expenditure, energy and experience. He was born blessed with privileges that many have held against him. Some may criticise him for a lack of verifiable philanthropy, but no one can accuse Sir George Bullough of not living life to the full. If nothing else – and there was a great deal else, like the provision of a hospital ship in the Boer War that is easily overlooked – his legacies include a life that radiated colour in drab times, and continues to do so to this day.

APPENDIX A

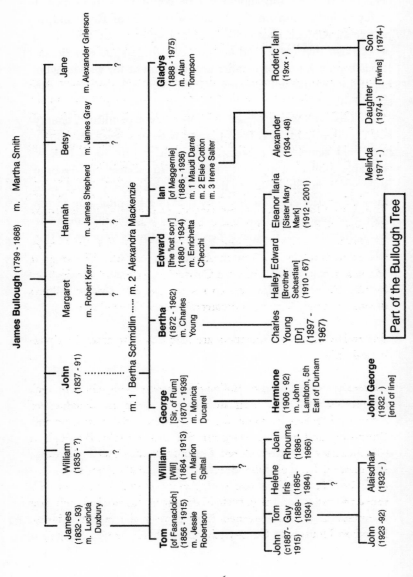

Part of the Bullough Tree

APPENDIX B

SUMMARY OF THE LIVES AND RELATIONSHIPS OF OTHER BULLOUGH FAMILY MEMBERS.

Hotels feature prominently in the family history. An uncommon number of Bullough men died in them: John in the Metropole, London; Sir George in the Château de Courcet, Pas de Calais; Tom in the Imperial, Bath; William in The Palace, Aberdeen. Ian escaped with his life from all such lodgings but was caught committing adultery in one, as was Tom Guy, in the Crown, Penrith.

Excluding war deaths, few of the principal men lived to old age: John, 54 (possibly 52); Edward, 54; Ian, 50; William, 49; Tom, 56; Tom Guy (Tom's son), 45; Sir George (exceptionally), 69. Unlike Monica, 98, Bertha, 90, Gladys, 87 and Hermione, 86.

Divorce was also common: John divorced Bertha, Sir George was co-respondent in Monica's divorce from Charles Charrington, Monica was 'intervener' in Lord Cowley's divorce, Ian was divorced by Lily Elsie, Tom Guy was co-respondent in Advocate Gillies's divorce, and may have been divorced by his wife, Marjorie.

The following family members are listed by first name in alpha-betical order:

Alexandra Marion, John Bullough's second wife, Sir George's stepmother. She was born in 1865, the youngest daughter of Kenneth Mackenzie, agent for the National Bank of Scotland, Stornoway, and his wife Margaret. She married John Bullough in 1884 and they had two children, Ian and Gladys. After John's death she married Lt. Col. John Beech in 1892 and they honeymooned in Cairo. Described in one source as a veterinary surgeon who proved so valiant on the battlefield that he was offered a combatant commission, he distinguished himself with the Scottish Horse Battalion Household Cavalry and the 20th Hussars in campaigns

Eccentric Wealth

in Egypt. They lived at Fasgath, Glenlyon. John Beech had family connections with Ballentemple, Co. Cork. Alexandra endured many heartbreaks. A son, aged 3, died in 1905. Within a year in World War One her husband died at Louth, Lincolnshire – I believe while serving the war effort – and her eldest son was killed in France during a night attack. After the war another son died, aged 22. (A fourth died of malaria in Kenya in 1933, aged 25.) Alexandra died on 5 August 1928, aged 63, and was buried at Innerwick, Glenlyon. She was always a popular figure in the glen.

Bertha Bullough: John's daughter by his first marriage, and Sir George's sister. Not much is known about her. She was born on 8 April 1872 and was ten years old when her mother (also Bertha) left for a new life in Switzerland. Two months after her father died she married Charles Florance Young (born 1865) of Melbourn, Cambridge, on 23 April 1891, when she was 19. The wedding took place in Eastbourne. In 1883 he had been managing director of the family brewing company, Youngs of Wandsworth, but stepped down in favour of a younger brother – a family schism appears to have developed. They had one son, also named Charles Florance, who became a doctor. Around 1902, Bertha published her translation from German of *The Danaid: An Episode from the Franco-German War*, thereby revealing some shared linguistic ability with that of her (half-?) brother, Edward. She attended Sir George's funeral in 1939. Bertha's husband died in 1934, and Bertha in 1962, aged 90. I do not know why they chose to be buried in a Macrae graveyard in Wester Ross (Clachan Duich New, Kintail), or why their son, Dr Charles Florance Young, was not buried alongside, where so much space is still available, but ended up beyond a fence in the congested cemetery of Clachan Duich Old. He never married, and his death in 1967 ended the line.

Bertha Schmidlin and her family: Bertha Wilhelmine Schmidlin was born on 18 September 1848 in Germany at Altmannshofen Castle, Aichstetten, in the Allgäu region north of Lake Constance. As teenagers Bertha and her sister, Marie, worked at the Giessbach

Hotel (see below) and both are mentioned in the diary of a frequent guest, the polymath John Ruskin, particularly the more beautiful Marie. Bertha married: 1. Otto Stephani on 17 October 1865, but he died 'after a long illness' four months later. 2. John Bullough on 11 February 1869. They separated in 1879 and Bertha returned to Thun, Switzerland, visiting England for the divorce proceedings. It was alleged she was having an affair with one Albert Nentwig, but the divorce was awarded solely on the grounds of John's misconduct. By 1883 she and baby Edward had moved to Dresden. She married again, her third husband being a judge called Friedrich Strüver, who was much younger. They had four children together. Bertha died on 12 November 1913 and was buried in Dresden.

Recent research by Thomas Krebs in Switzerland reveals Bertha's father, Eduard Emil Schmidlin, to have been a most unusual man. Born in Rottenburg am Neckar in 1808, he took part in a student political uprising, the Frankfurter Wachensturm, in 1833 and spent ten months in prison. He then became a gardener at Zeil Castle and married. The family moved to Switzerland, where Eduard became head gardener at the famous Giessbach Hotel, a legendary beauty spot popular with writers and artists. The main attraction was a series of waterfalls which Eduard illuminated – a great novelty at the time – and around which he landscaped a garden. From gardening he moved into hotel management, running the Giessbach for many years, and latterly the Bellevue Hotel in nearby Thun, until his retirement in 1882. He joined Bertha in Dresden, dying there in 1890.

Eduard wrote more than ten books on gardening (one was reprinted in the 1990s) and appears to have been fluent in English, as he also translated one book from English into German. He is credited with being among the first to challenge the elitist image of gardening at the time and to popularise it as an interest for all, not just the wealthy.

Edward Bullough: the 'forgotten son' of John by his first wife Bertha (*née* Schmidlin). The mystery is related in the main text, but he was either Sir George's full brother or his half-brother (if Albert Nentwig was the father). Edward was born in Bertha's adopted hometown of Thun, Switzerland, on 28 March 1880. He may never have seen his nominal father, John. Edward was brought up in Dresden, attended the prestigious Vizthum Gymnasium and went down to Cambridge in 1899, graduating in 1902. His gift for languages was exceptional, being fluent in German, English, Russian, Italian, Spanish and Chinese. He was also deeply interested in psychology. In 1912 he published his most famous work, *Psychical Distance as a Factor in Art and an Aesthetic Principle*, an essay which is still influential over a century later. As well as teaching, writing books on Russian and Italian, *The Scotsman* (11 July 1913) reported he was investigating 'thinking horses' – the controversial claims by several people who said they had taught the animals to understand English grammar and arithmetic. (His findings were not published.) He was a negotiator at the surrender of the German Fleet at the end of World War One, having worked for the Intelligence Department of the Royal Navy Volunteer Reserve, and was an interpreter at the signing of the Peace Treaty in Kiel. He was a fervent Freemason before he joined the Catholic Church in 1923.

In 1908 he married Enrichetta Checchi, a daughter of the internationally famous Italian actress, Eleanora Duse. (When Senora Duse died in 1924, even Mussolini sent a wreath to her funeral.) They had two children who both changed their names upon devoting their lives to the Dominican Order: Halley Edward (1910–1967), born in the year of the comet, became Brother Sebastian, and Eleonora Ilaria (1912–2001) became Sister Mary Mark.

Edward died at Woodchester Priory from septicaemia following a minor operation on 17 September 1934. He was 54. Whether misguided or not, the obituaries were unequivocal in stating he was John Bullough's son.

Gladys Bullough: John's daughter by his second marriage (to Alexandra), Sir George's half-sister. She was born at Meggernie on 24 November 1888. In her father's will she was left £20,000, payable in full on her twenty-first birthday, and the life interest on £30,000 being retained in trust. She went to court in 1909 and won the right to the full £50,000 without conditions. On 17 July 1915 she married Alan Hawtin Tompson, a sheep-farmer in Nairobi and a 2nd Lieutenant, 4th Battalion Grenadier Guards, aged 35. He was killed two months later on 27 September. I have no other details about her life, except that she did not remarry and died in 1975, aged 87.

Hermione Bullough: Sir George and Lady Bullough's only child. Born 5 November 1906. On 4 March 1931 she married John Frederick Lambton, 5th Earl of Durham (his second marriage) and became the Countess of Durham. Their son, the Hon. John George Lambton, was born in 1932. Hermione died in 1992, aged 86. The Hon. John George celebrated his twenty-first birthday with a party at Kinloch Castle. He inherited the Longholes Stud, Newmarket, which he continues to run. One of his most successful horses was Wake Up Maggie. He has no children.

Ian Bullough: John Bullough's son by his second wife, Alexandra Marion, and Sir George's half-brother. He was baptized 'John', always referred to as 'Ian', but reputed to be known as 'Ion' among the family. A handsome bon-viveur, playboy, car-racer and decorated soldier. Despite an age difference of sixteen years, Ian and Sir George continued to visit each other's estates and spend time together. Ian was born on 13 February 1886. When his father died five years later, Ian inherited Meggernie Castle and estate, and a half-share in Howard & Bullough. The inheritance was held in trust for him, Alexandra being his principal guardian, and Sir George assisting in the administration (and enjoyment) of Meggernie. Ian was educated at Eton and Cambridge. His 'coming of age' party was reported in detail in the *People's Journal* (16 March 1907). A few months earlier he had become a Captain in the Coldstream Guards, but resigned his commission a year later. He began racing cars at Brooklands. Between 1909 and 1911 he owned a 10hp Tsotta Fraschini ('2-seater aluminium scuttle dash body') registration ES563. He appeared to take no part in the running of Howard & Bullough.

In 1909 he married Maudi Darrell, a 'well-known musical comedy actress' whose father, Hugh Didcott, was the '"father" of music-hall agents'. At 26, she was three years older than him. Within a fortnight she contracted blood poisoning, underwent eight operations but never really recovered, dying eighteen months later. A year after her death, in 1911, he married the well-known actress and 'Gaiety girl' Lily Elsie (real name Elsie Cotton) and they honeymooned in Paris and the south of France. Ian had connections with Oakgrove, County Cork, where he was Master of the Muskerry Foxhounds, and with another Irish property, Warrenscourt, Lissarda. During World War One he served as a Major with the Scottish Horse and was awarded a MC for 'heroic conduct'. In 1919 he put Meggernie on the market and it sold in 1922. The couple moved to Drury Lane Farm (later renamed Drury Lane House) at Redmarley, Gloucestershire, where they were close neighbours of Sir George (in the Down House). When the latter stood down as Master of the Ledbury Hunt, Ian took his place three years later. Ian owned a large stud at the farm.

Lily Elsie was reported suing for divorce in the gossip column of a New Zealand newspaper as early as 1913, but their marriage lasted 19 years, ending in 1930 when they divorced on the court evidence of Ian's 'misconduct' in a hotel with 'an unidentified woman'. Perhaps this was a contrived 'admission' for expediting divorce proceedings, as the couple had long been living apart. The same year Ian (43) married for the third time, his bride (25) being Irene Salter, a 'masseuse' he appears to have met on a passenger ship from Brisbane. They lived at Inverawe House, Argyllshire, and had two sons, possibly twins – Ian's sole progeny, it seems – named Alexander, who was born in 1934 and died fourteen years later, and Roderic Iain, still living. Ian died in an Edinburgh nursing home in 1936 after a minor operation, aged 50, and was buried at Innerwick, Glenlyon. His obituaries said very little about his life, but were expansive on his father's achievements. Sir George was a pallbearer at his funeral. He left an estate valued at £228,943 gross.

James (2) Bullough: eldest son of James (1) and Martha, and brother to John. James was born in 1832. He and his next brother, William (born 1835), each inherited cotton mills, while John was left the Globe Works. James married Lucinda (*née* Duxbury) and they had two children – Sir George's cousins – Tom and William (Will). He died on 16 Jan 1893.

Monica, Lady Bullough, the family of: Her father was Gerard Gustavus Ducarel, the 4th Marquis (or Count) de la Pasture. The marquisate was created by Louis XVI in 1768, and the second Marquis emigrated to England in 1791. Gerard married Léontine ('Lilly') Standish on 4 July 1864. They were living in Christchurch, New Zealand, when Monica Lilly, their only child, was born on 8 April 1869. Léontine died the same day, almost certainly of post partum haemmorrhage. Gerard was running a high pasture sheep grazing with his brother, Henry, in the Magdalene Valley, but he appears to have left New Zealand shortly after his wife's death. Monica was brought up at Somerford Manor in Cheshire. Her father married Georgina Mary Loughman, daughter of a judge, on 20 May 1873. (Curiously, it took at least five years for the first child to appear in both his marriages.) The children of this second marriage were:

1. Charles Edward Mary [sic], born 1879. Was Captain in the Scots Guards, died of wounds in Flanders on 29 October 1914. He left a widow, Agatha.

2. Gerard Hubert, born 1886, became the Marquis de la Pasture on his father's death in 1916. His marriage to Evelyn Morris was reported as 'about to take place' in *The Times* of 14 March 1910. He served with the King's African Rifles and was wounded in 1917. In 1918 he married Ida Mosley.

3. Mary Helen. No information.

4. Margaret Mary. Two months after her brother's wedding she married his best man, Major the Hon. Hugh Bampfylde.

Gerard and his brother Henry were both living at Cefn Ila, Usk, Monmouthshire at the time of their deaths – the younger Henry in 1908 and Gerard in 1916. Around 1911 Henry's wife became a famous novelist and playwright, writing under the name Mrs Henry de la Pasture. She married again and became Lady Clifford. Her daughter wrote novels under the name 'Miss E. M. Delafield'.

Tom Bullough: Eldest son of James (2), and Sir George's cousin and friend, though fourteen years older. He was born in 1856 and became a director of Howard & Bullough, remaining active until his retirement in 1904. Like Sir George and his brother William, he appears to have rented the Rhyddings in Accrington for a time. He, George and William (Will) frequently shot and fished together. He was best man when his uncle, John, married Alexandra, and was left a sizeable legacy in the former's will, only to be denied it when it was realised he had inadvertently witnessed the testament being signed. He appears to have relocated to the Oban area in the 1880s, first as a tenant of Barcaldine Estate, then at various addresses, including Dungalan and Benvillin House. The latter he presented to the town of Oban. In 1901 he bought the estate of Fasnacloich at the head of Loch Creran and built a new mansion. A noted philanthropist, he donated land and £12,000 for a tuberculosis sanatorium to be built in Oban, and gifted to Accrington the 50-acre Bullough Park in memory of his grandfather. His legacies were many, and include the Bullough Cup (shinty) which is still competed for to this day. He was made a JP for Argyll in 1904. He owned a yacht called *Waihi* (after a gold-mining region of New Zealand).

In 1891 he married Jessie Robertson from Orbost, Skye, at Meggernie Castle. Their eldest son, John Leodius (born 1893), abandoned his studies at Cambridge to enlist, and was killed at the battle of Loos in 1915. Tom Guy (born 1899) married Marjorie Chinnery-Haldane in 1922, was cited in the divorce proceedings of an Edinburgh advocate, Arthur Gillies, in 1932, and died in 1934, aged 45. Helene Iris (1895–1984), the eldest daughter, married Henry Blakeney. Little is known about the youngest daughter, Joan Rhouma (1896–1966).

Tom Bullough died of pneumonia at the Imperial Hotel in Bath, where he used to stay each year, on 10 March 1915. He was 59, and left an estate valued at £704,643. He and his family are buried at Fasnacloich.

William (Will) Bullough: Tom's younger brother and a cousin of Sir George. Born in 1864, he was six years older than Sir George. He had worked as an apprentice in all departments of Howard & Bullough, then was a 'traveller for the firm' before becoming a director. He lived at the Rhyddings at the turn of the century and was married to Marion (*née* Spittal, from Galashiels) who presumably was responsible for the following advert in *The Scotsman* of 14 May 1898: 'Butler (single-handed), age 35–40, required immediately, wage offered £40–£50: unmarried, abstainer; must have exceptionally good references. Apply, stating all particulars, also enclosing photo, to Mrs Bullough, The Rhyddings, Accrington, Lancashire.' Another of their houses in Accrington was named 'Kinloch'. They too felt the pull north, to Aberdeenshire, living for time at Aboyne. Will was a keen angler on the Dee. At the time of his death he owned a London residence at 48 Sloane Square, and was described in his obituary as 'of the Palace Hotel, Aberdeen', which is where he expired on 15 March 1913, at the age of 49. His estate was valued at £187,835 19s 7d.

APPENDIX C

RUM AND BULLOUGH TIMELINE

3000 million yrs BP	Rum evolves; some of world's oldest rocks
59 million yrs BP	Rum's volcano active; later 1 km erodes
30,000 yrs ago	Last major Ice Age begins
16,000 yrs ago	Last major Ice Age ends, 4000-yr ice melt
12,000 yrs ago	Rum experiences minor ice return
8,500 yrs ago	Rum's human settlement – 1st in Scotland
4,000 yrs ago	Evidence of farming on Rum
677	St Beccan, a hermit, dies on Rum
c. 1000	Monks from Iona settle at Kilmory
1266	Norse lands won back by Scots
1493	Lords of the Isles power broken by James IV
?	Rum owned by Clanranald
?	Rum owned by Maclean, laird of Coll
1549	Donald Munro: 'heigh montanes . . . little deires'
1625	Franciscans visit: 'so wild and mountainous'
1677	Timothy Pont: 'Rhum' [nb spelling] & 'foullis'
1694	Blaeu Atlas of Scotland, 1654 – 1st map of Rum
1698	Martin Martin: 'inhabitants mainly Protestant'
c. 1726	Maclean of Coll enforces Protestantism
1728	152 persons over age of five – Rum's pop. c. 180
1733	John Kay invents the flying shuttle
1739	Dr Maclean, bankrupt, forced off Rum
1741	Report on number of Catholics: 'Rhum' spelling
1764	James Hargreaves 'invents' the spinning jenny
	Rum visited by 'mad minister' Rev John Walker
	Rum's pop. 304
1769	Richard Arkwright invents the water frame

Appendix C

1771		Pennant's description of poverty on Rum
1773		58 Rum familes are defiantly Catholic
1785		Edmund Cartwright: 1st power-driven loom
1787		Red deer extinct on Rum by this date
1795		Rum's pop. peaks at 443
1796		Statistical Account: 'kingdom of the wild forest'
1797		Edward Daniel Clarke's description of Rum
1799		Most likely date of birth of James Bullough
1803	30 Oct.	James Bullough baptized
1808	8 July	Eduard Emil Schmidlin (Bertha's father) born
1812		Luddite riots in Lancashire and Yorkshire
1818		First power looms introduced to Lancashire
1820 or 1824		John MacCulloch's description of Rum
1822		Rum's pop. c. 350; 443 also quoted
1824		James Bullough marries Martha Smith
1820s		Steam power replaces water (Lancashire)
1825		Rum leased to Dr Lachlan Maclean
1826		Power Loom Riots: more in 1829
	11 July	Rum pop cleared to N Scotia; 50 remain
1827		5 Skye families imported to work 8,000 sheep
1828		50 pop. who remained (1826) now emigrate
1830 or 1832		Trees planted (nr PO) – oldest trees on Rum
1832		James Bullough's first son, James, born
1835		James Bullough's 2nd son, William, born
1837	10 Dec.	James Bullough's 3rd son, John, baptised
1838		John Bullough born (ref: marriage certificate)
1839		John Bullough born (ref: tomb date)
		Dr Maclean, bankrupt, forced off Rum
1841		Rum's pop. 69 males, 55 females. Total 114
1842		Riots: James Bullough flees Blackburn
1843		Kilmory grave gives 'Rhum' spelling

1844		James Bullough invents the 'Loose Reed'
1845		James Bullough in mill-owning partnerships
		Hugh Miller visits Rum
		2nd Marquis of Salisbury buys Rum for £24,455
		Salisbury reintroduces deer to Rum
1847		Rum's population now 118 in 21 families
1848	18 Sep.	Bertha Schmidlin born in Germany
1849	June	New dam starts on Rum – destroyed by 5 Dec.
c. 1850		James Bullough trading as James B. & Sons
		First school opens on Rum
1851		Rum's population 74 males, 59 females. Total 133
1852		New dam project on Rum – washed out in 1854
		James Bullough patents the 'Slasher'
		58 Rum islanders cleared by Salisbury
1853		John Howard & James Bleakley start factory
1855		Salisbury dismisses all Rum shepherds
		Howard & Bullough's Globe Works founded
		James Bullough invents the Self-Acting Temple
1857	June/July	Cawnpore Massacre – Indian Mutiny
1861		Rum's population 74
1862		John Bullough joins H&B, aged 25
		Rum's population c. 60; 6 families resident
24 Nov.		Estimates of 100 fallow and 60 red deer on Rum
1863		Rum grazings let to a Captain Campbell
	16 April	James Bullough retires, John a partner of H&B
1866		John Howard dies; H&B wages bill is £8,000 p.a.
1868	31 July	James Bullough dies: John in sole charge of H&B
	to 1888	John Bullough patents 26 of his inventions
		Marquis of Salisbury dies, Rum for sale (1870)
1869 or 1870		Captain Campbell buys Rum
1869	1 Feb.	John Bullough marries Bertha Schmidlin

	8 April	Monica Ducarel born in New Zealand
1870	28 Feb.	George Bullough born in Accrington
1871		John Bullough adopts the 9-hour working day
		Rum's population 81
		Globe Works wage bill is now £30,000 p.a.
1872	8 April	Bertha Bullough (George's sister) born
1873	Sep.	Rum; diphtheria claims five Matheson children
1874		Globe Works wage bill now £40,000 p.a.
c. 1875		Bullough family moves to Rhyddings Hall
1876	5 April	Millowners of Accrington thank John Bullough
		John Bullough buys patent for Rabbeth Spindle
1878		Production of Rabbeth Spindle; 2000 employed
1879		John Bullough rents shooting on Rum; £800 p.a.
1880	28 March	Edward Bullough ('forgotten' son) born
	10 Aug.	Bertha separates from John (official date)
1881		Census: John & Bertha at Accrington
		Rum's population 'nearly 90'
	Nov.	People at Kinloch drown in storm and floods
1882 or 1886		Capt Campbell dies, Rum passes to nephew
		Rum's population 70; served by Hebridean
1883	16 Jan.	Bertha & John Bullough's divorce finalised
		The Limping Pilgrim on his Wanderings, E. Waugh
	27 Sep.	John Bullough buys Meggernie for c. £150,000
1884	8 Sep.	John Bullough marries Alexandra Mackenzie
	Sep.	George Bullough enters Harrow
1886	13 Feb.	Ian (John or 'Ion'), George's half-brother, born
		Last report of fallow deer seen on Rum
	5 June	Rum advertised for sale: plentiful deer/grouse
1887		George Bullough leaves Harrow
1888	18 May	Rum bought by John Bullough for c. £35,000
	24 Nov.	Gladys (George's half-sister) born

	26 Dec.	First entry (George) in Rum Deer Book
1889	19 March.	Monica Ducarel marries Charles Charrington
1890		Mr Martin is the shooting tenant on Rum
		Dorothea Elizabeth born to Monica & Charles C.
		80,000 trees planted & game imports to Rum
	Feb.	John Bullough buys 55-foot yacht *Mystery*
	5 Feb.	Eduard Emil Schmidlin, Bertha's father, dies
1891		Globe Works now has a weekly wage bill of £2000
	25 Feb.	John Bullough dies in London, aged 54
	27 Feb.	Coffin arrives in Accrington; memorial service
	28 Feb.	George Bullough's 21st birthday
	23 April	Bertha (George's sister) marries Charles Young
	May	Post Office opened on Rum
		Rum's population 53
		H&B converted to a limited private company
	2 Aug.	John Bullough's body exhumed, on Rum 4 Aug
	20 Oct.	Tom Bullough marries Jessie Robertson
	19 Dec.	George & Mitchell travel continent on H&B work
1892	12 Aug.	George and Mitchell shooting at Meggernie
	29 Sep.	George & Mitchell start World Tour, to Ceylon
	4 Nov.	Board SS *Taroba* for Madras – tour India
	1 Dec.	Alexandra Bullough marries Lt-Col. John Beech
1893		H&B expand into America at Rhode Island
		Tom Bullough's first son, John Leodius, born
	16 Jan.	James Bullough (George's uncle) dies, aged 61
	9 Feb.	Board SS *Africa* for Rangoon – tour Burma
	7 March	Board SS *Orient* for Australia – tour S. Australia
	June	*Maria* (later *Rhouma*) built on the Clyde
	7 July	Board SS *Port Pirie* for South Africa – tour SA
	?	Ship to Madeira

Appendix C

1894	5 June	Arrive Port Chalmers (NZ) on SS *Tainui*
	1 Aug.	First Sino-Japanese War starts over Korea
	Nov.	Depart NZ via Sydney for connection to Noumea
		H&B becomes a public company
1895	18 Jan.	Arrive Sydney from Noumea on *Ville de la Ciotat*
		To Batavia, Ceylon, Singapore, China, Japan
	April	The 4th National Industrial Exhibition, in Kyoto
	17 April	Treaty of Shimonoseki ends Sino-Japanese War
		Travel from Japan to Honolulu & USA
	31 July	Arrive Liverpool fm NY – end of World Tour
		Tom Bullough's 1st daughter, Helene Iris, born
		Deer population on Rum estimated at 800
	7 Oct.	George buys the *Maria*, renames her *Rhouma*
1896		Departs for West Indies on Rhouma(till 2 May)
	10 Aug.	Tom Bullough's daughter, Joan Rhouma, born
	31 Oct.	Monica Charrington in Lord Cowley's divorce
	27 Dec.	823-ton barque *Midas* wrecked at Kilmory
1897	22 Jan.	Adverts for tenders to build Kinloch Castle
	Feb.	*Rhouma* dep. for W Indies & Azores, 15,387 mls
	10 July	*Rhouma* returns from W. Indies cruise
	26 Aug.	*Times* reports zebra crossed with Rum pony
	25 Sep.	*Oban Times*: work has started on Kinloch Castle
		Bertha Young's only son, Charles Florance, born
1898		George buys Bishopswood Estate, Ross-on-Wye
	7 May	*Oban Times*: *Rhouma* at Key West, and for sale
1899		Edward Bullough studies at Cambridge
		Tom Bullough's 2nd son, Tom Guy, born
		George's dogs win at Birmingham & London
	11 July	George V-Commodore of Royal Clyde Y. C.
		Report that George holds annual ball in Madeira
	11 Oct.	Boer War begins; ends May 1902

	12 Oct.	Mitchell marries Miss O'Moore on *Rhouma*
	26 Dec.	*Rhouma* departs Oban for Cape Town
1900		Telegraph cable from Ardvasar to Rum laid by SS *Monarch*
	c. 25 Jan.	*Rhouma* arrives Cape Town as a hospital ship
	16–18 Oct.	George's dogs winning at Crystal Palace
	4 Nov.	*Rhouma* returns from Boer War, arrives Rum
	early Dec.	*Rhouma* departs for W Indies, Madeira and Med.
1901		Kinloch Castle completed sometime this year
	10 Dec.	George created a Knight Bachelor
		Tom Bullough buys Fasnacloich
1902		Rum Bess wins at Crufts
		Sir G. & Monica C. cruise Tangiers, W Indies
		Edward Bullough graduates Trinity College
	2 Sep.	Edward VII's 'coronation cruise' passes Rum
	Oct.	Monica C. and her father visit Kinloch Castle
	17 Nov.	C. Charrington divorces Monica; Sir G. is cited
1903		Sir G. buys the 43-ft, 18-ton *Kinloch*; sold 1908
	8 April	Archie Cameron born
	24 April	*Rhouma* in Nice
	25 May	Monica Charington's divorce finalised
	24 June	Sir G. & Monica marry at Kinloch Castle
	29 Oct.	Sir G is president of the Scottish Kennel Club
1904		Tom Bullough retires as chairman of H&B
	17 Feb.	Duke of Atholl vs Sir G. for £2000 rent arrears
	15 Apr.	Tom Bullough appointed a JP for Argyll
	7 Sep.	Monica shoots first stag. 8 pt, 14 st.
1905–1906		Kinloch Castle altered to Monica's designs
	June	Post Office now uses 'Rhum' spelling
		700 brace grouse shot on Rum
1906		Two more floors built on west side of castle

		Sir G. becomes a Fellow of Zoological Society
	9 May	Thomas Young is gardener at Kinloch Castle
		Sir G. buys orchestrion for £2000
	5 Nov.	Hermione born at 14 Stratton Road, Piccadilly
1907		Ian Bullough's 21st, joins Coldstream Guards
1908–22		Sir G.'s main residence is Down House, Worc.
1908–21		Sir G. is Master of the Ledbury Hunt
1908		Sir G. sells the boat *Kinloch (I)*. Buys *Kinloch II*
		11 corncrake shot on Rum
	9 June	Ian Bullough is racing his car at Brooklands
	18 July	Ian Bullough resigns from Coldstream Guards
		Sir G. a capt., Scottish Horse Imp Yeomanry
	12 Oct.	Henry Philip Ducarel, Lady B's uncle, dies
		Edward Bullough marries Enrichetta M. Checchi
1909		Lady B's 40th & Sir G.'s 39th portraits painted
		Sir G. resigns as parliamentary candidate
	24 March	Ian Bullough marries Maudi Darrell
		Tom Bullough donates Benvillin House & £12,000
	24 July	Oban's Country Chest Hospital opens
	Dec.	Gladys Bullough claims £50,000 inheritance
1910		Edward Bullough's son, Halley Edward, born
	14 April	Percy Hills is now gardener at Kinloch Castle
	24 Sep.	Sir G. shoots finest & record stag, 19st 6lbs
	Oct.	Threat to close PO on Rum, but averted
	31 Oct.	Ian Bullough's first wife, Maudi dies
1911	13 Sep.	R. Wallace Brebner appointed factor on Rum
	7 Nov.	Ian Bullough's 2nd marriage to 'Lily Elsie'
		Sir G. resigns Scottish Horse Imp Yeomanry
1912	16 March	H&B hit by many strikes, reduce hours & men
	24 June	*Rhouma* sold & later renamed *Giuliana*
	13 July	Sir G. resigns as Chairman of H&B

	21 Oct.	Edward Bullough's daughter, Eleanora I, born
1913		Sir G. buys *Triton*, renames her *Rhouma II*
	15 March	William Bullough (Sir G's cousin) dies
	12 Nov.	Death of Bertha (Sir G's mother) in Dresden
1913–39		Sir G. owns more than 60 race horses
1914–36		Sir G. member of National Hunt Committee
1914	17 March	Duncan Macnaughton starts work as stalker
	July	3-month strike starts at H&B; 4,000 locked out
	4 Aug.	Britain declares war on Germany
	13 Aug.	Sir G. subscribes £1000 to National Relief Fund
	19 Aug.	Protests & violence force H&B to close, briefly
	Oct.	*Rhouma II* requisitioned for war effort
	29 Oct.	Capt. de la Pasture, Scots Guards, killed
	Nov.	H&B makes munitions, employs 5,000 (1915)
		Sir G. Major/Superintendent Remount Division
	22 Dec.	Sir G.'s last visit to Rum for five years
1915		Sir G. serves on Trades & Textiles Committees
	10 March	Tom Bullough of Fasnacloich dies
	17 July	Gladys Bullough marries Alan Tompson
	Sept.	Tom Bullough's eldest son, John Leodius, killed
	27 Sept.	Gladys's husband, Alan Tompson, killed
	6 Nov.	Alexandra 2nd husband Lt-Col. John Beech killed
1916	21 Jan.	Sir G. created a baronet, resigns Remount duties
	28 Jan	Gerrard Ducarel, Lady B.'s father, dies
	18 Oct.	Alexandra's son, Robert Clyde Beech, killed
1917	21 March	Ballymacad wins the War National
	7 Dec.	GH de la Pasture (now Marquis) wounded
1918	23 July	Monica's half-sister marries Hugh Bampfylde
1919		Edward Bullough publishes book on Italian
		Sir G. buys Golden Myth for 1,400 guineas
	April	*Rhouma II* returned by RN after war requisition

Appendix C

	1 May	Verdict in jewellery fraud, Phillips vs Brooks
	27 June	Ian Bullough awarded Military Cross
	1 Aug.	Sir G. visits Rum for first time in 5 years
	27 Aug.	Ian Bullough advertises Meggernie for sale
1920		Sir G. gives up steeple chasing for flat-racing
		Sir G. sells *Rhouma II* – still afloat to this day
	14 July	Archie Cameron faces dismissal from Rum
c. 1921		Sir G. starts Park Lodge Stables, Newmarket
		Sir G. quits as Master of the Ledbury Hunt
1922	21 Feb.	Meggernie sold to Sir Edward Wills for £120,000
	24 June	Monica & Hermione with alsatians at dog shows
	24 June	Golden Myth wins double Gold at Ascot
		Campanula wins 1,000 guineas
		Sir G. gives up control of *Accrington Gazette*
1923–till his death		Sir G. stalks deer each season
	Aug.–Sep.	Edward Bullough joins RC Church
1924		Heating system at castle extended upstairs
	30 Aug.	Sir William Bass first shoots deer on Rum
1920s	(mid)	H&B reach peak of size, employing 6,000
1925		Heaviest sea trout caught, 8lb 2oz
1926	12 Aug.	Hermione's huge drink order! (20th birthday?)
1920s	(late)	Cotton industry decline. Rum imports fish/deer
1928		Warren Hill residence built at Newmarket
	5 Aug.	Alexandra (Sir G.'s step-mother) dies
	6 Sep.	Hermione's 'coming of age' party on Rum
	16 Oct.	*Giuliana* (*Rhouma*) retired from Italian navy
1929	16 July	Lily Elsie divorces Ian Bullough (adultery)
	2 Sep.	Hermione shoots first stag, 15st 4lbs
	16 Sep.	Heaviest stag killed on Rum, 21st 6 lbs
1930		Ian Bullough marries 3rd wife, Irene Salter
	Apr.	Rum advertises for a shooting tenant (fails)

	15 July	Tom Guy Bullough cited in divorce case
1931	4 March	Hermione Bullough marries Lord Lambton
		H&B merger: Textile Machinery Makers Ltd
	Apr.	Rum advertises for a shooting tenant (fails)
	1 Sep.	Sir G. considers selling Rum privately
	26 Oct.	Last letter in archives from factor Brebner
1932		Hermione's son, John George, born
1934		Edward Bullough dies, aged 54
		Ian Bullough & Irene have twins
		Tom Guy Bullough dies, aged 45
	16 Feb.	Bertha's husband, Charles Florance Young, dies
		Record 101 stags shot on Rum
		Campanula wins 1000 Guineas
1936	6 June	Ian Bullough dies, aged 50
1938		Hon. John George Lambton (age 6) visits Rum
	5 Oct.	Sir G. shoots last stag, 15st 12lbs
1939–45		H&B produce munitions, employing 6,000
1939	26 July	Sir George Bullough dies, aged 69
1948		Ian Bullough's son, Alexander Ian, dies at 14
1952	20 May	Jessie Bullough (Tom's widdow) dies
1953		Hon. John George Lambton's 21st on Rum
1954		Lady Bullough's last visit to Rum, aged 85
1957	28 Feb.	Rum sold to Nature Conservancy for £23,000
1962	21 July	Bertha Young (George's sister) dies, aged 90
1964	6 Nov.	Duncan Macnaughton dies
1966		Tom Bullough's daughter, Joan Rhouma, dies
1967		Lady Bullough dies at Newmarket, aged 98
		Brother Sebastian (Edward's son) dies
	19 Nov.	Dr Charles Florance Young (Bertha's son) dies
1970		H&B, now Platt International, employ 2,000
1975		Sir G.'s half-sister Gladys [Tompson] dies

Appendix C

1975	Platt, Saco, Lowell takes over H&B works
1982	Platt International crash – Globe Works continue
	Irene Bullough (Ian's 3rd wife) dies
1984	Tom Bullough's daughter, Helene Iris, dies
1991	Lady Bullough's daughter, Dorothea, dies
1992	Hermione, Countess of Durham, dies, aged 86
	John Bullough (Tom Guy's son) dies
	Rhum' spelling changed back to 'Rum'
1993	Globe Works cease production after 138 years
1996	Kinloch Castle Friends Association started
2001	Sister Mary Mark (Edward's daughter) dies
2003	Castle featured on BBC 'Restoration' programme

INDEX

Index